# How to Be a Global Nonprofit

# How to Be a Global Nonprofit

## Legal and Practical Guidance for International Activities

### LISA NORTON

WILEY

John Wiley & Sons, Inc.

Published by John Wiley & Sons, Inc., Hoboken, New Jersey.

Published simultaneously in Canada.

For general information on our other products and services or for technical support, please contact our Customer Care Department within the United States at (800) 762–2974, outside the United States at (317) 572–3993 or fax (317) 572–4002.

Wiley also publishes its books in a variety of electronic formats. Some content that appears in print may not be available in electronic books. For more information about Wiley products, visit our web site at www.wiley.com.

***Library of Congress Cataloging-in-Publication Data:***

Norton, Lisa, 1956–
  How to be a global nonprofit: legal and practical guidance for international activities/ Lisa Norton.

    p. cm.
  Includes index.
  ISBN 978-1-118-45222-6 (cloth/website); 978-1-118-53467-0 (ebk); 978-1-118-53468-7 (ebk); 978-1-118-53472-4 (ebk)    1. Nonprofit organizations—Law and legislation—United States.    2. Nonprofit organizations—Law and legislation.    I.    Title.
  KF1388.N68 2013
  346.73'064—dc23

                                                                        2012037488

Printed in the United States of America

10 9 8 7 6 5 4 3 2 1

To Harvey, my husband of 20 years, who has been my
greatest cheerleader throughout this project,
and to my four children,
Wendy, Nat, Naomi, and Ruby,
who suffered through innumerable discussions of this topic.

# Contents

# List of Case Studies

# Preface

It was not very many years ago that international philanthropy was the province of large organizations like the Red Cross, UNICEF, and Save the Children. Americans who wanted to help people overseas gave to those organizations and others like them. For donors who wanted a more personal connection, some organizations offered individual child sponsorship, which allowed donors to see the direct impact of their giving.

In recent years, while large global organizations have continued to attract funding, there has been a new groundswell of small and medium-sized organizations, formed by growing numbers of individuals who want to do more than write a check or even sponsor a child. This phenomenon was described by Nicholas Kristof in a *New York Times Magazine* article in which he coined the term "Do-It-Yourself Foreign Aid," to identify a revolution that "starts with the proposition that it's not only presidents and United Nations officials who chip away at global challenges."

Kristof noted that the young idealists he was describing are sometimes naive about what it takes to solve social problems, and don't always appreciate the need to work collaboratively with the local populations they intend to serve. This book focuses on another set of issues not readily apparent to the passionate leaders of the Do-It-Yourself Foreign-Aid Revolution: the myriad and diverse legal considerations that must be taken into account in planning and operating any nonprofit organization with cross-border activity.

A new army of international philanthropists is boldly forging ahead, creating nonprofit organizations, raising funds in the United States and sometimes abroad, traveling overseas, building relationships with foreign individuals, organizations, and governments, and even hiring local employees. The new international nonprofits they create often have all, and sometimes more, of the passion and commitment found in their larger counterparts. What they often lack are the resources to engage staff and consultants to ensure that they comply with U.S. and foreign laws while keeping their eyes on the mission.

While it is widely recognized that the Internet and social media have eliminated jurisdictional boundaries in so many ways, legal boundaries are alive and well. Individual countries enact and enforce their own laws and work hard to protect their tax revenues. In fact, as we will see throughout this book, legal and tax barriers imposed by individual countries impede the cross-border activities of nonprofits to a far greater degree than they affect international trade.

The operations of nonprofit organizations, in the United States and abroad, are shaped by a variety of laws: notably, those addressing legal structure and governance (such as formation of nonprofit corporations); taxation (including income, estate, sales, excise, property, import duties, and more); anti-terrorism; exports; currency; corruption; immigration; and labor. In some countries, restrictions on the freedom of association preclude or hamper nonprofit organizations. When an organization operates across borders, whether by making grants or directly operating programs, the interaction among legal requirements of two or more countries quickly becomes highly complex.

This book is intended primarily for nonprofit organizations that qualify for U.S. federal tax-exempt status, as so-called *501(c)(3) organizations,* and operate and/or fund non-U.S. programs. While there are many categories of U.S. tax-exempt organizations, the 501(c)(3) is the only one (with narrow exceptions) that can attract tax-deductible funds in the United States. While this type of organization may directly operate or fund foreign programs, those foreign programs must also serve 501(c)(3) purposes. A broad range of organizations falls into the 501(c)(3) category, including, among others, those that are engaged in traditional charitable activities such as humanitarian aid, disaster relief, development, global health, the environment, and scientific research.

We will see in this book that any particular foreign country may or may not afford tax-exempt status to an activity that would qualify for it in the United States. Moreover, if in addition to operating foreign programs, an organization is raising funds in one or more foreign countries, it will need to deal with yet another set of rules and restrictions on the use of those funds.

At times, this book uses the word *charitable* to refer to the range of activities that may be performed in any particular country by an organization that qualifies for tax-exempt status. In some countries, notably throughout most of Europe, the term *public benefit* is used instead.

An organization that raises funds in the United States and conducts activities in a foreign country must not only comply with the laws of two countries, but must also consider the interaction of those laws and their effect on operational decisions.

If your organization contemplates venturing beyond U.S. borders, you need to address a number of questions:

Will the foreign project be managed and operated by U.S. staff and volunteers, or will you hire locally? If you send U.S. citizens overseas, will your organization be able to compensate them for additional taxes and housing costs? Will U.S. people even be able to obtain visas? If you hire locally, will you need to form a separate nonprofit corporation (or the local country equivalent)? How will you manage cash flows and investments between countries in two or more currencies?

In addition, oversight of foreign operations and funds is essential, but it means there will be people traveling to places that are often difficult and expensive to get to. Here are some fundamental questions to be addressed:

- How will your organization ensure the security of people traveling to remote and sometimes dangerous locations?
- What kinds of communications technology will you need to maintain contact among various locations, and what will that cost?

As nonprofit organizations expand internationally, they frequently underestimate the resources required to manage a multinational structure. A passionate founder can quickly find that he or she, together with board members who joined to support the mission, are spending most of their time on administrative matters. Failure to devote the necessary resources to legal, tax, treasury, and other so-called *overhead* functions will cause an organization to fail, yet funders are often unwilling to support these functions adequately.

All too often, in my legal practice, I have encountered passionate individuals who have barreled down the road, starting up operations, only to run into legal or practical problems that could have been avoided with awareness of some fundamentals. While this book cannot substitute for individualized legal advice, it arms the would-be global nonprofit with knowledge of critical considerations.

Knowledge of the basic legal and practical issues that face international nonprofits will help you make important decisions to give your organization the best chance of success in pursuit of its mission. You will also gain an understanding of the resources required to pursue your mission. By knowing how and where you can run into trouble, you will know when to seek help.

Over Thanksgiving dinner, a friend asked me to describe this book. When I finished, he commented that it sounded like I was trying to discourage people from starting international nonprofits. My purpose is not to deter people from pursuing their passion, but rather to help them find the most effective way to achieve their goals. In truth, many nonprofit organizations fail, particularly in the international arena, because their founders were not prepared to raise the funds and devote the resources necessary to grapple with the puzzling array of legal and practical hurdles described in this book.

In many cases, available resources could have been used more effectively by working with, or through, an existing organization, rather than starting a new one. We will see, in the case study of Families with Children from China, that it may be possible to have your cake and eat it too. If you can find the right foreign partner, you may be able to participate in the development and implementation of projects without having to operate them directly.

At the same time, people start international nonprofits for many valid reasons. Throughout this book you will encounter inspiring stories of successful organizations. Case studies of Ashesi University and Half the Sky Foundation show that sometimes a founder may succeed with an audacious project where there is simply no one else willing to take it on. The case study of Lumana provides an example of a young person who was determined to create opportunities for other young people to gain hands-on experience that wasn't available to them through established organizations.

Whatever motivates you to consider starting a global nonprofit, my goal is to help you make informed decisions about what it will take, and how best to pursue your mission. There are so many global issues waiting to be addressed, and so many people with passion. My sincere hope is that adding a touch of realism will help those passionate people succeed in making a difference in the world.

## How to Use This Book

While all readers are invited to read this book cover-to-cover, many will hone in on certain chapters. I have included case studies throughout the book to illustrate the variety of ways U.S.-based organizations, from the largest to the smallest, have approached entering the international arena, and how they have dealt with a variety of legal and practical concerns.

If you are new to the realm of international nonprofits, you may find it useful to begin with Chapter 1, which provides an overview of the ways an organization can engage in international activities. On the other hand, if you have an established organization with international activities, you may find Chapters 8 and 9 useful as checklists of U.S. and foreign issues you need to consider.

This book addresses legal and practical considerations for organizations that are exclusively grantmakers, as well as those that directly engage in foreign activities. Chapters 2 and 3 provide an overview of U.S. legal requirements for organizations that make cross-border grants, and Appendix B lists a number of resources for those organizations. Many organizations that directly operate foreign programs also engage in some form of grantmaking, and therefore need to be concerned with the rules for international grantmaking. However, for most organizations either Chapter 2 or 3, but not both, will be relevant, as they address two distinct types of 501(c)(3) organizations, so-called *public charities* and *private foundations*.

The remainder of this book (Chapters 4 through 10) is devoted to those organizations that choose to go an extra step, or more, by operating directly in one or more countries outside the United States. Chapter 4 explores some alternatives to acting alone when creating a foreign program, and then looks at alternative ways of structuring foreign operations. Chapter 5 takes that a step further, exploring the creation of a separate foreign organization, or so-called *legal entity*, and the considerations involved in structuring the relationships among separate operations in multiple countries.

Chapter 6 looks at legal, tax, and practical considerations related to staffing foreign operations with any combination of U.S. and foreign employees and volunteers.

Chapter 7 takes it all a step further, looking at raising funds in foreign countries.

Chapters 8 and 9 provide a checklist of U.S. and foreign (respectively) legal and practical concerns. If you have already read the earlier chapters, or already have an established foreign presence, this will take you a step further. Chapter 9 provides an overview of significant foreign laws and practical issues you are likely to encounter and gives specific country examples.

Finally, Chapter 10 puts it all together with a story. This is the story of one organization that went from start-up to global nonprofit in a short 13 years. That is not for everyone. But if you have a compelling mission and extraordinary passion, and you're prepared to devote the resources to getting it right, you too may create a global nonprofit.

No part of this book requires that the reader have a legal background. Rather, this book provides a basic overview of the legal landscape for international nonprofit activities so that nonprofit founders, directors, and managers can make informed decisions about how best to structure operations and plan for the use of scarce resources. For those who are interested in more depth (such as lawyers and others with some knowledge of nonprofit law), I have included references and citations to facilitate further research.

In some places, I felt it was important to go into greater depth to help set the stage for fundamental decisions about structuring operations. For example, Chapter 6 discusses the implications of U.S. income tax treaties at some length. While this is intended as helpful background, if you find it to be too much information, you can simply skip those sections. You may, however, want to make a note of the issue so you can discuss it with your lawyer.

## Disclaimer

This book is not a substitute for obtaining individualized legal advice. It does not provide legal, tax, accounting, or other professional advice. No attorney-client relationship is established. Rather, the purpose of this book is to help an organization, its founders, directors, officers, and advisors, in making decisions about how to structure international activities.

The publisher and author make no representations regarding the accuracy or completeness of the contents of this book, and specifically disclaim all warranties of fitness for a particular purpose.

The proper interpretation and application of U.S. and foreign laws are highly dependent on specific facts. Laws also change constantly. An organization will need to seek individualized legal advice in the United States and each foreign country in which it operates.

Descriptions of U.S. laws in this book are intended to provide general information that can be used to help guide an organization in making decisions about its operational model, and in understanding the resources required to launch and operate an international nonprofit.

References to foreign laws are provided for purposes of illustrating, in general, the kinds of foreign constraints an organization may face, and how U.S. and foreign requirements interact. Descriptions of foreign laws in this book should not be relied on in forming or operating a nonprofit organization.

This book does not provide a comprehensive overview of U.S. and foreign laws that may apply to the activities of a particular organization. Although I have endeavored to provide an overview of the fundamental U.S. and foreign legal considerations to be taken into account by any international nonprofit organization, additional U.S. and/or foreign laws may be critical to any particular organization.

Websites referenced in this book may have disappeared, or their contents may have changed, between the time the book was written and the time it is read.

This book does not address the ethics of foreign aid, or issues around determining what is and is not appropriate in a particular foreign context.

## Internal Revenue Service Circular 230 Disclosure

This book is intended for general informational purpose and is not intended to provide tax advice. As provided in Treasury regulations, nothing in this book is intended or written to be used, and cannot be used for the purpose of (1) avoiding penalties under the Internal Revenue Code, or (2) promoting marketing or recommending to another party any plan or arrangement addressed herein.

## Notes

1. Nicholas D. Kristof, "The D.I.Y. Foreign-Aid Revolution," *New York Times Magazine*, October 24, 2010, 49, available at www.nytimes.com/2010/10/24/magazine/24volunteerism-t.html.

2. A so-called *501(c)(3) organization* is one that qualifies for U.S. federal tax-exempt status under section 501(c)(3) of the Internal Revenue Code (I.R. C.), 26 U.S.C. § 501(c)(3). To qualify for 501(c)(3) status, an organization must be formed for one of the following purposes: religious, charitable, scientific, testing for public safety, literary, educational, or fostering amateur national or international sports competition, or the prevention of cruelty to children or animals. Additional requirements apply. For a description of the requirements and process for obtaining federal tax-exempt status under section 501(c)(3), *see* IRS Publication 557, *Tax-Exempt Status for Your Organization* (December 2, 2011), available at www.irs.gov/app/picklist/list/publicationsNoticesPdf.html.

# Acknowledgments

I would like to acknowledge and thank so many people who provided invaluable input, insights, helpful comments, and support, without which this book would not have been possible.

I extend my deep appreciation to the representatives of the 10 nonprofit organizations who consented to be interviewed for case studies: Cathy Reilly of Agros International; Matthew Taggart and Nina Marini of Ashesi University; Aileen Kroger of Families with Children from China, Inc. of Greater New York; Jenny Bowen of Half the Sky Foundation; Sammi Raynor of Lumana; Allan Paulson and Linda Mason of Pangea Giving; Ruth Jones of Social Venture Partners International; Timothy Schottman of SightLife; Lillian Thorgersen of World Association for Children and Parents; and Timothy Burgett of World Vision International.

I also thank a number of individuals who generously donated their time to provide helpful comments and suggestions: Putnam Barber, Edward Diener, Mary Lou Fahey, Dorothy Foster, Bookda Gheisar, Kristi Helgeson, Ellen Jesse, Joelle Keene, Harvey Motulsky, Jeanette Ruby, and Thomas Schroeder.

I sincerely thank my publisher, John Wiley & Sons, and editors, Susan McDermott, Jennifer MacDonald, and Stacey Fischkelta.

# CHAPTER 1

# So You Want to Be a Global Nonprofit?

## 1.1 What Do You *Really* Want to Accomplish?

Why are you passionate about getting involved with global issues? Have you observed a need that tugs at your heartstrings? Do you want to make a measurable impact? Do you want to experience the personal rewards that come from helping people in need? Do you feel driven to make a difference by doing something no one else is doing?

These are questions to ponder before launching a nonprofit organization that works across borders. The answer to each of these questions may lead you to a different kind of organization. For example, you may be able to have the greatest impact by funding existing programs, while avoiding the administrative costs of operating your own. If you desire a more personal experience, you might consider collaborating with an existing organization by providing volunteer support as well as funding. On the other hand, you may have a strong vision that requires launching your own program in a foreign country. In that case, you must be prepared to devote resources to deal with a host of administrative, legal, and practical matters before you even start operating.

## 1.2   Spectrum of International Activities

You can think about international nonprofit activities on a spectrum, from minimum to maximum levels of foreign engagement. On the minimal end of the spectrum lies the U.S. charity that makes grants to U.S. or foreign organizations that operate, or support operations, in foreign countries. On the other end lies the truly global organization that has offices, employees, and donors around the world. As you move along the spectrum of international activities, you will encounter more complex legal issues and practical challenges. An organization may start at the minimal end and evolve in complexity over time, or it may decide to jump in with both feet from the outset.

### Example: Assisting Orphans in Foreign Countries

To illustrate how a single charitable purpose can be served by operating at different points along the spectrum of international activity, here are four examples of U.S.-based 501(c)(3) organizations that chose different paths to assist orphanages in foreign countries:

1. *Making grants through a foreign intermediary.* Families with Children from China, Inc., of Greater New York (*FCC*), was formed by a group of American families who had adopted children from China and wanted to create educational and cultural programs for adopted children and their families. Recognizing that many of its member families felt a strong desire to help improve the lives of orphans in China, FCC established a program for supporting children in orphanages throughout China by making grants to a China-based organization, the Amity Foundation. Each year, FCC appeals to its members for funding, and works with the Amity Foundation to identify projects and monitor the use of funds it contributes. By using a local country intermediary, FCC is able to further its mission, to improve the lives of children in Chinese orphanages, with minimal administrative costs.

   FCC's experience is discussed further in a case study later in this chapter.

2. *Making grants directly to foreign programs.* Friends of the Orphans (*FOTO*) seeks to improve the lives of orphaned, abandoned, and disadvantaged children by providing support to a network of orphanages throughout Latin America and the Caribbean. FOTO maintains a direct and close relationship with the network of orphanages it supports.

   In addition to providing funds, FOTO actively recruits and places volunteers with specific skills to assist in particular orphanages. FOTO does not maintain its own offices in countries where the orphanages are located. The volunteers FOTO sends are directly responsible to the orphanages, rather than to FOTO.

3. *Operating programs in foreign countries.* World Association for Children and Parents (*WACAP*) is an international adoption organization that also provides support to orphans in a number of countries. In some countries, WACAP maintains a registered office and staff, while in others it avoids the need to establish an office by working with a local NGO or government agency. Ethiopia and Russia are two countries in which WACAP operates directly through a licensed office and locally based staff.

A case study of WACAP appears in Chapter 4.

4. *Raising funds outside the United States.* Half the Sky Foundation (*HTS*) was founded by adoptive parents who wanted to improve the lives of children living in orphanages in China. HTS began by working directly in Chinese government-owned orphanages, helping to train caregivers and teachers. After operating in China for several years, HTS received permission to register its own office in China.

In addition, HTS recognized that its potential base of support extended beyond the United States, as families in a number of other countries had adopted children from China. Many of those families would want to help the children left behind. Within 13 years following its founding, HTS had formed separate fundraising organizations in Canada, Hong Kong, the United Kingdom, and the Netherlands, and was awaiting approval in Australia, allowing it to attract tax-deductible contributions from residents of those countries.

HTS's evolution into a global organization is the subject of Chapter 10.

Each of the organizations described above has to be concerned with a variety of U.S. laws that apply specifically to international activities and, at least to some extent, with the legal requirements of one or more foreign countries. The legal and practical considerations, both U.S. and foreign, become increasingly complex as your organization becomes more directly and deeply involved in operations outside the United States.

The remainder of this chapter provides an overview of the basic models for conducting international activities, and a framework for identifying the legal and practical considerations you'll need to know about. The remaining chapters further explore these models, and delve more deeply into important legal and practical issues.

## 1.3  Overview of International Grantmaking

While international grantmaking entails less complexity, and less administrative cost, than does running a full-fledged operation in a foreign country, grantmaking itself runs across a spectrum of activity. As you become more directly engaged with foreign organizations, you will face more legal and practical complexity.

For purposes of this discussion, international grantmaking includes any form of support that is intended for use outside the United States for a charitable (501(c)(3)) purpose. Grantmaking may take the form of providing cash or gifts in kind. Grants may be made directly to individuals, local nongovernment organizations (*NGOs*) that provide direct services, or to foreign governments.

If you are contemplating international grantmaking, you need to think about whether you want to work with an intermediary organization, which may be based in the United States or in a foreign country. Alternatively, you may want to provide funds directly to organizations that operate their own programs in foreign countries.

An intermediary organization is one that provides funds to, and typically monitoring of, programs operated in one or more foreign countries by foreign organizations or governmental bodies. Working with an intermediary can be a great way for a nonprofit to enter the international arena. You will avoid the need to manage personnel remotely, to comply with local laws, and to deal with all of the administrative complexities of delivering services, or even sending funds, overseas. At the same time, this can be a way for you to learn about how to work in a particular geographic area. By working with an experienced organization whose mission is similar to yours, you can learn a lot about what a particular population needs, and how to serve those needs most effectively.

Ultimately, you may decide that working with one or more U.S. or foreign intermediaries, or even funding foreign organizations that directly operate programs, strikes the right balance. This can afford your organization an opportunity to make a real impact without enormous administrative effort and costs. You can leverage what others have already learned, giving your dollars maximum impact.

The U.S. legal requirements for international grantmaking differ depending on whether the grantmaking organization is classified as a so-called *public charity* or *private foundation*. Chapter 2 deals with public charities, while Chapter 3 deals with private foundations.

If you desire more direct involvement, by operating your own foreign programs, you will need to be prepared to devote significantly more time and resources. You will face practical, and often complex, questions about how best to deliver services to the intended population. You will also need to deal with a host of legal and practical issues, in the United States and abroad. Chapters 4 through 7 explore models for operating foreign programs directly, while Chapters 8 and 9 address additional legal and practical considerations you are likely to encounter, in the United States and abroad.

## Funding through a U.S.-Based Intermediary

At one end of the grantmaking spectrum, your organization may choose to support a U.S.-based 501(c)(3) organization that makes contributions to foreign organizations. This can be a good way to start if your organization has no existing relationships in the country you want to work in. By working with a U.S.-based organization, you can learn a lot about the opportunities and challenges involved in supporting programs in a particular country. In fact, you don't even need to have formed your own 501(c)(3) organization to get started this way.

There are some large U.S.-based organizations that support a variety of interest fields and provide a wide range of services. These organizations frequently operate as so-called *donor-advised funds* (*see* section 2.5), accepting contributions from donors who make non-binding requests that the funds be granted to particular foreign organizations. For example, Give2Asia (www .give2asia.org) operates in more than 20 countries throughout Asia, and maintains staff and/or advisors in each country. Give2Asia will provide you with advice and assistance to decide which programs you wish to support. It also devotes resources to seeking out worthy recipients of aid, vetting those organizations and monitoring the use of funds. This relieves your organization of the legal, and practical, need to exercise extensive oversight, allowing you to devote your scarce resources to the programs you are supporting.

A few other large, U.S.-based intermediaries are Charities Aid Foundation (www.cafamerica.org), Tides Foundation (www.tides.org), and United Way International (worldwide.unitedway.org).[1] Of course, you may also know of a smaller 501(c)(3) organization that funds, or even directly operates, in the geographic area where you want to work. You can start out by funding such an organization as a way to learn about the local environment.

A U.S. intermediary will most likely charge administrative fees. These fees may include a one-time set-up fee, and an annual fee based on a percentage of assets held in a fund a donor has created. While the fees may seem high, you should consider what it would cost your organization to administer a cross-border grantmaking program. After assessing the costs of complying with the requirements outlined in Chapter 2 or 3 (as appropriate to your organization), you may find that working through a U.S. intermediary is a cost-effective way to achieve your purposes.

While funding through a U.S.-based intermediary is a relatively easy way to get started with supporting programs outside the United States, the trade-off is that you will not experience a direct relationship with the foreign programs you want to support. Moreover, these U.S. intermediary organizations cannot make a legally binding commitment to direct your funds to the foreign organization or project you select. You can only recommend that the organization use your contribution in the way you desire. This is explained further in Chapter 2.

## Funding through a Foreign Intermediary

If you choose to fund a foreign, rather than a U.S. intermediary, you will need to form your own U.S.-based 501(c)(3) organization in order to attract contributions that are tax-deductible for U.S residents. A foreign country intermediary can serve as the eyes and ears on the ground for your organization by helping to vet potential projects, and it can assist with monitoring the use of funds.

There are multitudes of foreign intermediary organizations that have developed expertise in providing aid to service providers in their local countries.[2] Many of these foreign intermediary organizations operate like community foundations, and can direct contributions to particular fields of interest. These intermediaries have staff and/or advisors, as well as experience in the countries they serve. If your organization does not have the resources to carefully vet and monitor the local country organizations you support, an intermediary organization may give you the greatest bang for your buck. Or, it may allow you to start pursuing your mission while learning what you need to know about working in the country of your choice.

Of course, even if you choose to work with a large, well-respected foreign intermediary, your organization will need to adopt policies and procedures to ensure that your funds are used for the intended purposes, and to comply with U.S. laws (discussed in Chapters 2 and 3). Stories of disappearing funds are rampant in the world of international aid. Two notorious examples of extensive misuse of charitable funds occurred in 2011 in China, where, as reported by the South China Morning Post, two of China's largest charities, the Red Cross Society of China and the China Charity Federation, were found to have improperly channeled charitable funds to private business interests.[3]

The following case study is an example of one organization that did its homework and found a foreign intermediary that served its objectives. The result was a long-term relationship in which the U.S. funder participated in project development, and even initiated projects. Sustaining such a relationship is not an easy task, but neither is operating a foreign program of your own. The key point here is to think about what you are prepared to take on, and how you can best achieve your objectives with the resources you have.

## Case Study: Families with Children from China

Families with Children from China, Inc., of Greater New York (www.fccny .org), known as FCC, is a 501(c)(3) organization, based in New York City, formed during the mid-1990s by a group of families who had adopted children from China. These families wanted to provide support to other adoptive families and educate the public about adoption. In addition, a number of FCC's early members had visited Chinese orphanages while adopting their children, and they wanted to help improve orphanage conditions for children left behind. To explore alternatives for providing assistance to children in Chinese orphanages, a group of FCC members formed a committee they called the *Charitable Initiatives Committee*.

## Setting Criteria

Before they began to research alternative ways of providing assistance, FCC's Charitable Initiatives Committee established certain criteria that would help guide their decision-making:

- *Be culturally sensitive, and listen to what the need is.* A number of FCC members had previous experience in the Peace Corps and other foreign development efforts, and believed it was critical to avoid imposing their own notions of what was needed. These members wanted to work with Chinese orphanage directors to help bring about improvements that the orphanage personnel would embrace.
- *Be realistic about time and travel commitments.* The committee recognized that FCC members were busy professional parents with young children. It would not be feasible to sustain a program that required FCC members to spend significant time in China, or even one that required full-time management from the United States.
- *The impact must be visible.* FCC members wanted the ability to see a direct impact on the lives of children.

## Exploring Alternatives

Having set criteria, the committee began to look at alternative ways of providing assistance to Chinese orphanages. The group quickly dismissed the possibility of operating their own program in China. Not only would that require time commitments and resources FCC didn't have, but also the group recognized that there was no member with experience running a nonprofit organization with international activities. Starting one was simply too much to take on. In addition, FCC's members wanted to work in cooperation with existing orphanage programs to be sure that they were responding to the local perception of what was needed.

The committee considered providing medical or baby supplies to orphanages. However, it would be impossible to be sure that the supplies actually reached the children in need, and therefore it would not be possible to see the impact.

Finally, the committee arrived at the idea of partnering with an organization that was already working within Chinese orphanages. The group surveyed U.S.-based adoption agencies to see whether any of them had started such a program, but did not find any (although in subsequent years a number of adoption agencies would have such programs). Eventually, the committee learned about the Amity Foundation (*Amity*), an independent (*NGO*) charitable foundation based in China that promotes education, health, and social services within China.

It appeared that FCC could satisfy its criteria by funding projects operated by Amity. Amity was run by Chinese nationals who would be sensitive to cultural norms and could easily communicate with orphanage directors to understand the children's needs. FCC members would not have to make undue time commitments, and Amity's reports would provide visibility into the impact of FCC's funding.

## Performing Due Diligence

As of the time FCC contacted Amity in 1996, Amity's program in Chinese orphanages was quite small. However, Amity had been operating other programs in China since 1985, and it had a proven track record in delivering social services. FCC was able to confirm this through the Ford Foundation, one of the few American foundations operating in China at that time.

Having determined that FCC could work with Amity to address the needs of Chinese orphanages, and with confidence that Amity was a sound organization, FCC decided to proceed with raising funds from its members.

## FCC's Experience Working with a Chinese Foundation

In its first year, FCC raised over $50,000 from its members and made a grant to Amity for orphanage projects. The funds were used to provide surgeries and pay school fees for some children. In addition, Amity started a foster care program whereby children would live with foster families instead of remaining in an orphanage. Based on the report Amity provided at the end of the first year, FCC was pleased to see that its funding had made a direct impact on the lives of children.

In 1997, as FCC contemplated a second grant to Amity, the chair of FCC's Charitable Initiatives Committee made a site visit to see the Amity orphanage programs, and to meet Amity and orphanage personnel. The FCC representative was impressed with the level of knowledge and dedication of Amity's staff, and recommended that FCC continue to fund orphanage projects operated by Amity.

During its second and subsequent grant cycles with Amity, FCC became more deliberate about selecting the projects it would fund, aiming to maximize its impact. FCC was particularly pleased that Amity was interested in working to improve conditions in Chinese orphanages by helping to bring best practices to orphanage care. For example, Amity would hold conferences, within China, bringing volunteer caregivers (called *Grandmas*) together to provide training and sharing of best practices.

Amity personnel also attended conferences held by internationally renowned childcare experts, bringing ideas about best practices back to the orphanages. One such idea led to improvements in foster care among orphanages where Amity worked. When Amity proposed a project that would introduce a new model of foster care, FCC responded enthusiastically. FCC was already aware that foster care in China was often no better, if not worse, than orphanage care. With financial support from FCC, Amity introduced a model of foster care that included education and support for foster parents, as well as oversight and social services intended to ensure that children in foster care received proper nutrition and health care.

Often, a disadvantage of working through an intermediary organization is a loss of ability to influence the selection and implementation of projects. In particular, smaller funders can find themselves overshadowed by those who provide large grants and command greater influence. In the case of FCC and the Amity Foundation, this did not turn out to be the case.

In fact, FCC proposed at least three separate projects to Amity, which agreed to develop and implement the projects. In one instance, FCC identified a need for nursing care in orphanages and asked Amity if it would work with orphanage directors to implement a nursing program for children with medical needs. In another instance, FCC members who had adopted children from Wuhan wanted to assist the orphanage there in connection with its fiftieth anniversary. Although Amity had not been working in that orphanage, or even in that province, Amity agreed to initiate a project there with a mere $10,000 of funding from FCC. In a third instance, a family whose adopted daughter had passed away, wanted to raise funds and provide assistance to the orphanage their daughter had lived in. Again, although Amity was not working in that orphanage, it was willing to work with the orphanage director to address its needs.

FCC views Amity as a true partner, having worked together for 16 years to improve the lives of children living in Chinese orphanages. As FCC's funding began to decline in recent years, due in part to the U.S. economy, FCC became concerned that the programs it had developed with Amity might be too dependent on FCC funding. However, that turned out not to be the case. Amity has been able to sustain its orphanage programs by developing new sources of funding, for example from wealthy Chinese individuals living in China, Taiwan, and Hong Kong.

It is no accident that FCC's funding relationship in China has been so successful. The Charitable Initiatives Committee was deliberate about setting criteria and seeking out a partner that fit those criteria. FCC began cautiously, and evaluated the results as it went. While the committee members were realistic about their time and resource limitations, they were engaged and attentive, carefully building trusted relationships.

## Directly Funding Foreign Programs

If you want to be more involved with foreign projects, you may want to fund one or more foreign organizations that directly operate programs. Here again, you will need to form your own U.S.-based 501(c)(3) organization in order to attract contributions that are tax-deductible for U.S residents.

You might consider forming a so-called *American friends of* organization, for the primary purpose of supporting a particular foreign NGO. Alternatively, your U.S. organization may want to support multiple foreign organizations. In either case, the U.S. grantmaking organization is required to vet its grantees and the projects it funds, and to monitor the use of grant funds. Your U.S. grantmaking organization may choose to become involved in the planning and implementation of the foreign projects it funds, and in some cases may even obtain the right to appoint and remove some or all of a foreign grantee's board members. Alternative ways of structuring such legal relationships are discussed in Chapter 5.

---

## Case Study: Pangea Giving (Pangea)

Pangea (www.pangeagiving.org) is a Washington state-based 501(c)(3) organization that operates as an international giving circle. Its mission is to raise awareness of global issues, study ways to address them, and help people in economically disadvantaged countries around the world.

Pangea was formed by a group of people who, in the wake of the September 2011 terrorist attacks, wanted to become better global citizens. Within less than a decade, they grew into a 50-member organization with a grant portfolio of approximately 20 grantees in Latin America, Africa, and Asia. Through their concerted efforts to educate themselves about world issues and international grantmaking, the members of Pangea have become highly knowledgeable about the substantive issue areas they fund, and the specific needs of populations living in the areas they target. Equally important, as a group they have worked to understand how to have the greatest possible impact with their modest dollars, and how to ensure that the funds they give are used for the intended purposes.

Pangea's strategy is to make a significant impact through small grants to carefully selected foreign organizations that can show demonstrable success in tackling specific problems in rural communities. Every Pangea member must make a relatively modest minimum annual contribution of $2,000, although some members contribute more. Out of the total raised each year, approximately 10 percent is devoted to administrative costs and the remainder, approximately $125,000, is awarded in grants. The average grant is approximately $6,000, and a typical grantee has a budget of $100,000 or less.

---

What makes Pangea successful? Some of the critical success factors for Pangea are:

- *Highly engaged members.* Pangea's members, on the whole, have significant time and resources to devote to the process of selecting and monitoring grant recipients. They also have a love of travel. Members regularly travel to far-flung corners of the world to visit prospective grantees, and to monitor the use of grants. Collectively, they spend many hours identifying prospects, reviewing proposals, and monitoring results.
- *Collaborative decision making.* The Pangea model of grantmaking is highly collaborative. There is a committee, or *pod,* dedicated to each of the three regions (Latin America, Africa, and Asia) in which Pangea makes grants. Pod members fully vet proposals, meet to discuss the applicants, and ultimately make recommendations to the full membership. Sometimes, but not always, one or more pod members conduct a site visit during the due diligence process. At an annual meeting of members, the pods present their recommendations to the full membership, which then votes, usually to approve the pods' recommendations, but occasionally rejecting a recommendation or requesting more information. This lengthy process helps ensure that grant proposals receive careful review.
- *Research and member education.* The members of Pangea recognize that, in order to have a positive impact in a foreign country, it is critical to understand the most critical needs of a local population and how they can be addressed. Equally important is understanding what has and has not worked in a particular area, and why. Pangea places strong emphasis on educating members so that the entire group can make informed funding decisions.
- *Relationships with U.S. and foreign NGOs.* From the outset, Pangea members appreciated the importance of developing a network of relationships with various U.S. and foreign-based NGOs working in the regions that Pangea targets. Pangea understands that the small community-based organizations it funds do not operate in isolation, but fit into a larger web of assistance in a particular region.
- *A realistic perspective on the group's strengths and limitations.* Pangea concedes that it is ambitious in funding organizations in three very distinct regions of the globe. At the same time, the members know that to be knowledgeable and effective, they need to narrow the geographic focus within each region, and target specific issue areas. The group has limited its reach in Latin America to Guatemala, southern Mexico, and Haiti. In Africa, it focuses on Kenya and Tanzania, and in Asia, Pangea concentrates on Nepal, Cambodia, and the Thai-Burma border.

- *Gradual start-up and slow growth.* During the organization's early years, Pangea's members decided that its resources should be spent directly on grantmaking and education, rather than on creating a legal structure. For that reason, Pangea initially found a U.S. 501(c)(3) organization that was willing to act as an intermediary for grantmaking purposes. Pangea members would conduct full due diligence and recommend grants to the intermediary organization, which would then review Pangea's materials and decide whether to approve the grants. Funds would flow to the intermediary organization, which would then formally make grants upon the recommendation of Pangea.

By working with an intermediary organization during the initial phase, Pangea had time to test its model and develop a solid membership base, thereby ensuring financial sustainability before committing the resources required to create and sustain a separate 501(c)(3) organization.

## 1.4   Directly Operating Foreign Programs

Direct foreign operations run across their own spectrum, with foreign country activities ranging from collaboration with a foreign organization to operating an independent program. At some point, your organization may engage a foreign consultant to oversee the operation. Later, perhaps it will hire a full-time employee. This may require registrations or permissions. Once registered, the organization may have tax obligations, or may obtain tax-exempt status. It may have to withhold employment taxes and pay social taxes on behalf of its employees. Even if the organization is exempt from income taxes on contributions it receives, it may have to pay value added taxes (*VAT*) on purchases it makes. There may be import duties on goods shipped into the country.

If you are hiring outside the United States, or even sending U.S. staff or volunteers, you may need or want to create a separate, foreign nonprofit corporation, or something similar to a nonprofit corporation under the particular foreign country's laws. You will still need to maintain a separate U.S. 501(c)(3) organization, assuming you want to raise funds from U.S. taxpayers. You may want the organization you founded in the United States to have some form of control over the foreign operations. Or, you may want the foreign organization to operate autonomously but coordinate with the U.S. organization in setting strategy. You can usually achieve the relationship you want, but how you do it will require knowledge of the foreign country's laws, and how they interact with U.S. legal considerations. You will need to work with both U.S. and foreign attorneys. This is discussed in Chapter 5. Now, you can envision your hard-won contributions going to pay legal fees before you have even started to operate a program!

By the time you have calculated all of the costs of maintaining a local office, and considered the costs of hiring attorneys, and perhaps other consultants, to help you comply with foreign requirements, you may conclude that you're better off partnering with an established organization. Or, you may decide it makes sense to launch your own foreign operation because your organization is uniquely suited to deliver the program you envision.

Regardless of where you end up, working through all of these issues in advance will help your organization to decide what is the most efficient way to make use of the resources it has.

The following case study is an example of one organization that decided to widen its reach beyond the United States, by contributing its knowledge and expertise, to help foreign organizations to replicate its programs in their own countries.

## Case Study: SightLife—Scaling Local Operations for Global Impact

SightLife (www.sightlife.org) is a U.S.-based 501(c)(3) organization whose mission is to eliminate corneal blindness through the process of eye banking, which is the recovery and placement of eye tissue used in cornea transplants. Since it began operating in 1969 (initially as the Northwest Lions Eye Bank), SightLife has provided corneal tissue for transplant throughout the western United States. By 2009, SightLife was the leading eye bank in the United States, filling 100 percent of the need in the U.S. regions it served. At the same time, SightLife recognized that it was serving only a tiny portion of the 10 million people in need of cornea transplants throughout the world.

### Determining How to Serve a Larger Population

SightLife's CEO, Monty Montoya, and the board of directors, realized that by working with partners in foreign countries, SightLife could make far more progress toward curing corneal blindness throughout the world than it could by expanding its own eye bank operations across the globe. Beginning in 2009, SightLife embarked on an effort to leverage its knowledge and experience in eye banking by identifying foreign partners that could make use of SightLife's support to develop scalable, self-sustaining programs.

In its 2010 Annual Report, SightLife estimated that, by the end of 2011, SightLife's worldwide partners would be serving more transplant patients than those served directly by SightLife, and eventually the number served by worldwide partners would eclipse SightLife's own numbers by 100-fold, and even 1,000-fold.

## Moving from Local to International Organization

Eye banking is a local process. It requires surgeons to perform transplants, and hospital facilities that can support them. A local eye bank must work with hospitals to identify potential donors, employ counselors to reach out to families of potential donors, employ technicians to recover corneal tissue, and maintain a network of surgeons who can perform transplants.

SightLife had operated locally for 40 years. The plan developed in 2009 called for SightLife to become an international organization by helping foreign partners to develop local programs in their own countries. SightLife would support the creation and growth of effective and efficient eye banks by providing strategic, technical, and financial assistance with every aspect of the eye banking process. Funding would be conditioned on meeting specific milestones. The package of support that SightLife developed to support its foreign partners became known internally as *eye bank in a box*.

## Deciding Where to Go

With limited resources, and with requests for assistance coming from all parts of the globe, SightLife quickly realized that it needed to be intentional about where it could have maximum impact. It hired Tim Schottman, a former Starbucks executive, to serve as Chief Global Officer, leading the global expansion. Tim approached global expansion as if it were a business initiative, beginning with an analysis of some past projects, not all of which had been successful, to come up with a set of criteria for evaluating geographical areas and potential partners.

SightLife conducted market research to determine need, measured by estimates of corneal blindness by country throughout the world. The next step was to focus on the supply side. In each country where the need was great, was there an adequate supply of hospitals and eye surgeons to harvest corneal tissue and perform transplants?

The analyses revealed that approximately 7 million people in India suffer from corneal blindness in one or both eyes, and that India has a functional health care system with an existing network of approximately 400 corneal surgeons. The combination of those conditions led SightLife to identify India as the country where an investment of resources could have the greatest impact in restoring sight to millions of people.

Having identified its primary geographical focus, SightLife developed a set of criteria for identifying partners that could make the best use of SightLife's support, scale their operations, and ultimately become self-sustaining. The criteria required, for example, that an eye bank have a professional manager to oversee operations.

Having laid careful groundwork for success, in 2010 SightLife established partnerships with five eye banks in India. In addition to providing funding, SightLife helped install managers, facilitated the hiring of eye donation counselors, and provided training for managers and counselors.

## Establishing a Presence in India

Although SightLife would not directly operate eye banks in India, its engagement with Indian eye banks demanded that SightLife maintain a permanent presence there. This would require forming a separate Indian organization, similar to a U.S. nonprofit corporation. SightLife decided to form a so-called *section 25 company*, a commonly used form of Indian nonprofit organization, with SightLife as the sole member. While the board is comprised of Indian nationals, SightLife, as sole member, has the ultimate power to appoint and remove board members.

In India, as in many developing countries, foreign organizations often face challenges trying to identify all of the requirements to establish operations. Requirements are not always formalized in laws or regulations, and government officials may have significant discretion. Consulting with multiple attorneys can result in conflicting advice. Precious time can be wasted when government bodies reject applications because of simple failures that could have been avoided.

SightLife faced all of these challenges in establishing a nonprofit company. In particular, the process for obtaining permission to receive foreign grants was confusing and cumbersome. India's Foreign Contribution Regulation Act (*FCRA*) requires that all nonprofit organizations in India wishing to receive funds from outside India must register with the government, agree to accept foreign contributions only through designated banks, and file reports that include information about the source and intended purpose of the funds.

Having operated as a local organization for 40 years, it is, as of this book's publication, still a new a challenge for SightLife to work with a foreign affiliate that has its own board of directors. SightLife continues to work toward striking the optimal balance between central control and local autonomy, while meeting legal requirements in both countries.

The next step for SightLife's Indian company will be to become registered to receive tax-favored contributions from within India. SightLife believes that, among India's wealthier individuals, there is capacity and willingness to contribute to projects aimed at curing corneal blindness.

## Hiring a Country Director

Hiring a full-time director to manage SightLife's Indian operations was more of a practical than a legal challenge. Bringing SightLife's American management model into India proved to be difficult. Based on its own experience, SightLife knew that it needed a strong manager who would not be subservient to doctors, but finding such an individual within India seemed impossible. Ultimately, SightLife was able to transcend the cultural divide by hiring an Indian national who had been educated in the United States and, in fact, had become a U.S. citizen. The individual was able to obtain a visa to work for SightLife in India.

## Developing Information Systems

SightLife views the development of information technology (*IT*) systems as a critical piece in helping its foreign partners scale their operations. Having consistent, accurate data from its partners is essential to SightLife's operational consulting and performance comparisons. It is standard practice today for any multinational business to have systems that facilitate shared, real-time measurements. It is still rare, however, to find such systems across a network of nonprofit organizations. To this end, SightLife is developing a web-based, operational IT system that will track all corneal tissue and provide analysis and performance tracking for all of its partner eye banks.

In addition to developing an operational system, SightLife is developing a national distribution system in India that links surgeons needing corneal tissue with eye banks that have tissue to share, creating an efficient exchange, and improving tissue utilization.

## Moving into Additional Countries

While SightLife intends to focus most of its international efforts on India for the next few years, it is also working to build a network of potential future partners in other countries where the need is great. By 2011, SightLife had alliances in Nepal and Ethiopia, and was exploring opportunities in Latin America.

As SightLife gains experience working in foreign countries, it will continue to develop alliances throughout the world in furtherance of its vision, to eliminate worldwide corneal blindness.

## 1.5  Global Fundraising

On the farthest end of the international activities spectrum lies a complex multinational organization that not only operates its own foreign programs, but also raises funds in one or more countries outside the United States. You may be considering this model if you already know people in other countries who support your mission.

You will probably want your donors to be eligible for whatever tax benefits their resident countries afford. The level of tax benefit available for charitable giving varies widely among countries. In addition, every country that provides tax benefits for charitable contributions is concerned about making sure those contributions are used for the intended purposes. Those concerns are heightened when funds are going outside their borders. As a result, some countries afford tax benefits only for charitable donations that are used within the particular country. Others impose a variety of requirements on a domestic organization that directly receives the contribution.

In most countries, a donor must contribute directly to a separate organization, established under the laws of the donor's resident country, before the funds can flow to a foreign recipient. This means that your organization must either create a separate nonprofit organization in the donor's country, or identify an existing NGO that is willing to raise funds for your foreign program. Each has its pros and cons. Establishing a separate nonprofit corporation (or something similar under a foreign country's laws) adds significant complexity for your organization, but provides you with more control over fundraising strategies and communications.

Once again, you can see that working through the issues ahead of time will allow you to create the structure that provides optimal efficiency for your organization, and helps you avoid taking on complexity that you may not have the resources to manage. Global fundraising is discussed further in Chapter 7. In Chapter 10 we look at how one organization, Half the Sky Foundation, developed a multinational fundraising structure.

## 1.6  Legal Considerations: A Basic Framework

As you think about where you want to operate along the spectrum of international activities, it is important to understand how you can best serve your mission within the context of applicable U.S. and foreign laws. These legal considerations are summarized here and addressed in greater detail in later chapters.

### Obtaining and Maintaining U.S. Tax-Exempt Status

Assuming you wish to attract tax-deductible contributions from U.S. taxpayers, you will need to qualify as a particular type of federal tax-exempt organization, commonly referred to as a 501(c)(3) organization. This book does not delve into all of the requirements and restrictions that apply to 501(c)(3) organizations, nor how to become qualified. There are many resources available to help you with that, and several are listed in Appendix B. This book does, however, address the special rules that apply to 501(c)(3) organizations that engage in international activities.

Keep in mind that 501(c)(3) status means that your organization is exempt from U.S. federal income tax. In most cases, state income tax exemption (in states that have income taxes) follows, either automatically or upon filing of an application. Note, however, that a 501(c)(3) organization may be subject to various non-income taxes, such as employment, property, sales, and/or excise taxes, at the U.S. federal, state, and even local levels. In some cases, you need to apply separately for exemption from these other taxes. In others, there is no applicable exemption. In some states, exemptions from property taxes, and/or sales and use taxes, apply to specific activities, but not to the entire scope of activities that can qualify for federal income tax exemption under 501(c)(3).

**CROSS-BORDER GRANTMAKING**    If your 501(c)(3) organization is sending funds or goods to a foreign country, you will need to adopt procedures to be sure that the contribution is used for the purposes for which your organization was granted tax-exemption (so-called *501(c)(3) purposes*, sometimes referred to as *charitable purposes*). The particular procedures you need to adopt for cross-border grantmaking depend on whether your 501(c)(3) organization is classified as a so-called *public charity* or *private foundation*. These classifications, and the applicable procedures, are discussed in Chapters 2 and 3.

**FOREIGN ACTIVITIES**    If you are directly operating foreign programs, you can still qualify as a 501(c)(3) organization. It is well established that an organization can qualify for 501(c)(3) status even though all or part of its activities are conducted outside the United States.[4] In fact, by directly conducting foreign programs, you will be in a good position to monitor and control the use of the funds your organization devotes toward carrying out its purposes. At the same time, your organization's foreign, as well as domestic, activities must comply with all of the 501(c)(3) requirements. It can be particularly challenging to enforce internal policies and procedures to ensure that your foreign operations comply with 501(c)(3) requirements, such as:

- Avoiding supporting any terrorist activities.
- Avoiding the provision of improper benefits to insiders, or other private interests.
- Avoiding participation in excessive lobbying or prohibited election-related communication.

You will also want to monitor whether, and the extent to which, your organization engages in any business activity that could trigger U.S. and/or foreign tax. All of these considerations are discussed further in sections 4.8 and 4.10.

In addition, it's important to keep in mind that a 501(c)(3) organization is tax-exempt only in the United States. If you establish an office and hire employees in a foreign country, you should not assume that your organization will qualify for tax-exempt status in that country. It may qualify for exemption from some but not all applicable taxes, and you may have to comply with cumbersome requirements.

## Foreign Legal and Practical Concerns

Once you begin to operate directly in a foreign country, for example by sending staff, hiring locally, and/or registering an office, you will need to understand how that country's laws affect your operations. However, even if you are merely considering funding a foreign NGO, you may run into restrictions and unforeseen expenses. Indeed, in recent years there has been a trend toward increasing numbers of countries enacting, or considering, laws that restrict the operation and funding of nonprofit organizations within their borders, particularly those that receive foreign support.[5] When exploring the feasibility of operating in a foreign country, you should inquire not only about the laws that apply to your organization, but also about proposed legislation.

Listed further on are some important questions you need to ask before launching operations in a foreign country. Each of these topics is addressed in greater detail in later chapters.

It would be impossible to summarize the laws of all foreign countries, and doing so would be fruitless given the rapid pace of change, particularly in developing countries. Rather, this book aims to arm nonprofit organizations and their leaders with the questions they need to ask up-front in order to shape their international activities to best fit their purposes and available resources.

**DOES THE FOREIGN COUNTRY RESTRICT THE INFLOW OF FUNDS OR GOODS?** In recent years, there has been a disturbing trend among a significant number of countries to restrict foreign funding of local country NGOs. These restrictions come in a variety of forms, including prohibitions on the receipt of foreign funds for particular purposes, requirements that funds be channeled through governmental entities or banks, government approval requirements, and the imposition of prohibitive taxes on the receipt of foreign funds.

For example, Venezuela prohibits the receipt of foreign funding by organizations that have political purposes. Some countries permit their NGOs to receive foreign funding, but require advance governmental approval.

India, China, Indonesia, Egypt, Jordan, Eritrea, Belarus, and Uzbekistan fall into this category. Some of these countries, including India, Uzbekistan, and Eritrea, go even further, to require that foreign funds be routed through government-owned ministries or banks.[6]

Local country embargoes may prevent the importation of specific goods into a particular country. An organization that sends goods overseas must also investigate whether the goods will be subject to import duties or VAT, and if so, whether there is a way to reduce or eliminate those costs.

**WILL THE FOREIGN COUNTRY ALLOW THE KINDS OF ACTIVITIES YOU WANT TO CONDUCT?**   If your organization intends to operate its own programs in a foreign country, you will need to investigate whether your activities are permitted. Restrictions on a nonprofit's activities in a particular country can take a variety of forms. In some countries, foreign organizations are subject to restrictions on their ability to operate. Azerbaijan, Turkmenistan, and Uganda are examples of countries that make it very difficult for foreign nonprofit organizations to operate within their borders.[7]

Some countries prohibit certain kinds of activities, such as the promotion of democracy and/or human rights. In some countries, policies tend to change quickly, and your organization can find itself shut down, or worse, overnight. Laws and policies may even differ from region to region within a particular country.

It is critical to talk with NGOs that are already working in a particular location to understand the environment and assess the risks.

**WHAT REGISTRATIONS AND LICENSES WILL YOU NEED?**   Even if a particular country's laws allow the activities you want to conduct, you may need a registration or license. You will need to investigate applicable requirements, and what it will cost to obtain and maintain licenses and registrations. In the United States, as well as in Canada and much of Europe, we take for granted that we have the right to create organizations as long as we satisfy the legal filing and registration requirements. This is not true everywhere. There are many countries in which government officials have broad discretion to permit or deny applications to form organizations, and they can use that discretion to prevent the establishment of any organization they perceive as a threat. China falls into this category.

**SHOULD YOU CREATE A SEPARATE NONPROFIT ORGANIZATION IN A FOREIGN COUNTRY?**   Once you have a registration or license in a foreign country, you have an official presence in that particular country, and your organization may be subject to a number of legal requirements as well as potential liabilities, including taxes. At this point, you should explore whether you are better off forming a separate foreign nonprofit organization (such as something similar to a nonprofit corporation under the foreign country's laws), to collaborate with the U.S. organization. If you form a separate foreign nonprofit organization, how much control might you lose? Are there requirements regarding local control of the organization? There is no one-size-fits-all approach to this, but it is important to think it through up-front.

**HOW WILL YOU STAFF YOUR FOREIGN OFFICE? CONSIDER EMPLOYMENT LAWS AND VISA REQUIREMENTS** If you decide to hire employees to work in a foreign country, you need to understand how that country's employment laws may affect your organization. Is it difficult to lay people off? Will you be subject to severance pay requirements? If you decide to send U.S. residents to work in a foreign location, you will need to understand and allow time for meeting visa requirements. If you are staffing foreign operations with U.S. individuals, taxes and expenses may add significantly to the overall costs.

**DOES THE FOREIGN COUNTRY HAVE ANTI-TERRORISM RULES THAT APPLY TO NONPROFIT ORGANIZATIONS?** Anti-terrorism rules, in the U.S. and many foreign countries, have become a significant force that shapes the way international nonprofit organizations operate. U.S. anti-terrorism laws, discussed in Chapter 8, have served as a model for many other countries. Some countries have adopted regulations and guidelines that are similar, although not identical, to those of the United States, while in other countries nonprofit organizations are subject to very different restrictions. Nonprofit organizations need to pay close attention to the requirements of each country in which they operate or provide funding.

**DOES THE FOREIGN COUNTRY HAVE ANTI-BRIBERY RULES?** It may seem obvious to you that bribery is illegal and unethical, but you may be surprised to discover that many foreign countries, along with the United States, have anti-bribery laws that are quite complex, often with severe consequences for violations. At the same time, you may well be operating in an environment where bribery is the norm, and it's very difficult to get anything done without it. Don't fall into the trap of thinking that your mission justifies the means. Before launching a program in a foreign country, you need to understand the laws that apply to you, and assess whether you can be effective in that environment.

**DOES THE FOREIGN COUNTRY RESTRICT LOBBYING OR POLITICAL ACTIVITY?** Many countries restrict lobbying and political activities by nonprofit organizations, particularly those that receive foreign support. Do not assume that a particular country's definitions of lobbying and political activities are the same as those applicable to 501(c)(3) organizations (described in Chapter 8). You could find yourself entirely within the IRS restrictions, yet in violation of some foreign restriction. Penalties can be harsh. No organization wants to be ejected from a country, or worse, have an employee jailed there. If you are working in a high-risk country, you will be well advised to talk with other NGOs to understand the environment.

**HOW CAN YOU PROTECT TRADEMARKS AND OTHER INTELLECTUAL PROPERTY IN A PARTICULAR FOREIGN COUNTRY?**   You will need to consider whether you have valuable trademarks, copyrighted materials, or other so-called *intellectual property*. If so, you may need to take steps to protect your organization from others who might seek to use and profit from your valuable intellectual property.

**ARE YOU SUBJECT TO PRIVACY PROTECTION REQUIREMENTS?**   Many countries, notably throughout Europe, regulate the collection, use, and transfer of personal information. Nonprofit organizations may become subject to these laws, for example, when they maintain databases of members or beneficiaries of their programs.

**WHAT FOREIGN TAXES APPLY, AND HOW CAN YOU MINIMIZE THEM?**   As your organization moves along the spectrum of international activities, it is more likely to become subject to a variety of foreign taxes. Some taxes may be an unavoidable cost of operating, and others may be legally avoidable with some careful planning.

Creating a regular presence in a local country, for example by leasing an office, hiring an employee, or even sending U.S. staff or volunteers for extended periods, may subject a U.S.-based organization to that country's income tax. Individual employees that spend extended time in a foreign country, as well as locally hired employees, may become subject to individual income tax, and the organization may have income tax withholding and/or social tax obligations. Organizations that send goods in kind to foreign countries may also have to deal with customs duties.

Many countries have *value added tax* (VAT) regimes. These taxes are often unfamiliar to Americans. A U.S.-based organization that engages in purchasing or selling in a foreign country may well need to familiarize itself with VAT compliance requirements.

**HOW CAN YOU FIND THE RIGHT LAWYER IN A PARTICULAR FOREIGN COUNTRY?** Once you have decided to operate in a foreign country, you will need to consult with a lawyer. Taking the time to find the right lawyer in the right location can save you significant time and money.

Keep in mind that, in many countries, local laws and policies may play just as big a role, if not bigger, than national-level laws and policies. Find a local lawyer who works in the locality where you intend to operate. You should also talk to other organizations working in that area to find out about unwritten practices and requirements.

## Affording Tax Benefits for U.S. or Foreign Donors

It's important to be aware, that (with very limited exceptions, discussed in Chapter 7) U.S. tax law affords an income tax deduction only for funds contributed to a 501(c)(3) organization formed in the United States (that is, under the laws of any state or the District of Columbia, or any U.S. possession). On the other hand, U.S. citizens and residents are eligible for estate and gift tax deductions for charitable gifts and bequests made directly to foreign organizations, subject to certain conditions.[8]

In addition, to ensure that donors' contributions are eligible for income tax deductions, a U.S. 501(c)(3) organization must avoid acting simply as a mere pass-through for contributions destined overseas. Your organization may have donors who want you to commit to regranting their contributions to a specific foreign organization or individual. You will need to put some procedures in place to be sure that your organization retains sufficient control over the funds so that you can be sure they are used for 501(c)(3) purposes. This is discussed further in Chapter 2.

If your 501(c)(3) organization is sending funds outside the United States, you will probably want to form the organization as a nonprofit corporation and not a charitable trust. This is because, due to a historical quirk in the federal tax law, U.S. corporations that make contributions to 501(c)(3) organizations can take income tax deductions only if the recipient organization is a corporation and not a trust.[9] So, unless your organization is a family foundation, you will probably want to retain flexibility in the event that some corporation wants to contribute funds to further your overseas mission, and/or in the event that your donors are eligible for matching contributions from their corporate employers.

If you seek to raise funds in multiple countries, you need to consider how you can ensure that your donors are eligible for whatever tax benefits are afforded by their country of residence. Most countries provide some form of tax benefit for charitable giving, but the level of tax benefit, and therefore value of tax benefit to the donor, varies widely among countries. Not all countries afford tax benefits for contributions that are destined for overseas projects, and those that do often impose restrictions on the use of the funds, the destination, and/or the way the fundraising organization is controlled or operated.

If you want to raise funds from non-U.S. citizens or residents, in most cases you should not ask them to contribute directly to your U.S. 501(c)(3) organization. Rather, with limited exceptions, you will need to explore creating a separate foreign organization (such as something similar to a nonprofit corporation under the laws of the foreign country) in the country in which you want to raise funds. Alternatively, you may be able to work with an established organization to raise funds in another country.

The key point here is, do your homework. If you want to raise funds from non-U.S. donors, find out whether tax benefits are important. Then determine whether, and how, you can create a structure that affords tax benefits for donors who support your cause.

These issues are explored further in Chapter 7.

## Complying with U.S. Laws that Regulate International Activities

While a myriad of U.S. laws could come into play, we will focus on those that most commonly apply to international nonprofits. These requirements become more complex as you move along the spectrum of international activities. A nonprofit organization that is formed in the United States is subject to various U.S. laws that regulate its activities, even when the activities are entirely outside the United States.

Following is a list of important U.S. legal considerations for U.S.-based international nonprofit organizations. Each of these is discussed in more detail throughout this book. Of course, any particular nonprofit organization may be subject to a variety of additional federal, state and local laws and regulations.

**ANTI-TERRORISM REQUIREMENTS**   All organizations that have international activities, including grantmakers, must take steps to avoid supporting terrorist activities, even inadvertently. Since the terrorist attacks of September 11, 2001, a number of federal laws, regulations, and policies have been implemented, providing severe sanctions against U.S. organizations and individuals that provide funds or assistance to terrorist organizations. Under some of these programs, a U.S. charitable organization may have its assets frozen, or may face civil or criminal penalties, for unknowingly providing funds, in-kind donations, or even humanitarian assistance to foreign terrorist organizations.

**EXPORT CONTROLS AND ANTI-BOYCOTT LEGISLATION**   The U.S. federal government imposes a complex web of restrictions on the exportation of certain goods and technologies to foreign countries. Some of these restrictions are country-specific. Some exemptions are available for humanitarian aid, but it may be necessary to obtain a license.

**U.S. ANTI-BRIBERY LAW**   It can be very difficult to operate in many developing countries, where bribery is a way of life. You may hear the phrase, *everybody does it*. Regardless of where you draw your ethical lines, U.S. law imposes criminal penalties for bribing foreign officials. The mere fact that something is common practice in a particular country does not mean you can do it without risking serious sanctions.

**U.S. RESIDENTS WORKING OVERSEAS**   U.S. citizens and permanent residents (as well as those who meet certain residency tests for U.S. federal income tax purposes) are subject to U.S. federal income taxes, even on income they earn while working outside the United States. They may also have to pay taxes in a foreign country. When thinking about how to staff foreign operations, for example with U.S. or local country nationals, you need to take into account U.S. and foreign tax considerations. It may turn out to be very expensive to staff foreign operations with U.S. individuals, due to taxes as well as travel and other expenses.

## 1.7   The Importance of Vigilance

No matter how important your mission is, and no matter how much effort you devote to properly structuring your organization, things can go horribly wrong if you don't have the right people and processes in place. Just ask Madonna, the celebrity singer, or Greg Mortenson, the best-selling author of *Three Cups of Tea,* which describes his experiences while building schools in Afghanistan.

Madonna raised millions of dollars from celebrities in the United States for the laudable purpose of creating a girls' school in Malawi, where very few girls ever attend high school. Yet, despite the good intentions and success in raising funds, the project had to be abandoned after running out of funds amidst allegations of mismanagement and misuse of funds by the charity's executives, both in the United States and in Malawi. Instead of a showcase school, she was left with a lawsuit by former employees in Malawi, and a possible IRS investigation.[10]

Greg Mortenson founded the 501(c)(3) organization, Central Asia Institute (*CAI*), to build schools in Afghanistan, and wrote about CAI's charitable activities in his best-selling book, *Three Cups of Tea.*[11] However, Mortenson and CAI came under fire in 2011 amidst reports that many of the schools he claimed his organization built in Afghanistan were either nonexistent or empty. In some cases, buildings were built, but there was no follow-through with real educational programs.[12]

In addition, the Montana Attorney General launched an investigation into the use of funds contributed to CAI, and ultimately found that funds had been misused for purposes such as Mortenson's personal travel. A settlement with the Montana Attorney General allowed CAI to continue operating, but Mortenson was required to resign as executive director, and the entire board was replaced. Mortenson was required to repay $1 million to CAI to reimburse it for the misuse of funds for personal purposes.[13]

For our purposes here, the lesson is that it's not easy for U.S.-based organizations to manage projects in foreign countries, no matter how well intentioned. To be sure, no nonprofit organization is immune from the risks of misappropriation of funds, loss of focus, or just plain poor execution of programs. However, organizations that operate in the international arena have additional challenges in carrying out their missions. It takes extra vigilance, and resources, to monitor programs that are conducted in foreign countries. The legal landscape, both U.S. and foreign, becomes more complex as operations expand overseas. Meanwhile, board members who are passionate about the mission, but unfamiliar with the foreign terrain, may be all too willing to defer to a knowledgeable founder or chief executive.

## Choose Board Members Carefully

You can see that, when you are operating in the international arena, there's a lot to be on top of. While it may be tempting to choose your board members for their fundraising abilities alone, that strategy will not ensure success for your organization. Madonna, Greg Mortenson, and many other celebrities were great fundraisers, but lacked the vigilance needed to keep their organizations out of trouble. You need board members who pay attention and ask probing questions.

## Follow the Money

Whether your organization is making cross-border grants, or directly operating programs abroad, you need to be vigilant about how funds are being used. Misuse of funds can, of course, incur the wrath of donors, but can also trigger legal problems at the state level, and even loss of federal and/or state tax-exempt status. The IRS and many states' attorneys general are scrutinizing the activities of nonprofit organizations engaged in international activities. Your organization cannot afford to be lacking in so-called *internal controls*, or processes for ensuring that funds are used for their intended purpose.

If your organization is making grants to programs operated by a foreign NGO, you need to insist, up-front and in writing, on financial and narrative updates. Investigate and develop relationships so that you know you are working with people you can trust. Even with that, there is no substitute for first-hand observation. So, if at all possible, have staff, board members, or volunteers make periodic site visits to ensure that your grants are being used for the intended purposes, and the programs you are supporting are operating as expected.

The same concerns exist if your organization is directly operating programs abroad. You will have to rely on people who are on the ground, possibly in a remote location. They may be collaborating NGOs, U.S. staff or volunteers who spend time overseas, or locally hired staff. In any case, the use of funds, and operation of programs, must be monitored. Do not be tempted to expand your operations for the sake of a great mission, at the expense of devoting the necessary resources for careful monitoring of operations.

## 1.8 So, You *Still* Want to Be a Global Nonprofit?

If you are still passionate about pursuing your mission after reading this chapter, then you are ready to learn more. The following chapters provide the information you need to decide which model of international activities is right for you, and will arm you with the questions you'll need to ask as you plan your project. With some careful, up-front attention to legal and practical matters, you are more likely to succeed in turning your vision into reality.

## Notes

1. You can find a more extensive list of U.S. intermediaries on the website of the United States International Grantmaking Project, available at www .usig.org. For a list of organizations that fund projects in Africa, *see* Buchanan, Rob and Jayne Booker, *Making a Difference in Africa: Advice from Experienced Grantmakers* (Arlington, VA: Council on Foundations, 2007), 103, available for purchase at www.africagrantmakers.org/index. asp?PageURL=126#advice_grantmakers.
2. A useful resource for identifying foreign country intermediaries is the website of Worldwide Initiative for Grantmaker Support (WINGS), available at www.wingsweb.org.
3. As reported by Rick Cohen, "Chinese Press Targets Charitable Irregularities in Henan," *Nonprofit Quarterly*, September 7, 2011, available at www .nonprofitquarterly.org/updates/15601-the-chinese-press-targets-charitable-irregularities-in-henan.html.
4. *See* Rev. Rul. 71-460, 1971-2 C.B. 231; Rev. Rul. 68-117, 1968-1 C.B. 251.
5. *See* Douglas Rutzen, "Practice Note: Egypt and the Catalyst Constraint," *International Journal of Not-for-Profit Law* 14, no. 1–2 (April 2012), 49–51, available at www.icnl.org/research/journal/vol14iss1/index.html.
6. "Defending Civil Society," co-authored by International Center for Not-for-Profit Law and World Movement for Democracy Secretariat at the National Endowment for Democracy, *International Journal of Not-for-Profit Law*, 14, no. 3 (September 2012) ("Defending Civil Society Report") 27–29, available at www.icnl.org/research/journal/vol14iss3/art1.html; David Moore and Douglas Rutzen, "Legal Framework for Global Philanthropy: Barriers and Opportunities," *International Journal of Not-for-Profit Law* 13,

no. 1–2 (April 2011), 17–23, available at www.icnl.org/research/journal/vol13iss1/index.htm.

7. Defending Civil Society Report, *supra* note 6, at 17.

8. IRC §§ 2055(a)(2), 2106(a)(2)(A)(ii), 2522(a)(2).

9. IRC § 170(c).

10. *See* Claire Provost, "Madonna's Folly in Malawi," *The Guardian*, March 30, 2011, available at: www.guardian.co.uk/commentisfree/2011/mar/30/madonna-malawi-charity. Subsequently, in 2012, Madonna announced that she was partnering with an existing organization to build multiple schools in Malawi. Meanwhile, millions of dollars that had been contributed for the original project remained unaccounted for. *See* David Smith, "Madonna's new school pledge angers Malawi officials," *The Guardian*, February 23, 2012, available at www.guardian.co.uk/music/2012/feb/23/madonna-schools-pledge-angers-malawi-officials.

11. Mortenson, Greg and David Oliver Relin, *Three Cups of Tea: One Man's Mission to Fight Terrorism and Build Nations . . . One School at a Time* (Perfection Learning, 2007).

12. *See* CBS 60 Minutes segment, "Questions Over Greg Mortenson's Stories," April 17, 2011, available at www.cbsnews.com/2100-18560_162-20054397.html?tag=contentMain;contentBody.

13. *See* Matt Pearce "'Three Cups' Author Must Pay $1 Million to Charity," *Los Angeles Times*, April 5, 2012, available at www.latimes.com/news/nation/nationnow/la-na-nn-greg-mortenson-central-asia-institute-20120405,0,3566022.story.

# CHAPTER 2

# International Grantmaking by Public Charities

C hapters 2 and 3 focus on U.S. requirements that pertain to international grantmaking. In these chapters, we are dealing with 501(c)(3) organizations, formed under U.S. laws, that make grants directly to foreign recipients. If you are making grants to a U.S. intermediary you generally will not need to be concerned with these rules, although the U.S. intermediary will.

There are a number of good sources of information for international grantmakers, including the Council on Foundations (www.cof.org) and its U.S. International Grantmaking Project (www.usig.org). Additional resources are listed in Appendix B. By contrast, there is very little information available for U.S. organizations that directly conduct activities outside the United States. For this reason, the greater part of this book (Chapters 4 through 10) is aimed at organizations that are, or are contemplating, operating foreign programs directly. At the same time, most U.S. organizations that operate foreign programs also engage in some cross-border grantmaking, and therefore need to understand the basic rules discussed in this chapter or Chapter 3 (whichever applies).

For purposes of Chapters 2 and 3, the term *grantmaking* is used to refer to any contribution of funds or in-kind donation (books, clothing, medical supplies, technology, or anything else) made for charitable (that is, 501(c)(3)) purposes. The discussion contemplates that contributions are made to foreign organizations. As a general rule, a U.S. 501(c)(3) organization may also provide charitable aid directly to foreign individuals, subject to the rules discussed in Chapters 2 and 3.[1]

A 501(c)(3) organization is permitted to support foreign programs, and in doing so it may use tax-deductible contributions received from U.S. taxpayers.[2] We will see in Chapter 7 that not all countries allow this kind of cross-border giving, and many impose significant restrictions. The United States does, however, impose certain restrictions on cross-border giving to ensure that funds are used for 501(c)(3) purposes. It is critical that your organization comply with these rules; failure to do so could jeopardize your donors' tax deductions, and possibly even jeopardize your organization's tax-exempt status.

## 2.1  Public Charity or Private Foundation: Why Does It Matter?

A 501(c)(3) organization is classified as either a *public charity* or *a private foundation*. All 501(c)(3) organizations are exempt from federal (and often state) income tax and, if established under U.S. laws, can attract tax-deductible funds. However, those 501(c)(3) organizations that are classified as private foundations are subject to a variety of additional restrictions. Contributions to private foundations also receive less generous tax deductions than contributions to public charities. There are many resources that explain all of the requirements and restrictions applicable to private foundations, some of which are listed in Appendix B.

The remainder of this chapter focuses on the U.S. rules applicable to cross-border grantmaking by public charities. Chapter 3 addresses the rules applicable to cross-border grantmaking by private foundations. As discussed in Chapter 3, if your organization is classified as a private foundation, you will face more burdensome requirements in making cross-border grants.

## 2.2  What Is a Public Charity?

An organization may qualify for public charity status by satisfying any of several alternatives. In practice, each of these alternative tests is quite technical.[3] With few exceptions, to avoid being treated as a private foundation an organization must apply to the IRS for recognition as a public charity, generally with its initial application for tax-exempt status. If your organization receives funding from a large number of individual donors, it may be easy to determine that you qualify for public charity status. In many cases, however, it will not be readily apparent whether the organization qualifies as a public charity. It is often advisable to work with an attorney or accountant to make that determination.

An organization can qualify as a public charity by satisfying any of the following alternatives:

- Broad public support test.
- Mission-related revenue test.
- Automatic public charity status.
- Supporting organization.

Each of these is described in the following paragraphs.

## Broad Public Support Test

A broadly supported organization is one that receives at least one-third of its total revenue from gifts, grants, or other contributions from governmental units or the general public.[4] This would include, for example, the charitable organization that receives donations from a broad base of individuals, does not receive fees for services, and does not rely substantially on a few large donors.

This test is quite technical in practice. An organization that relies on a small number of large donors may not meet the one-third requirement. However, some organizations can take advantage of a more flexible *facts and circumstances* test by showing that at least 10 percent of the organization's support comes from government units and the general public, and that the organization makes significant efforts toward reaching out to a broad base of donors.[5]

## Mission-Related Revenue Test

Some organizations receive broad support, not just through contributions, but because they earn revenue, such as service fees and ticket sales proceeds, through the pursuit of their charitable purposes. Some examples of this type of organization are providers of health services, museums, and performing arts organizations. Of course, these organizations must qualify for 501(c)(3) status in the first place, but charging fees for services generally does not preclude that.

To meet this test, an organization must receive more than one-third of its support from a combination of gifts, grants, and contributions or membership fees from governmental units and the general public, plus revenue earned in furtherance of the organization's tax-exempt purposes.[6] In addition, the organization must not earn more than one-third of its support from investment income. This second test prevents an organization from qualifying for public charity status by relying heavily on endowment funds for ongoing support.

## Automatic Public Charity Status

Certain categories of 501(c)(3) organizations are automatically treated as public charities. These include schools (including colleges and universities), churches, and hospitals.[7] It is critical to pay attention to technical definitions and requirements to be sure you qualify under any of these categories. For example, in order to qualify as a school for this purpose, an organization must satisfy certain criteria including maintaining formal instruction, regularly enrolled students, and regular faculty, and adopting certain nondiscrimination policies and procedures.

## Supporting Organization

A 501(c)(3) organization that is supported by a small group of donors may be unable to qualify as a public charity under one of the previous three tests. Such an organization may nevertheless qualify for public charity status as a so-called *supporting organization*.[8] A supporting organization is one that is formed to support one or more other public charities. It must meet certain specific criteria, establishing that the supporting organization has a close relationship with the organization or organizations it supports.

Prior to a 2006 change in the U.S. federal tax law, this was a common way of obtaining public charity status for a U.S. 501(c)(3) organization (a so-called *American friends of* organization, described in section 2.4) formed to support a foreign charity. Today, the primary use of a supporting organization in international grantmaking is to support a U.S. intermediary public charity, which in turn, supports one or more foreign organizations.

## 2.3 Basic Rules for Foreign Grantmaking

Any organization that makes cross-border grants must develop policies and procedures to ensure that funds are used for their intended purposes. The rules that will help shape your policies and procedures are predominantly federal tax requirements, some of which are written into the Internal Revenue Code, Treasury Regulations, written IRS rulings, and court opinions.

In addition, in recent years the U.S. government has become increasingly concerned about the possibility that cross-border grants may be diverted away from charitable purposes, and even into the hands of terrorists. Federal tax laws require that your grants be used solely for 501(c)(3) purposes. If you transfer funds that end up supporting terrorist activity, which, of course, is not a 501(c)(3) purpose, your organization may face severe penalties. *See* section 8.1.

Your application for federal income tax exemption may well be met with a list of questions, and even demands, aimed at assuring the IRS that the funds you send outside U.S. borders cannot be diverted for improper purposes. Once exempt, you may face similar questions if your organization is audited by the IRS. For these reasons, any organization that intends to engage in international grantmaking is well advised to seek legal advice in preparing and organizing documents, such as articles of incorporation and bylaws, developing written grantmaking policies, and preparing the application for tax-exempt status.

## Establish Objective Selection Criteria

To ensure that all grants your organization makes are in furtherance of its 501(c)(3) purposes, the board of directors should adopt a policy that establishes criteria for selecting grantees. This is good governance practice, and it is also something the IRS will look for in your application for recognition of tax-exempt status.

Written selection criteria may be more or less detailed, depending on the nature of the grantmaking organization and the kinds of organizations it supports. Keep in mind that the primary reason for having such criteria is to ensure that your organization's funds are devoted to the proper purposes.

Selection criteria should, at the least, specify the purposes for which grants may be awarded, consistent with the 501(c)(3) purposes of the grantor. In addition, criteria should aim to determine that the grantee is capable of carrying out the purposes of the grant. Selection criteria should also include a process for vetting prospective grantees, described in the following paragraph.

## Know Your Grantee

Before agreeing to make a grant, it is critical that your organization has vetted the prospective grantee sufficiently to determine that:

- The grantee is capable of carrying out the purposes of the grant.
- The grantee will not, purposefully or inadvertently, use the funds to support terrorist activities or any other noncharitable purposes.

The scope of the vetting process can vary greatly, and will depend on a variety of factors including your relationship with or knowledge of the prospective grantee, the grantee's geographical location, and the nature of the grantee's activities.

**CONFIRM THE GRANTEE'S ABILITY TO CARRY OUT THE PURPOSES OF THE GRANT** Here are some questions you should ask when assessing whether a prospective grantee is capable of carrying out the purposes of a grant:

- *Does the grantee have legal authority to engage in the contemplated activities?* Review the grantee's legal registration and organizing documents. If the answer is unclear, you may want to seek local legal advice.
- *Are there any restrictions on the grantee's ability to receive funds or goods-in-kind from foreign sources?*
- *Does the grantee have the practical ability to carry out the contemplated project, given the amount of the proposed grant and the grantee's existing resources?* This inquiry can include confirmation that the grantee has adequate financial resources, staff, facilities, and access to utilities.
- *Does the grantee have the ability to provide reports on the use of the grant?* Look at whether financial systems are capable of tracking the use of grant funds, as well as whether the grantee has adequate communication technology and English language ability.

**DETERMINE THAT FUNDS WILL NOT BE DIVERTED FOR TERRORIST PURPOSES** Unfortunately, there is no procedure you can follow that will automatically protect your organization from potentially severe consequences should your grant funds end up in the hands of terrorists. Rather, you need to assess the risk and determine the appropriate scope of pre-grant inquiry. It is not always clear how much vetting of prospective grantees is required. For example, is it necessary to check potential grantees against official terrorist lists, even if you have a close, long-standing relationship? You need policies to ensure compliance with the law, and to protect your organization from misuse of resources, without imposing unnecessary burdens on your thinly stretched staff and/or volunteers.

Section 8.1 summarizes some helpful and important guidelines to help you avoid inadvertently supporting terrorism. These include voluntary guidelines issued by the U.S. Treasury Department, which should be considered in determining the appropriate scope of inquiry for any proposed grant.

## Do Not Act as a Pass-Through for Contributions to Foreign Organizations

A U.S. taxpayer cannot (subject to very limited exceptions discussed in section 7.6) deduct a contribution made directly to a foreign organization, even if the recipient organization has obtained 501(c)(3) status. For this reason, the IRS has long disallowed deductions to a U.S. 501(c)(3) where the U.S. organization acts as a mere pass-through. That is, if an individual makes a contribution to a U.S. organization, subject to a restriction requiring that the funds be re-granted to a foreign charity, that contribution is not deductible because it is viewed as an individual contribution to a foreign organization.[9]

The IRS does, however, allow a U.S. organization to use tax-deductible contributions to fund foreign organizations, as long as the U.S. organization retains *discretion and control* over the funds. Simply stated, this means that the U.S. organization must take responsibility for evaluating whether and how the funds will be used by a foreign grantee to ensure that the funds are used for charitable purposes and are not diverted for any improper purposes.

If your organization intends to provide funding to foreign organizations, the IRS will generally require, when reviewing your application for tax-exempt status and upon audit, that your bylaws include:

- A statement that your organization will retain discretion over funds contributed to it, and control over whether and how to disburse the funds.
- A statement that the board of directors has exclusive control over making foreign grants.
- A statement that a foreign grantee must agree to make periodic reports to ensure that the funds are used for their intended purposes, and to return any funds not spent.

This does not always mean that the board has to review and approve each individual grant. In larger grantmaking organizations, the board may establish detailed criteria, and delegate to staff the authority to make grants that comply with the criteria up to a specified dollar threshold.

The IRS has provided two general models for cross-border grantmakers that are public charities (and not private foundations):[10]

## U.S. ORGANIZATION SOLICITS FUNDS FOR ITS GENERAL PURPOSES, THEN SELECTS FOREIGN GRANTEES AND PROJECTS

The U.S. organization receives contributions for its charitable purposes and decides to make grants to one or more foreign organizations to carry out the purposes of the U.S. organization. The U.S. organization can advise its donors that it makes grants to certain foreign organizations, but must not make any binding commitments to donors regarding foreign grants. That is, the U.S. organization must have *control* over the funds it receives, and must have *discretion* as to their use, so that it can determine how to ensure they are used for charitable purposes.

For example, consider a hypothetical U.S. organization, the purpose of which is to supply warm winter clothes to young children living in poverty. The organization might decide to devote some of its funds to supply coats for children in a foreign orphanage, and it might do that by making a grant to a foreign-based organization that provides assistance in the particular orphanage. Before making a foreign grant, the organization must vet the grantee, review the grantee's proposed use of funds, and enter into a written agreement regarding the use of grant funds.

**U.S. ORGANIZATION SOLICITS FUNDS AFTER VETTING AND SELECTING A SPECIFIC FOREIGN PROJECT**   Your U.S. organization may decide to solicit funds from U.S. donors for a specific foreign project conducted by a specific foreign organization. As a variation on the example immediately above, the U.S. organization would identify and vet the foreign organization and its project, and would then solicit funds from U.S. donors for that project. In this case, additional requirements apply:

- Prior to soliciting funds, the project must be carefully vetted to ensure that it will serve your organization's charitable purposes, and that the funds will not be diverted for any improper purposes.
- Donors must be clearly informed that the U.S. organization maintains discretion and control over the funds, such that your organization can redirect the funds to another project, or even to some other organization, if you determine that the contemplated project is not consistent with 501(c)(3) requirements.

## Funding through a Foreign Intermediary

Note that the rules discussed earlier apply regardless of whether your organization is funding an organization that directly conducts foreign projects, or is funding a foreign intermediary organization (described in section 1.3). If you are making grants to a foreign intermediary, you should:

- Before disbursing funds, vet and approve the foreign project in which the funds will be used (identify the ultimate beneficiary and use of the funds).
- Disburse funds only as needed for the approved project.
- Require periodic reports so that you can monitor how the funds were used by the ultimate beneficiary for the approved project.
- Monitor the use of funds by the ultimate beneficiary.

## Use Written Grant Agreements

Any organization that engages in cross-border grantmaking should insist upon receiving written grant requests from prospective grantees, and entering into written agreements confirming the terms of a grant. Not only does the IRS ask about these procedures, but these procedures are also commonly recognized as best practices that help ensure that your organization's resources are being used in furtherance of its charitable purposes.

**ITEMS THAT SHOULD BE INCLUDED IN WRITTEN GRANT AGREEMENTS** Every grant agreement should, at a minimum, include the following:

- A description of the way grant funds will be used. The grant agreement may incorporate by reference the terms of the grant proposal, which may include a budget for the project to be funded.
- A requirement that any deviation from the agreed use of funds must be approved in advance, in writing, by the grantor.
- A prohibition against any use not permitted under 501(c)(3), including any use of grant funds for political activities.[11]
- A prohibition against the use of grant funds for any lobbying activity, or a specific limitation to ensure that the grantee's lobbying activities do not cause the grantor to exceed its own lobbying limits (*see* section 8.5).
- A requirement that the grantee segregate and separately account for the use of grant funds.
- Periodic (at least annual) reporting by the grantee to demonstrate that the funds are used for the agreed purpose.
- The return of unused grant funds upon completion of the project, or as of a specified date.
- The grantor's right to withhold grant funds if it determines that the grantee is not in compliance with the grant agreement.
- The grantor's right to terminate the grant agreement, terminate funding, and receive a return of unused funds in the event funds are misused.

**ADDITIONAL ITEMS TO CONSIDER** You may wish to include the following, where appropriate:

- The right of grantor to conduct periodic site visits.
- A certification that the grantee will not provide material support to terrorist activities.[12]
- A description of each party's rights (if any) to publicize and/or use logos or other intellectual property of the other.
- A description of the ownership and rights to use any intellectual property created with the grant funds.
- The right of the grantor to withhold grant funds to comply with U.S. withholding tax requirements, if applicable.
- A right of the grantor to withhold taxes if required by law.
- A restriction against the use of grant funds for travel to, or activities in, the United States. The purpose of this is to avoid the possibility of triggering a requirement that the grantor withhold taxes from the grant funds.

- In the event U.S. tax withholding is required, a provision for *grossing up* grant funds, that is, adjusting the grant so that the grantee receives the entire grant amount and the grantor absorbs the cost of withholding.

This list is not comprehensive. Any particular grantor-grantee relationship may include a host of additional provisions.

## Monitor Your Grants

It is critical to monitor the use of grant funds. This doesn't necessarily mean that your organization must send staff, board members, or volunteers to visit the grantee, although that is always desirable. When feasible, site visits are an excellent way to confirm that a grantee is using funds for the intended purposes. At the least, you need to make sure that you receive financial and narrative reports that are adequate, given the level of resources and degree of risk, to assure your board that the funds are being used for the intended purposes.

## The Critical Role of the Board of Directors

Regardless of where in the United States your organization is established, the board of directors is legally responsible, under state law, for ensuring that the organization devotes its resources in furtherance of its purposes. The board need not, and in all but the smallest organizations should not, participate in day-to-day management. However, to satisfy its oversight responsibility the board must see that the organization adopts and complies with appropriate policies and procedures to ensure against any misuse of funds.

The risk that funds may be diverted for improper purposes is, in general, greater when organizations make cross-border grants. It is more difficult to gather information about grantees, and once obtained, such information may be difficult to interpret due to legal, cultural, and language differences. Monitoring of remote activities can be challenging.

In addition to state law requirements, as discussed above, the IRS requires that the board have exclusive control over the making of cross-border grants.

To satisfy both state law and IRS requirements, boards need to assess the level of risk inherent in their organizations' grantmaking, and develop policies and procedures establishing selection criteria and monitoring procedures appropriate to the level of risk. As a general rule, the board, or a board committee, should review and approve individual grants. For larger organizations that make many grants, the board may authorize staff approval of grants, up to a specified dollar limit, based on objective, written criteria. Some organizations choose to set forth in bylaws the board's specific responsibilities in overseeing the grantmaking process, and this can be useful in obtaining IRS determination of exempt status.

## 2.4   American Friends of Organizations

A common structure for Americans who want to support a particular foreign organization is the so-called *American friends of* organization.[13] This term was coined because often the name begins with *American friends of,* or *friends of,* and ends with the name of the foreign organization it supports (such as, for example, American Friends of the British Museum). While a *friends of* organization is typically formed primarily to support a single foreign organization, it should have some additional purposes or activities. For example, the bylaws may contemplate supporting additional foreign organizations, and/or the *friends of* organization may engage in some activities in the United States beyond fundraising.

While the IRS has approved many *friends of* organizations as 501(c)(3) public charities, all of the requirements described in this chapter with respect to cross-border grants apply. A *friends of* organization must be careful to act independently of the foreign organization it supports. It must review requests for funding, and make funding decisions, on a project-by-project basis. Funding a specific foreign project may include an allowance for administrative, so-called *overhead,* expenses of the foreign organization.

The U.S. organization may solicit funds for a specific project it has approved, but it must advise donors that it maintains discretion and control over the funds, as described in section 2.3. This means that the U.S. organization must advise donors that it has the right to withhold and redirect funding in the event that a project is not conducted in accordance with 501(c)(3) requirements.

In order to maintain its independence, and to avoid any perception that the *American friends of* organization is controlled by the foreign charity, a majority of the directors of the U.S. organization should not also be directors, officers, or employees of the foreign organization.[14] It is also important to maintain a separate website for the *friends of* organization so that it's clear to visitors that they are being asked to contribute to a U.S. organization, not directly to a foreign organization, and that the U.S. organization does not directly operate the foreign projects being funded by U.S. donors. The U.S. organization's website may contain a link to that of the foreign organization, but visitors should know which organization's website they are visiting.

## 2.5   Special Rules for Donor-Advised Funds

One way to avoid the burden of complying with foreign grantmaking requirements is to contribute to a U.S. intermediary organization using a donor-advised fund. Simply stated, a *donor-advised fund* is an account that a donor creates with a so-called *sponsoring organization*.[15] The sponsoring organization must be a public charity, and frequently is, but is not required to be, a community foundation or large financial institution. The donor makes an irrevocable contribution, which triggers a tax deduction (to the extent otherwise allowed by law). The donor can then make recommendations regarding the use of the contributed funds, but the sponsoring organization must maintain discretion and control over the funds, and therefore cannot have a legal obligation to comply with the donor's wishes.

Donor-advised funds that make cross-border grants are required to comply with the so-called *expenditure responsibility* requirements that apply to private foundations, described in Chapter 3. For this reason, many sponsoring organizations refuse to make cross-border grants. Those sponsoring organizations that do make cross-border grants typically need to charge relatively high fees to cover the costs of legal compliance.[16]

## 2.6  Other U.S. Intermediaries

You can greatly simplify your grantmaking process by contributing to a U.S. intermediary organization which itself is a public charity (and not a donor-advised fund). However, it's important to be aware that any U.S. intermediary is subject to the discretion and control requirements explained earlier. This means that, at best, you will be able to make recommendations regarding the ultimate recipients of your funds. The intermediary organization must have the ultimate authority to determine how the funds are disbursed. You need to decide how much control and involvement you want to have in the grantmaking process.

## 2.7  Review and Further Considerations

Before venturing into cross-border grantmaking, it's important to properly classify your 501(c)(3) organization as a *public charity* or *private foundation*. This chapter has focused on U.S. federal tax requirements related to cross-border grantmaking by public charities. The following chapter provides an overview of U.S. federal tax requirements for private foundations making cross-border grants.

Whether your organization is characterized as a public charity or private foundation, it's important to be aware that additional U.S. legal requirements and restrictions may come into play. Chapter 8 lists a number of additional legal and practical considerations that may apply to cross-border grantmakers.

In addition, you need to know whether the recipient's country imposes any restrictions on the receipt of funding or importation of goods in-kind. These considerations are addressed in Chapter 9.

# Notes

1. A private foundation that wishes to provide scholarship assistance must obtain advance approval from the IRS. I.R.C. § 4945; Treas. Reg. § 53.4945-4.
2. As explained in Chapter 1, in order to be eligible to attract tax-deductible contributions, a 501(c)(3) organization must be formed under U.S. (not foreign) laws.
3. *See* IRS Publication 557, *Tax-Exempt Status for Your Organization* (December 2011), 33, available at www.irs.gov/app/picklist/list/publicationsNoticesPdf .html?value=557&criteria=formNumber&submitSearch=Find.
4. I.R.C §§ 509(a)(1) and 170(b)(1)(A)(vi); Treas. Reg. § 1.170A-9(f).
5. Treas. Reg. § 1.170A-9(f).
6. I.R.C. § 509(a)(2).
7. I.R.C. §§ 509(a)(1) and 170(b)(1)(A)(i)-(iv). Also included in this category are: organizations formed to hold and administer endowments for public colleges and universities, governmental units, and organizations organized and operated for purposes of testing for public safety.
8. I.R.C. section 509(a)(3).
9. The IRS has not clarified whether this would also jeopardize the U.S. organization's tax-exempt status. In any event, no organization wants to jeopardize a donor's tax deduction, and misleading donors about the tax-deductibility of contributions may cause further trouble for the organization.
10. *See* Rev. Rul. 63-252, 1963-2 C.B. 101 (Jan. 1, 1963), and Rev. Rul. 66-79, 1966-1 C.B. 48 (Jan. 1, 1966).
11. As a technical matter, the grant agreement would typically make reference to section 170(c)(2)(B) of the Internal Revenue Code.
12. For a discussion of the pros and cons of requiring such a certification of grantees, *see* Andrew Schulz, "The Debate Over Anti-Terrorism Certification," *International Dateline, a Publication of the Council on Foundations* 74 (Third Quarter 2005), available at www.cof.org/templates/ content.cfm?ItemNumber=2036&navItemNumber=2527.
13. For a detailed explanation of the rules and restrictions applicable to so-called *American friends of* organizations, *see* Lieber, Penina Kessler and Donald R. Levy, eds., *Complete Guide to Nonprofit Organizations* (Kingston, NJ: Civic Research Institute, 2005), ¶10.3[3], and Cumulative Supplements. See also Edie, John A., Jane C. Nober and Jacob T. Clauson, *Beyond*

*Our Borders: A Guide to Making Grants Outside the United States*, Fourth Edition (Council on Foundations: Arlington VA, 2012).

14. The IRS has, on occasion, ruled that a U.S. 501(c)(3) organization may have a board that overlaps completely with that of a foreign organization. *See* PLR 200551024 (Sept. 30 2005), where the foreign organization met the requirements of 501(c)(3). IRS Private Letter Rulings such as this do not have legal precedential value, and cannot be relied on. Today, it is likely to be difficult, if not impossible, to obtain recognition of 501(c)(3) status where there is complete overlap among the boards of a domestic and foreign organization.

15. I.R.C. § 4966(d)(2) defines a *donor-advised fund* to mean a fund or account: (i) which is separately defined by reference to contributions by a donor or donors; (ii) which is owned and controlled by a sponsoring organization; and (iii) with respect to which a donor (or any person appointed or designated by such donor) has, or reasonably expects to have, advisory privileges with respect to the distribution or investment of amounts held in such fund or account by reason of the donor's status as a donor.

    This definition, along with restrictions applicable to donor-advised funds, was enacted into law as part of the so-called *Pension Protection Act of 2006*, Pub. L. No. 109-280, 120 Stat. 780 (2006).

16. *See*, for example, Charities Aid Foundation America, available at www.cafamerica.org.

# CHAPTER 3

# International Grantmaking by Private Foundations

The term *private foundation* is a U.S. federal tax law concept. It does not designate a form of nonprofit organization under U.S. state laws. Tax-exempt organizations that can receive tax-deductible contributions from U.S. taxpayers are formed under the laws of a state of the United States (or of the District of Columbia or a U.S. possession). They are typically formed as nonprofit corporations, charitable trusts, or unincorporated associations. *See* Chapter 5. Any of these forms of tax-exempt organization may be classified for U.S. federal (and often state) tax purposes as a so-called *private foundation*.

## 3.1 What Is a Private Foundation?

Typically, a private foundation is a 501(c)(3) organization that has a small number of funders, such as a family foundation. Technically, a private foundation is any 501(c)(3) organization that does not qualify as a so-called *public charity*. There are several ways an organization can qualify as a public charity, and these are described in Chapter 2.

In general, the consequences of being treated as a private foundation, rather than a public charity, are:

- The organization must comply with additional restrictions on operations. Notably, the so-called *self-dealing* rules prohibit a private foundation from providing any benefits to, or entering into transactions (such as sales, leases, or loans) with significant contributors and others (so-called *disqualified persons*) who have certain insider relationships to the organization.[1] Steep penalties, in the form of excise taxes, can be imposed on an organization and/or individuals for failure to comply with this and other restrictions. To avoid incurring this tax, it is critical to know who the disqualified persons are with respect to your organization.
- The organization is subject to an excise tax on investment income.
- Donors receive less generous tax deductions for contributions to private foundations than they receive when contributing to public charities.

A private foundation may be further classified as a *non-operating foundation* or an *operating foundation*.

## Private Non-Operating Foundations

Most private foundations are classified as non-operating foundations. These foundations typically function as grantmakers, and do not directly provide services or conduct other charitable (501(c)(3)) activities.

Every private non-operating foundation is required to disburse a minimum amount each year, in the form of so-called *qualifying distributions*. This minimum is approximately equal to 5 percent of the foundation's investment assets, although computing the required amount can be rather complex. A private foundation that does not distribute the minimum amount within a specified time period is subject to an excise tax.[2]

Qualifying distributions consist generally of grants, gifts, and so-called *program related investments* (described later) made for charitable purposes. These distributions may be to 501(c)(3) public charities, private operating foundations, governments, and to other organizations and individuals, subject to additional requirements. Qualifying distributions also include reasonable administrative expenses incurred by the private foundation in carrying out its charitable purposes and amounts paid to acquire assets used in carrying out the foundation's exempt purposes. If a private foundation has control over another 501(c)(3) organization, its grants to the controlled organization are qualifying distributions only if additional requirements are met.[3]

## Private Operating Foundations

A special type of private foundation is the so-called *private operating foundation*.[4] This is a 501(c)(3) organization that does not qualify for public charity status, typically because it has limited sources of support. However, unlike the typical family foundation, a private operating foundation directly conducts activities, such as providing charitable services, rather than functioning solely as a grantmaker. To qualify as a private operating foundation, an organization must not only be involved in some charitable activities beyond grantmaking, but also must meet certain technical tests.

Private operating foundations are subject to some, but not all of the restrictions that apply to non-operating foundations. For example, they are not required to make minimum distributions. In addition, contributions to private foundations are eligible for the more generous income tax deductions that apply to contributions to public charities.

## 3.2   Should a Private Foundation Make Cross-Border Grants?

Private foundations (including operating foundations) making grants to foreign organizations are subject to rather onerous requirements aimed at ensuring that the funds are used for 501(c)(3) purposes. Indeed, it has been suggested that smaller private foundations, such as family foundations, should limit their foreign grantmaking to organizations that have obtained IRS recognition of their 501(c)(3) status.[5]

If you are managing a private foundation that has an international purpose, you should carefully weigh the cost of compliance with these rules. You may decide that your resources are most efficiently used by granting to U.S.-based public charities that serve international purposes. If, on the other hand, you decide that it is important to maintain control over your foreign grantmaking, you will need to be prepared to devote additional resources toward complying with cumbersome U.S. tax requirements.

## 3.3   Permitted Grants and Disbursements

The focus of this chapter is on the U.S. tax rules that apply specifically to cross-border grantmaking by private foundations. This book does not delve into all of the other requirements and restrictions applicable to private foundations, as there are many resources available.[6] However, to set the stage for a discussion of cross-border grantmaking, we start with a brief overview of some fundamental rules that apply generally to grantmaking by private foundations.

While public charities are permitted to devote a minor portion of their resources toward noncharitable purposes, private foundations are subject to steep penalties, in the form of excise taxes, if any resources are considered used for noncharitable purposes.

One of these excise taxes is imposed on so-called *taxable expenditures.*[7] In general, a taxable expenditure is a grant that does not satisfy certain safeguards to ensure that it will be used exclusively for 501(c)(3) purposes. Reasonable administrative expenses, and expenses of acquiring and maintaining investments held for the foundation's charitable purposes, are not treated as taxable expenditures.

Taxable expenditures include distributions for purposes of influencing legislation (that is, lobbying, as defined for federal tax law purposes), for influencing the outcome of any public election, or carrying on any voter registration drive, subject to certain exceptions. These prohibitions on lobbying and election-related activities apply equally to domestic and foreign activities. While it is not always easy to apply these rules in the context of a foreign political regime, it is critical to make sure that foreign grantees do not use grant funds for any activity that could be considered lobbying or political activity for this purpose.

Another excise tax is triggered by so-called *jeopardizing investments,* such as equity investments or loans that are not made on commercially reasonable terms, thereby putting the foundation's financial health at risk.

To avoid being treated as a taxable expenditure or jeopardizing investment, a grant or investment of funds must fall into one of the following categories.

## Grants to 501(c)(3) Public Charities

A private foundation may make grants to any organization that has received an IRS determination letter confirming its status as a 501(c)(3) public charity (or private operating foundation), or that falls into a category of organizations that qualify for 501(c)(3) public charity status without obtaining an IRS determination letter.[8]

Many private foundations restrict their grantmaking to public charities because this allows them to focus resources on furthering their purposes without having to comply with the additional administrative requirements that come into play when making grants to other kinds of grantees. These requirements are discussed in the following paragraphs.

## Grants to Organizations Other Than Public Charities

A private foundation is also permitted to make grants to organizations that are not 501(c)(3) public charities, as long as the private foundation takes certain steps to ensure that the funds are used exclusively for 501(c)(3) purposes. The required procedure is referred to as the exercise of *expenditure responsibility.* Expenditure responsibility, which is used with respect to both domestic and foreign grantees, is explained in section 3.4. In addition, when a grantee does not qualify as a public charity (either by having an IRS determination letter or through equivalency determination described later), a grant will not be considered toward meeting the private foundation grantor's minimum distribution requirement unless the grantee also satisfies certain distribution requirements.

## Grants to Governments and Government Units

A private foundation may make grants to domestic and foreign government units, as long as the terms of the grant require that the funds be used solely for charitable purposes.

## Scholarships and Other Grants and Gifts to Individuals

A private foundation that makes grants to individuals for travel, study, or similar purposes must satisfy certain requirements to avoid the excise tax on taxable expenditures.[9] The grant must be a scholarship or fellowship, a prize or award, or a grant that has a specific objective such as the production of a report or improvement of a literary, artistic, or musical skill of the grantee. It must be awarded on an objective, nondiscriminatory basis, and the private foundation must obtain advance IRS approval of the grantmaking procedure.

Charitable gifts to individuals, other than for travel, study, and similar purposes, may be made without the need to obtain advance IRS approval. For example, a private foundation may provide relief from poverty or disaster directly to individuals. It is critical that the private foundation maintain detailed records to establish that the funds were used for charitable purposes.

## Program-Related Investments

A *program-related investment* (*PRI*) is typically a loan or equity investment (and may take other forms of investment) made by a private foundation or public charity, primarily for charitable purposes. While the private foundation typically expects to earn a return on the investment, the anticipated return is less, or the risk is greater, than that which a business entity would demand because the primary purpose for making the investment is charitable. As with grantmaking, a private foundation that makes a program-related investment in a foreign organization is required to make an *equivalency determination* or exercise *expenditure responsibility. See* section 3.4.[10]

A private foundation that contemplates making a program-related investment should seek legal advice in advance of doing so. IRS guidelines can be difficult to apply, and a program-related investment that fails to qualify can trigger an excise tax.

## 3.4   International Grantmaking: Special Requirements for Private Foundations

Most foreign organizations do not apply to the IRS for recognition of 501(c)(3) public charity status. When a U.S.-based private foundation makes a grant to a foreign organization that has not obtained an IRS determination of 501(c)(3) public charity status, the U.S. private foundation must take additional steps to make sure that the grant will not trigger an excise tax as a taxable expenditure. These additional steps take the form of so-called *equivalency determination* or *expenditure responsibility*, described in the following paragraphs.

In addition, for purposes of satisfying the minimum distribution requirement (described in section 3.1), a private foundation that makes a grant to a foreign organization may rely on an affidavit or opinion of counsel to determine that the foreign grantee meets the requirements for 501(c)(3) public charity status. The affidavit or opinion must set forth sufficient facts to allow the IRS to conclude that the organization meets those requirements.[11] See *equivalency determination*, following.

### Grants to Foreign Organizations: Equivalency Determination or Expenditure Responsibility

Assuming a prospective foreign grantee organization has not obtained an IRS determination of its public charity status, the private foundation may make the grant (and thereby avoid a tax on taxable expenditures) only if it either makes a so-called *equivalency determination* or exercises *expenditure responsibility*. An equivalency determination requires reaching the conclusion that the foreign organization would qualify as a 501(c)(3) public charity if it were established in the United States. The exercise of expenditure responsibility entails taking certain steps to see that the grant is used solely for charitable purposes.

A private foundation may choose whether to make an equivalency determination or exercise expenditure responsibility. Of course, if a prospective grantee does not meet the requirements for 501(c)(3) public charity status, expenditure responsibility will be the only option. Regardless of which one you choose, you will need to engage an attorney.

Grants to foreign governments are exempt from these requirements, but a private foundation contemplating such a grant must proceed with caution. Grants to certain international organizations designated by Executive Order are also exempt from these requirements. These special cases are discussed later.

It is important to keep in mind that the prohibitions against the use of grant funds for lobbying or election-related activities, or for any other noncharitable uses, apply in all cases. In addition, all cross-border grants and program-related investments must satisfy anti-terrorism requirements, discussed later in this chapter.

**EQUIVALENCY DETERMINATION** A private foundation may make a grant to a foreign organization that has not received an IRS determination of 501(c)(3) public charity status if it makes a good faith determination that the grantee would qualify. The determination must be based on either an affidavit of the grantee or an opinion of counsel of the grantor or grantee. The affidavit or opinion must set forth sufficient facts such that the IRS can determine whether the foreign grantee meets the requirements for 501(c)(3) public charity status.

This determination typically involves both legal and factual analyses. It is necessary to review the foreign organization's organizational documents (such articles of association and bylaws, or the foreign country's equivalent). You may need to have the documents translated into English. You may also need to obtain a translation and analysis of applicable foreign law. For example, if organizational documents do not sufficiently restrict the organization's activities or disposition of funds, you will need to look into whether those restrictions are imposed under applicable local laws. Determining whether an organization qualifies for public charity status may require an analysis of its support over a period of years. This can be a challenge where different accounting methods are used.[12]

Even after a thorough analysis of the facts, law, and numbers, it is not always clear whether a foreign organization meets the requirements for 501(c)(3) public charity status. Where there is ambiguity, even a carefully drafted legal opinion may not protect you from an IRS challenge and potential excise tax liability. For that reason, you may well prefer to exercise expenditure responsibility when the conclusion regarding equivalency is less than clear.

**EXPENDITURE RESPONSIBILITY** Making an equivalency determination is often difficult, and many private foundations find it easier to satisfy the alternative *expenditure responsibility* requirement. A private foundation that diligently complies with the expenditure responsibility procedures set forth in U.S. Treasury regulations will generally not be subject to penalties if the grantee misuses funds.[13]

At the same time, complying with the expenditure responsibility requirements for a foreign grantee, particularly drafting the required written agreement, will entail engaging an attorney familiar with applicable U.S. law, and possibly also consulting a foreign lawyer. Translation services may also be needed. Of course, all of this adds expense to your grant-making process.

Expenditure responsibility can only be used when a grant is made for a specific, preapproved project. You can include an allowance for administrative expenses to be incurred by the grantee in connection with the project. However, you cannot make a general operating grant using expenditure responsibility. If you want to make a general operating grant, you should explore whether an equivalency determination is possible. Note also that, while exercising expenditure responsibility ensures that a grant will not be a taxable expenditure, additional steps may be required in order for the grant to count toward the private foundation's minimum distribution requirement. This is the case if the grantee is classified as a private foundation (a foreign organization that does not establish public charity status), or if the grantee is controlled by the private foundation.

There are three parts to the exercise of expenditure responsibility:

1. *Pregrant inquiry.* The purpose of a pregrant inquiry is to gain reasonable assurance that the grantee will use the funds for proper purposes. The extent of an appropriate inquiry will vary depending on a number of factors, including the size and nature of the grant, and the grantor's familiarity with the prospective grantee. It is important to keep in mind that additional pregrant due diligence may be required to satisfy anti-terrorism requirements, discussed later.

2. *Written agreement.* The terms of a grant must be set forth in a written agreement. Treasury regulations set forth certain items that must be in the written agreement. The written agreement must set forth the purpose of the grant, and the grantee must agree:

   - To use grant funds exclusively for charitable (501(c)(3)) purposes.
   - To repay any funds not used for the purposes of the grant.
   - To submit full and complete annual reports.
   - To maintain records of receipts and expenditures and to make its books and records available to the grantor.
   - Not to use grant funds for purposes of lobbying (as defined in the Treasury regulations).
   - Not to use grant funds for purposes of influencing any election or carrying on any voter registration drive.
   - Not to make any grant that is not permitted to be made by a domestic private foundation.

   The last three items may be phrased in appropriate terms under foreign law or custom, accompanied by an affidavit or opinion of counsel stating that the agreement complies with these requirements.

3. *Reports from grantees.* A private foundation must obtain an annual report from the grantee providing details as to how the funds were used, and confirming that the grantee complied with all of the terms of the agreement.

   A private foundation that is required to exercise expenditure responsibility is also required to report certain information about the grant with its annual IRS return, and to maintain certain records including a copy of the grant agreement and reports obtained from the grantee.[14]

It is easy to underestimate the time and resources it can take to explain these U.S. requirements to a foreign grantee, and to reach an agreement that is acceptable to both parties. It can be quite challenging to draft a legal agreement, often requiring translation, that takes into account the legal requirements and cultural environment of the grantee's country, while satisfying U.S. rules.

## Grants to Foreign Intermediaries

If a U.S. private foundation is making grants to an intermediary organization that does not qualify as a public charity (by having an IRS determination letter or through equivalency determination), that U.S. grantor must require that the grantee comply with 501(c)(3) requirements for private foundation grantmaking, and this may include a requirement that the grantee exercise expenditure responsibility in making its own grants.

## Grants to Foreign Governments or Government Units

The equivalency determination and expenditure responsibility requirements do not apply to grants made to units of foreign governments. It is critical, however, to enter into a written agreement that prohibits the use of grant funds for any noncharitable purposes. Foreign laws, culture, and language differences can make it difficult to draft such an agreement. In addition, it is not always clear whether a foreign entity is a governmental unit. For example, a foreign university or hospital may or may not qualify as such. You will need to understand its legal structure to make that determination, and for that reason it is advisable to seek legal advice before making a grant to a foreign government unit.

## Grants to International Organizations Designated by Executive Order

A private foundation may make grants to certain international organizations designated by an Executive Order without the need to make an equivalency determination or exercise expenditure responsibility. This category includes the World Health Organization (*WHO*) and World Trade Organization (*WTO*), among others.[15]

## Cross-Border Program-Related Investments

A private foundation that makes a cross-border program-related investment is required to comply with expenditure responsibility procedures, assuming the investee does not qualify as a 501(c)(3) public charity (through an IRS determination letter or an equivalency determination). Treasury regulations set forth the specific items required to be included in a program-related investment agreement.[16]

If your private foundation is contemplating making a program-related investment, you should also consider whether any payments of interest or dividends from the investee will be subject to foreign withholding taxes, which could reduce your investment return. Many countries impose a withholding tax on outbound transfers of interest and dividends. If a withholding tax does apply, you should determine whether there is a bilateral income tax treaty between the United States and the investee's country of residence that would eliminate or reduce the tax. If a treaty provision applies, you may need to provide the foreign government with certain required documentation.

### Anti-Terrorism Compliance

Every grant and program-related investment made to a foreign organization or individual is subject to the U.S. anti-terrorism rules. Private foundations, like public charities, must take appropriate steps to minimize the risk that any cross-border distribution could be used to support any terrorist activity. This requires additional due diligence, which can be quite cumbersome. *See* section 8.1. Moreover, even if an organization takes appropriate steps to avoid inadvertently funding terrorist activities, it can still face government sanctions if its grant funds fall into the hands of terrorists. This is in contrast to the expenditure responsibility procedures, which if followed, protect a private foundation from penalties in the event that a grantee misuses funds.

## 3.5  U.S. Withholding Tax on Disbursements of Grant Funds

A private foundation or public charity that makes a cross-border grant may, under some circumstances, be required to withhold U.S. tax from the grant funds. A grantmaking organization that wants to avoid any potential withholding requirement can do so by including a provision in the grant agreement that prohibits the use of any grant funds for travel to or use in the United States. Withholding taxes are discussed further in section 8.11.

## 3.6  Review and Further Considerations

Chapters 2 and 3 have focused on U.S. federal tax requirements related to cross-border grantmaking by the two types of 501(c)(3) organization: public charities and private foundations. We have seen that it's critical to know whether your organization is a public charity or a private foundation because private foundations are subject to more rigorous requirements.

Public charities and private foundations alike need to be mindful of additional (non-tax) U.S. and foreign laws when making cross-border grants. Chapters 8 and 9 address additional U.S. and foreign legal requirements that may apply to grantmaking activities.

If your organization's international activities are confined to grantmaking, you may decide to skip Chapters 4 through 7. On the other hand, if you are contemplating moving beyond grantmaking by operating your own programs in a foreign country, you are well advised to continue to Chapter 4 and beyond. Whether you're staffing a foreign school, or merely sending a few volunteers or employees overseas for limited periods, it's important to be aware of the various legal and practical considerations that may affect your international activities.

In the next two chapters, we look at how to achieve the optimal legal structure for your organization in order to further your mission, while making the most efficient use of your resources and minimizing legal risks and liabilities.

## Notes

1. I.R.C. §§ 4941, 4946.
2. I.R.C. § 4942; Treas. Reg. § 53.4942.
3. I.R.C. §§ 4942(g), 4946. The controlled grantee organization must be a 501(c)(3) organization, and the grantmaking foundation must make sure that the grantee uses the funds within a specified period of time. This rule also applies when individuals that have certain relationships to the private foundation (so-called *disqualified persons*) have control over the grantee.
4. I.R.C. § 4942(j)(3).
5. *See* McCoy, Jerry J. and Kathryn W. Miree, *Family Foundation Handbook*, (Chicago, IL: CCH 2012), ¶7.02[B][3].
6. *See* Appendix B for a list of resources.
7. I.R.C. § 4945; Treas. Reg. § 53.4945. Other excise taxes are: a tax on net investment income (imposed on all private foundations), a tax on excess business holdings, and a tax on so-called *self-dealing*.
8. You should always obtain confirmation of a prospective grantee's public charity status. Note also grants to certain supporting organizations do not qualify. If a prospective grantee qualifies for public charity status as a supporting organization, you should seek professional guidance before moving forward.

9. IRC § 4945.
10. IRC § 4944(c); Treas. Reg. § 53.4944-3. In April 2012, the U.S. Department of Treasury issued proposed regulations to provide more guidance for organizations wishing to make program-related investments. These proposed regulations provide nine new examples, and may be relied on by grantmaking organizations even before they become final. Prop. Treas. Reg. § 53.49-44-3(b), examples 11–19 (April 19, 2012).
11. Treas. Reg. § 53.4942(a)-3(a)(6).
12. The IRS has set forth the required elements of an equivalency determination in Rev. Proc. 92-94, 1992-2 C.B. 507. Various grantmaker groups have called upon the IRS to update this Revenue Procedure in light of intervening changes of law. In addition, these groups have urged the IRS to approve, and allow grantmakers to rely upon, one or more central databases (referred to as *equivalency determination information repositories*, or EDIRs) of foreign organizations for which equivalency determinations have been made. This would make foreign grantmaking significantly more feasible for smaller private foundations. As of this book's publication, the IRS has not sanctioned any EDIRs. However, Proposed Regulations issued in 2012 would allow a private foundation to rely on opinions issued by certain advisors other than the foundation's (or the grantee's) own counsel. This may open the door to the use of a repository for equivalency determinations.
13. The requirements for exercising expenditure responsibility are set forth in Treas. Reg. § 53.4945-5(b).
14. Treas. Reg. § 53.4945-5(d).
15. These are organizations designated by Executive Order pursuant to the federal statute 22 U.S.C. § 288.
16. Treas. Reg. § 53.4945-5(b)(4).

# CHAPTER 4

# Going Deeper: Operating a Foreign Program

## 4.1 Are You Determined to Move Beyond Grantmaking?

We have seen in previous chapters that, as a grantmaker, you can develop very close relationships with foreign NGOs and you can certainly make a direct impact. Nevertheless, grantmaking may just not be sufficiently hands-on for you. It may be your personal passion to work in or direct a project. Or, maybe you have a unique vision, or see a need that no other organization is fulfilling.

In this chapter, we circle back to the question raised in Chapter 1: Do you really want to operate a nonprofit outside the United States? Before plunging ahead, you should step back and consider whether there is an alternative, such as partnering with an existing organization, that might allow you to more efficiently devote your resources toward your mission.

For many nonprofit founders, there are strong reasons to create something new, and if you decide to go that route you will need to determine how best to structure your foreign operations. A U.S. 501(c)(3) organization does not lose its 501(c)(3) status merely because it operates in a foreign country, nor does it lose the ability to attract tax-deductible contributions from U.S. residents. Indeed, you could even have all of your operations, including office, staff, and volunteers in a foreign country without losing 501(c)(3) status.[1] Of course, this may not be the most practical way to operate if you are raising funds from U.S. donors. This chapter will explore some alternatives and the considerations that go into deciding among them.

Chapter 5 will delve into the creation of a foreign *legal entity*, such as the foreign law counterpart to a nonprofit corporation or charitable trust. Chapter 6 will explore additional foreign legal, tax, and practical considerations in connection with staffing foreign operations.

## 4.2   Is Anybody Else Doing It?

As we see throughout the remainder of this book, moving along the spectrum of international activities is not as easy as packing your bags and getting on a plane. As your organization becomes more deeply embedded in a foreign country (not to mention more than one country), the complexity of legal and practical issues grows dramatically. You will be spending time and financial resources working through these issues. So, before you decide to go deep, consider whether and why you need to.

Two questions you might ask are:

1. Is anybody already doing what we want to do?
2. Does anybody else even see the need?

### Three Audacious Founders

Here are three examples of visionary founders who answered both of these questions with a resounding "no" and forged ahead to establish foreign-based programs:

EXAMPLE 1: JENNY BOWEN AND HALF THE SKY FOUNDATION   Jenny Bowen, founder of Half the Sky Foundation (HTS), adopted a daughter in China and had a first-hand view of the plight of children living in orphanages. Jenny wanted desperately to improve the lives of those children who could not be adopted and were destined to grow up in institutions. She had a vision that institutionalized children could live happy, fulfilling lives if caregivers could be recruited and trained professionally to address the children's emotional and intellectual needs. This was a matter of quality, not just quantity. That is, to implement the vision required funding, but also required working within orphanages to provide training, and ultimately to change attitudes about what could be accomplished. In those early days, there was no local organization with which HTS could partner. There was no choice for HTS but to hire and train its own employees to work in Chinese orphanages. Since orphanages in China are government-owned, Jenny had to convince governmental authorities of the merits of her idea. This was no easy task, but eventually she prevailed, and within a few short years, governmental authorities had fully embraced HTS's work.

**EXAMPLE 2: PATRICK AWUAH AND ASHESI UNIVERSITY**   Patrick Awuah, founder of Ashesi University in Ghana, grew up in Ghana and attended a liberal arts college in the United States. He stayed in this country to pursue a successful career in the high-tech industry, but eventually was pulled by his desire to help his native country. He believed that he could effect change in Ghana by establishing a new kind of university that would engender critical thinkers and leaders with strong ethics. At first, Patrick met strong resistance because his vision did not fit nicely with the established requirements for educational accreditation in Ghana. He persisted, and within several years Ashesi University had been accredited and its alumni were being recognized for their capabilities. Like Jenny Bowen of HTS, Patrick Awuah had no choice but to jump in with two feet and create a full-fledged foreign program. No one else was doing what he wanted to do, and no one even saw the need until he showed them.

**EXAMPLE 3: SAMMIE RAYNER AND LUMANA**   Sammie Rayner founded Lumana to serve a dual purpose: to bring microfinance services to rural Africa, and to create opportunities for young college graduates to gain experience in the microfinance sector. After graduating from business school with a certificate in international business studies, Sammie searched far and wide for a job or internship in the microfinance sector, and she discovered that there were very few opportunities for young graduates like herself. She also learned that only about 1 percent of microfinance funds were going to Africa, and almost none of those funds reached rural Africa. Undaunted by her youth and inexperience, Sammie proceeded to develop a network of contacts and advisors to help her develop and implement a plan to serve the dual mission. Within just two years, Lumana had served 233 clients with loans and had provided hands-on opportunities in Ghana for 20 interns.

## How Can You Find Out Whether Anyone Is Out There Doing What You Want to Do?

There are a variety of sources you can use to search for organizations that have purposes similar to what you are contemplating. Even if you are determined to launch your own program, it's worthwhile knowing what other organizations are doing. You may end up finding ways to conserve scarce resources by collaborating. Some resources for finding other organizations with purposes similar to yours are listed in Appendix B.

## 4.3   Are You Sure You Will Be Allowed to Do What You Want to Do?

Before your organization begins work in a foreign country, you need to understand what activities are permitted in that country, what the licensing or registration requirements are, and what legal structure is needed.

For American citizens, it is often easy to take for granted our constitutional rights to freely associate and communicate without government interference. Of course, U.S.-based nonprofit organizations, particularly 501(c)(3) organizations, accept certain restrictions as a condition to receiving tax-favored status, and certain activities are subject to federal or state regulation.[2] Nevertheless, the degree of freedom we enjoy in America, to form a variety of types of associations for a wide range of purposes, does not exist in a large number of countries.

In many countries, particularly developing countries, some or all of the kinds of activities that may be carried on by a U.S. 501(c)(3) organization within the United States are highly regulated, restricted, or even prohibited. Restrictions may be clearly set forth in statutory or administrative codes, or they may be a matter of bureaucratic discretion. Laws or administrative policies may prohibit or regulate specific activities, such as human rights activity or advocacy. In some cases, activities that are legal when carried out by a domestic organization may not be carried out by a foreign organization, or by a domestic organization controlled or funded by foreign interests. Penalties can be harsh. Tax legislation may also be used to influence behavior by providing preferential tax treatment or imposing tax penalties on particular activities.

In recent years, perhaps surprisingly, there has been a wave of restrictive legislation and policy in many countries, often aimed at limiting the ability of foreign NGOs to operate within a particular country or even provide funding to local organizations.[3]

These restrictions come in various forms, including broad prohibitions against foreign funding of local organizations, requirements that local organizations receive advance government permission for the receipt of foreign funding, prohibitions against foreign funding of certain types of local activities, requirements that foreign funds flow through government-controlled entities or banks, onerous tax burdens on the receipt of foreign funds, and a variety of other restrictions aimed at impeding the efforts of foreign organizations, their employees and volunteers.[4] Before you decide to launch operations in a particular country, make sure you investigate any proposed, as well as current, legislation. You don't want to incur the expenses of starting up, only to be shut down.

Here are a few examples of countries with such restrictive policies:

- Jordan, where government officials have complete discretion over whether to permit a branch of a foreign organization.[5]

■ India, China, Indonesia, Egypt, Algeria, Jordan, Eritrea, Belarus, and Uzbekistan where advance government approval is required for non-profits to receive funding from foreign sources.[6]

■ India, Uzbekistan, and Eritrea, where foreign funding is required to flow through government institutions.[7]

■ Russia, where nonprofit organizations are taxed on the receipt of funds from most foreign nonprofit organizations.[8]

■ Mexico, where, as a condition to obtaining status as a Mexican nonprofit or establishing a Mexican office, all non-Mexican members and directors must agree not to seek any protections from their own governments (for example, in the event that a non-Mexican individual is charged with a crime in Mexico).[9]

Recent experiences make Egypt an extreme example of a country that severely restricts, and even penalizes, the activities of foreign organizations. In April 2012, the Egyptian government rejected applications for registration submitted by eight foreign-based organizations, stating that the organizations' activities violated Egyptian sovereignty. Some of those organizations had humanitarian purposes unrelated to government affairs or the promotion of democracy. For example, one of the rejected organizations was Coptic Orphans (www .copticorphans.org), a faith-based organization, registered in the United States, Australia, Canada, and the UK, devoted to improving the lives of fatherless Egyptian children whose widowed mothers lack the resources to support them. In addition, earlier in 2012, Egyptian authorities brought criminal charges against employees of three American organizations working to promote democracy in Egypt, for allegedly receiving foreign funds illegally and operating without registration. While the American employees were ultimately released and sent back to the United States, as of the time of this book's publication the Egyptian employees of those organizations were facing trials and possible jail time.[10]

Given the continuous, and sometimes rapid, state of change in the legal environments of many countries (and particularly in developing countries), references here to specific country laws and policies are intended merely to illustrate the kinds of restrictions your organization could find itself facing when seeking to operate in a foreign country. The critical point here is, you cannot assume that activities that seem quite innocuous to you will be unregulated, or even permissible, in a foreign country.

## 4.4 Alternative Models for Operating a Foreign Program

Launching operations in a foreign country can be overwhelming for an organization. You may be able to avoid shouldering everything all at once by collaborating with an existing organization. Here are three alternatives:

1. *Find a U.S. sponsor organization.* If you can find an existing U.S. 501(c)(3) organization, with a similar or complementary mission, that is willing to serve as a host for your program, you will avoid much of the learning curve and administrative costs of starting up in a foreign country. Of course, you will still be charged for all of the operational costs of your program, probably with a markup.[11]

2. *Send staff and volunteers, plus funding, to assist or collaborate with a foreign organization.* One way to move beyond grantmaking is to collaborate with one or more of your organization's foreign grantees by sending U.S.-based staff or volunteers to work on projects in the foreign country. If you can arrange for the volunteers and/or employees to work directly for the foreign organization, you will be able to avoid a variety of issues that arise when a U.S. organization sends volunteers or employees to a foreign country (discussed in Chapter 6). Sending employees to work on a temporary basis for a foreign organization is referred to as *secondment*. You will need a lawyer to help structure this type of arrangement. Arranging for volunteers to be engaged directly by a foreign organization is less complex, although the individuals may have to deal with certain issues such as visas and insurance. *See* Chapter 6.

3. *Establish your own foreign country program.* If your organization intends to conduct a program directly in a foreign country, you need to think about who is going to be in that country delivering services and supervising the work. It is likely that you will send employees, or perhaps even volunteers, for extended periods. Alternatively, you may hire employees or independent contractors locally (in the foreign country). Maybe you will use some combination of these, and perhaps you will also collaborate with local country NGOs.

   The decisions you make about how to manage your foreign operations will necessarily be influenced by foreign country laws and regulations, so do your homework before making plans to conduct activities in a foreign country.

## 4.5   Establishing a Foreign Office

If your U.S. 501(c)(3) organization is sending people for extended stays and/or hiring locally, you may be required to register a local office. This means that your U.S.-based organization has an official branch in a foreign country. Some commonly used terms for this are *registered office*, or *branch*. These terms will be used interchangeably throughout this book. In some countries, including China, the term *representative office* is used to designate a form of legal registration that authorizes limited activities in the foreign country. In Chapter 5 we distinguish a local country branch or registered office from a legal entity, such as a nonprofit corporation or something similar under a foreign country's legal regime.

Registration, as a branch or otherwise, may afford your organization certain benefits under the laws of the foreign country, such as permission to hire employees. In some countries, registration is required as a condition to holding meetings, or even informal gatherings, and penalties can be harsh. This is true, for example, in Ethiopia, Uganda, Zambia, Zimbabwe, and also throughout much of the Middle East.[12]

The process for formal registration of an office or branch varies widely. The licensing process may be with a national or local governmental authority, or both. The nature of your operations may also dictate the kind of license and formal designation required. A registered office or branch may, in itself, be able to obtain nongovernment organization, or *NGO* status. For example, in South Africa, a nonprofit corporation established outside South Africa (including a U.S. nonprofit corporation) is permitted to register a branch that has the same status as a South African nonprofit corporation (the so-called *section 21 company* described in Chapter 5).[13]

Not all countries will allow a foreign organization to establish a branch. Some will allow it, but will impose significant burdens. For example, in Iraq, branches of foreign organizations must provide the government with detailed lists of their staff and members.[14]

Of course, once your organization is operating in a foreign country, it is subject to the laws of that country, including laws relating to employment, protection of intellectual property, and enforcement of contracts, to name just a few. In addition, some countries have laws that apply specifically to the activities of foreign organizations, and many impose restrictions on speech and association, which can be very surprising to Americans. Chapter 9 provides an overview of some foreign legal and practical considerations you are likely to encounter. It is critical to do your homework by seeking legal advice and talking with other organizations that operate where you want to go. Know what you are getting into before you devote valuable resources toward making it happen.

You should also be aware that registering a foreign office may or may not determine how your organization is taxed. Once you have an office, whether or not it is required to be formally registered, you need to know whether your organization is subject to taxes, including corporate (income) tax, value added tax (*VAT*), import tariffs, and possibly others.

You may well be eligible for tax-exempt status in the foreign country based on the nature of the work you do. Eligibility for tax-exempt status may be correlated with having a license to engage in certain activities (e.g., educational or charitable). You need to investigate all of this up-front. You may have to apply separately for tax exemption, if it is even available. Also, remember that there may be various types of taxes, and your organization may be eligible for exemption from some but not others, or you may have to make multiple applications. Some common types of taxes foreign countries may impose on your organization or its activities are described in Chapter 9.

## Foreign Office or Separate Legal Entity?

A foreign office or branch is not the same thing as a so-called *legal entity*, which is a separate organization (such as a nonprofit corporation) established under the laws of a foreign country. Foreign legal entities are discussed in Chapter 5.

A foreign branch (or office) of a U.S.-based nonprofit corporation is a part of that corporation. While a branch may have something referred to as a board or council, that group acts under the authority of the corporation's board of directors. Because a branch and its home office are legally one corporation, a U.S. nonprofit corporation that operates through a branch (or office) can find itself subject to liabilities attributable to the foreign operations.

To make matters even more confusing, the term *NGO* is frequently used to refer to a branch office, as well as a legal entity, that has registered or received permission to operate for some purpose outside of the governmental and business sectors. When someone tells you that an organization *has NGO status* or *has formed an NGO* in a foreign country, you cannot know, without more information, whether that refers to a branch or a separate legal entity.

For now, it's important to know that forming a separate legal entity in a foreign country can have very significant consequences, which may be desired or not (or a mix of both), depending on the country in which you are working, the nature of your activities, and a number of other factors.

Common reasons for preferring to operate in a foreign country through a branch rather than a separate legal entity include:

- You want the U.S. 501(c)(3) organization to have maximum control over the foreign operations.
- You want to solicit funds for your foreign projects without having to comply with the *discretion and control* requirement (see section 2.3).
- You want to avoid the costs of maintaining a separate legal entity.
- In some countries, it may be easier to work with government officials if you are operating through a branch of a foreign (U.S.) organization. You need to talk with U.S. organizations that are established in the country and locale you are targeting to determine whether this is relevant to your organization.

Factors that point toward forming a separate foreign legal entity, rather than operating through a foreign branch or office, include:

- You are required to do so. This may be a condition to hiring local residents (or to their eligibility for social benefits), or it may be due to the nature of your activities.

- You want to allow for local governance.
- Operating through a local entity may facilitate relationships with government officials, or make it possible to obtain funding from local country sources. For example, in the European Union (EU), some funding is available only for organizations incorporated in an EU country.
- Forming a separate legal entity may avoid subjecting the U.S. nonprofit organization to liabilities, including taxes, in the foreign country.
- Forming a separate legal entity may avoid disclosing the financial statements of your U.S. operations to foreign authorities.
- If you want to solicit contributions in a foreign country, it is likely that you will be required to form a separate legal entity in that country.
- You may want to engage in substantial foreign business activity, or in lobbying or political activity, or in other activities that are not in furtherance of the U.S. 501(c)(3) organization's tax-exempt purposes.
- If your foreign operations are likely to grow significantly, you may need a separate legal entity down the road. In that case, it may be more efficient to structure the foreign operation through a separate legal entity from the outset.

These considerations are discussed in Chapter 5.

## Branches versus Separate Legal Entities: Wikipedia

Wikipedia, the nonprofit 501(c)(3) organization that relies on volunteers to research, draft, and post factual information on the Internet, wrestled with whether to operate globally through branches or legal entities. It ultimately chose to operate through branches. For Wikipedia, the goal was to balance empowering local country volunteers against the need to maintain centralized control in order to ensure compliance with Wikipedia's fundamental policies. Separate legal entities would facilitate local empowerment, but would make it more difficult to maintain central control over policies. Maintaining legal entities also requires more resources, and Wikipedia would have had to hire paid staff. Ultimately, Wikipedia struck the balance by operating through branches (chapters) in foreign countries.[15]

## Case Study: World Association for Children and Parents (WACAP)

The following case study shows how one organization structures its operations differently from country to country, taking into account foreign legal requirements and other factors.

WACAP (www.wacap.org) is a U.S.-based 501(c)(3) organization that provides international adoption services. It finds permanent families in the United States for orphaned children who live in institutions or foster homes in (at the time of this book's publication) eight foreign countries: China, Taiwan, Thailand, Korea, India, Russia, Bulgaria, and Ethiopia. The nature of WACAP's work requires that in each of these countries the organization is licensed, or accredited, to place children for adoption.

In each country WACAP must have, or rely on an intermediary that has, a strong working relationship with childcare institutions (which themselves may or may not be government-owned) and/or with the government officials in agencies that have oversight over children's welfare and adoption.

WACAP structures its operations differently in each country. Ethiopia and Russia are the only countries in which WACAP maintains an office and directly employs local staff. In each of the other countries, WACAP's U.S.-based staff works directly with government officials and/or local country NGOs. These differences in operational structures are dictated by each country's conditions of accreditation for the provision of adoption services.

In each country, every individual child's adoption involves massive amounts of documentation. In many cases, the responsible government officials require that WACAP comply with multiple layers of documentation. The way WACAP is structured in each country affects the efficiency and cost of its local operations, although it must also be recognized that local cultural and legal factors play a very big role.

In general, operating through a local country office with local staff contributes to efficiency and confidence, but it is also very expensive. Where possible, working through a trusted local country NGO can provide a good balance between having some control on the one hand, while avoiding excessive costs on the other. Working directly with local government officials, without any local staff, works well when the local government officials have excellent English language skills, and are efficient and proactive. On the other hand, in locations where the government officials are overburdened, lack adequate technology and/or have limited English capability, WACAP finds that the process becomes cumbersome and can be extremely frustrating.

## WACAP's Experience in Ethiopia and Russia

Maintaining a local office, in both Russia and Ethiopia, requires, as a condition to providing adoption services, that the U.S. organization has 501(c)(3) status (or the equivalent in its home country) and maintains a local country office with employees. WACAP's legal status in each country is that of a foreign NGO. It is required to satisfy requirements applicable to NGOs in general, while also complying with specific conditions for licensing as an adoption organization.

As a foreign NGO in Ethiopia, WACAP has to produce annual audited financial statements for its local branch. Along with the audit requirement, there are strict document retention rules. WACAP is aware that if it cannot produce receipts for all local country expenses, it could lose its NGO status and its accreditation for adoption services.

In Russia, having foreign NGO status means that the government agencies with oversight responsibilities can visit the local office at any time, with or without notice, and request any documents. WACAP's U.S.-based senior staff and board of directors are mindful that any changes in the organization's governing documents, such as bylaws, must be registered with Russian authorities. The authorities will pore over legal documents, and minor inconsistencies can cause major problems. Among the government bodies that have authority to make inquiries is the prosecutor's office, which can shut down operations, temporarily or permanently, if it perceives irregularities.

When hiring and paying employees, WACAP employs local staff in both Ethiopia and Russia in order to satisfy the local office requirement in each of those countries. Maintaining local country staff is very expensive, but it also has its advantages. By employing people locally, rather than relying on third parties, WACAP is better able to ensure compliance with its own high ethical standards in the adoptions it handles.

Of course, managing employees in remote locations is challenging. WACAP has found it essential to develop relationships among other NGOs doing similar work in each country, in part as a way of identifying and vetting potential employees. U.S. staff must also make frequent trips to oversee the local operations.

Paying staff in foreign countries is also costly. In general, the only way to transfer funds from the United States is by wire transfer, which can be expensive. Reimbursing employees for out-of-pocket expenses (such as expenses of escorting families who travel to adopt) can also be burdensome. In Russia, WACAP has had to establish a separate bank account so that certain employees can access funds directly with a credit or debit card.

## WACAP's Experience in Korea and India

In Korea and India, WACAP does not maintain an office, but rather it works in each country directly with a local NGO that is licensed by the government to provide adoption services and act as an intermediary.

Working with a local country accredited NGO allows WACAP to avoid the costs of maintaining a local office and employees, while knowing that the intermediary organization is accountable to the local government. A disadvantage of this arrangement is that, relative to employing staff directly, WACAP has little control over the adoption process and often has little recourse in the face of long delays.

### WACAP's Experience in China

In China, WACAP's U.S.-based staff works directly with government agencies and, when permitted to do so, it works directly with government-operated orphanages. As in Korea and India, this avoids the costs of maintaining an office and staff. However, the absence of a local intermediary NGO means that WACAP's U.S-based staff has to communicate directly with government agencies. When WACAP was first exploring and starting up its program in China, U.S.-based staff members made repeated visits to meet and develop relationships with government officials. China's policies and procedures for adoption, and foreign NGOs in general, are continually changing. Today, even though WACAP has operated a program in China for nearly a decade, U.S.-based staff must travel frequently to maintain the relationships that are critical to continuing the program.

## 4.6  Do You Need to Do It Alone?

Once you've decided to operate a foreign program, you may consider whether it makes sense to cooperate with existing organizations. This could allow you to focus on your organization's core strengths, while relying on others to deliver ancillary services. Increasingly in recent years nonprofit organizations have developed mutually beneficial relationships with for-profit businesses as well as with other nonprofits.

The word *partnership* comes up frequently among international nonprofits, and it is used to refer to a wide range of relationships. In the legal context, a partnership is an arrangement between two or more individuals or organizations that agree to share profits and losses from a business venture. This is not necessarily what nonprofits mean when they say they have *partnered* with another organization. Rather, they may be referring to a formal arrangement between two or more organizations in which each agrees to undertake specific responsibilities for a common purpose. Or, an organization that says it is *partnering* with another may be referring to an informal form of cooperation.

Your organization may choose to cooperate with other organizations, as well as for-profit businesses and/or governmental bodies, in any number of ways. It is important, however, to think about whether and how you should formalize the relationship with a written agreement. Are you relying on the other party to do something that is important to your program, or is the other organization relying on your organization to do something? Are you paying or receiving payments for the performance of services or provision of goods? Are you allowing the other party to use your name or logo, copyrighted material or patents (so-called *intellectual property*), or to issue communications referencing your organization? A *yes* answer to any of these questions (among others) suggests that you should protect your rights with a written agreement.

It is beyond the scope of this book to delve into the vast array of cooperating relationships that international nonprofits have established with other nonprofits, for-profits, and governmental bodies. However, the following case study shows how one organization has successfully used relationships with other NGOs and for-profit businesses to benefit its programs and the people they serve.

## Case Study: Agros International

Agros International (www.agros.org) is a Washington state-based 501(c)(3) organization, formed in 1985, that works to break the cycle of poverty in rural villages of Central America and Mexico by enabling landless communities to achieve land ownership and economic stability. Agros works in villages where poverty has existed for generations, and it recognizes that breaking the cycle of poverty requires addressing a variety of root causes.

Once Agros makes a commitment to work with a particular community (usually because the community has sought Agros's assistance), Agros devotes 7 to 10 years to working with that community to help it grow from a loose organization of landless families into a self-governing, self-sustaining, and thriving community. Fundamental to that process is helping families to become landowners and teaching them to farm their land in an economically sustainable way. Agros purchases land and transfers it to landless families, extending long-term loans that are repaid as the families earn revenue through farming. To help those families develop economically sustainable agriculture, Agros employs agronomists who provide technical support with agricultural projects.

Agros understands that, while land ownership and economically sustainable farming are critical to breaking the poverty cycle, much more is required to develop sustainable communities. These communities, previously lacking structure, need to develop their own government and social systems, as well as to provide access to education, healthcare, adult literacy, and spiritual growth. To help develop the social infrastructure required for self-sustaining communities, Agros works with a range of local and international nonprofit organizations, government entities, churches, and community-based organizations.

## Collaborating with Nonprofit Organizations

Recognizing that building a sustainable community requires a team effort, Agros has developed a program it calls *Journey with a Village* (JWAV). In this program, Agros facilitates relationships among the communities it serves and other local and international nonprofit organizations, churches, government entities, and even for-profit businesses. These so-called *JWAV partners* provide funding and also help work with the communities to develop the needed social infrastructure.

Agros is very deliberate about selecting JWAV partners. The selection criteria ensure that the partner shares Agros's view of the mission and its faith-based approach, and that it has the financial capacity to provide the needed support. Agros enters into formal agreement with all of its JWAV partners.

## Working with For-Profit Businesses

Agros has also entered into mutually beneficial relationships with some for-profit businesses. As with its nonprofit relationships, Agros requires that its business partners share its vision of economic sustainability and support its faith-based approach. In addition, Agros requires written agreements to ensure clarity of the objectives and terms of its relationships with business entities.

One of Agros's key partners is *Camano Island Coffee Roasters* (CICR), a certified organic, shade-grown, and fairly-traded coffee company. CICR is a for-profit company that values sustainability for the land and people who grow coffee beans. At the same time, many of the communities served by Agros are in coffee-growing regions.

The sharing of a vision and values set the stage for a mutually beneficial relationship between Agros and CICR, beginning in the mid-2000s, whereby CICR contributes one dollar for every package of coffee purchased by its coffee club members. Agros, in turn, acknowledges CICR's contribution to its programs and allows CICR to publicize the relationship subject to certain parameters.

Many nonprofit organizations dream of finding a corporate sponsor, and large corporations are continually bombarded with requests from nonprofits. The Agros story illustrates that finding the right fit can make all the difference, and that fit just may exist close to home, within the small business community.

# 4.7 Staffing a Foreign Office: Consequences to the Organization

Organizations that are starting up a foreign country office frequently send U.S. employees for a transition period of, say, six months to a year. Once the operation is running smoothly, local employees are hired and the U.S. personnel go home. This can be an effective way of making the transition into a new country. It is also expensive. Sending U.S. employees to live in a foreign country is typically more expensive than hiring locally.

If your U.S. 501(c)(3) organization is sending employees, independent contractors, or volunteers overseas for extended periods, you need to be concerned with foreign country laws and regulations, including those that impose tax liabilities on the organization or individuals, immigration or visa requirements, and obligations to register or license your branch or office. At the same time, you need to be sure that your foreign activities do not jeopardize your U.S. tax-exempt status.

The remainder of this chapter focuses on the impact to your organization of sending employees to work in a foreign office. In Chapter 6, we explore legal, tax, and practical considerations for U.S. and foreign individuals who staff your foreign operations.

## How Do Foreign Activities Affect Your U.S. Tax-Exempt Status?

A 501(c)(3) organization may conduct some, or even all of its activities outside the U.S. without losing 501(c)(3) status or the ability to receive tax-deductible contributions.[16] In fact, by operating foreign activities directly, rather than through a separate related or unrelated organization (discussed in Chapter 5), the U.S. organization retains the power to control the use of funds in a foreign country.

Operating in a foreign country can, however, create special challenges. You need to be sure that your foreign activities are conducted in compliance with 501(c)(3) requirements. Overseeing the conduct of staff and/or volunteers in remote locations can be difficult, all the more so when cultural and language differences come into play. As a result, it is critical to adopt policies and procedures that ensure compliance with 501(c)(3) requirements, to monitor compliance, and to educate foreign-based staff and volunteers about U.S. 501(c)(3) requirements.

Challenges in overseeing foreign activities of a 501(c)(3) organization include:

1. *Complying with U.S. anti-terrorism requirements.* U.S. nonprofit organizations operating outside the United States need to be highly vigilant about avoiding even inadvertently supporting terrorist activities. Support of terrorist activity is not a 501(c)(3) purpose, and can result in loss of

tax-exempt status in addition to the imposition of other harsh sanctions. This is discussed in section 8.1.

2. *Avoiding improper benefits to private interests.* An organization does not qualify for 501(c)(3) status if it is found to be more than incidentally benefiting private interests.[17] This is referred to as the *private benefit doctrine.* Private interests are individuals or organizations that are not the intended beneficiaries of the organization's exempt purposes.

   A related concept, referred to as *private inurement*, prohibits the provision of any unearned benefits (for example, excessive compensation or compensation for services not really performed) to certain individuals in a position to have control or influence, including directors, officers, and other individuals with significant influence, such as program heads, along with family members of these people with influence.[18]

3. *Avoiding excessive lobbying and prohibited election-related communication.* A 501(c)(3) organization is also subject to the same limitations on lobbying, and a prohibition against political activity, whether its activities are conducted within or outside the United States. However, applying those rules in a foreign country context may not be straightforward. This is discussed in section 8.5.

4. *Avoiding bribery of foreign officials and other corrupt activity.* U.S. laws strictly prohibit bribing foreign government officials. Engaging in this type of activity can trigger severe sanctions, and can even jeopardize tax-exempt status. In many countries around the world, bribery is a way of doing business. If you conduct operations in such a country, you will need to implement firm policies and exercise oversight to ensure compliance with U.S. law. This is discussed in section 8.4.

5. *Monitoring unrelated business activity.* All U.S. 501(c)(3) organizations are required to pay U.S. federal (and in some cases state) income tax on income they earn from certain business activities that are considered unrelated to the organization's tax-exempt purposes. This is true regardless of whether the activities are conducted within the United States or in a foreign country. *See* section 4.9.

## 4.8   Will Your U.S. Organization Be Taxed by a Foreign Country?

Once you have decided to send staff or volunteers to work in a foreign country, you need to be concerned with whether your organization will have to pay taxes in that country. Keep in mind that your organization may be subject to a variety of taxes in any particular country.

## Value Added Tax (VAT)

Most countries (other than the United States) have *value added tax*, or *VAT*. For many organizations VAT can be a greater burden than income tax because VAT is charged on purchases while income tax, even if applicable, is computed based on an excess of revenue over expenses. Unlike income tax, which may be reduced or eliminated under a tax treaty (discussed in the following paragraphs), VAT is solely a matter of applicable foreign country law. If you are operating in a foreign country you will want to understand whether and how VAT applies to your organization's activities.

VAT and other common types of non-income taxes imposed by foreign countries are discussed in Chapter 9. The remainder of this chapter focuses on foreign income taxes.

## Income Tax

Income taxes can be a concern, particularly if you are charging fees for services or otherwise earning revenue in a foreign country from sources other than grants and contributions. Most countries, like the Unites States (and most states within the United States), impose income tax (sometimes referred to as *enterprise tax*, or *corporation tax*) on corporations and other entities that operate within their borders, once the level of activity reaches a certain threshold. The fact that your organization qualifies as tax-exempt under U.S. federal, and possibly state law, does not mean that another country cannot tax it.[19]

Some countries, such as South Africa, afford tax-exempt status to a branch of a foreign (e.g., U.S.) organization that is tax-exempt in its home country. Many countries, however, will not automatically consider your organization tax-exempt. This is particularly true if your organization receives some form of earned revenue, such as tuition or fees for services you provide in furtherance of your mission. There are even a few countries, notably among the former Soviet Republics, which tax contributions received from foreign sources unless certain conditions are met.[20]

Assuming your U.S. organization is not automatically tax-exempt in a foreign country, you may nevertheless be eligible to obtain tax-exempt status based on the nature of the work you do. You may have to apply for tax-exemption, if it's available, separately from registering a branch. Eligibility for tax-exempt status may be correlated with having a license to engage in particular activities, such as educational or charitable activities. You need to investigate this up-front.

If you cannot obtain tax-exempt status, you will need to know whether the activities you are conducting in the foreign country could trigger any income tax liabilities. When your activities within a country rise to the level that subjects the organization to income tax, that status is called a *taxable presence* or *permanent establishment*.

What level of activity in a country creates a permanent establishment? This varies widely among countries. The first question to ask is, *Is there a bilateral income tax treaty between the United States and that particular country?*

Bilateral income tax treaties are agreements, entered into between two countries, intended to clarify which country has the right to tax income from various activities. The goal (which is often but not always achieved) is to prevent any individual or organization from being taxed on the same income by two different countries. That would be double taxation. The United States has entered into income tax treaties with many, but far from all, foreign countries. Appendix C lists these countries.[21]

If a treaty exists between the United States and the country in which you are operating, the level of activity you can conduct in that other country before becoming subject to income tax there is typically greater than where no treaty exists. However, you still need to understand what activities will subject your organization to tax, particularly if your organization earns revenue from sources other than contributions and grants.

This chapter assumes that your organization is formed in the U.S. as a nonprofit corporation, rather than as a trust or unincorporated association. While a 501(c)(3) organization may be formed as a nonprofit corporation, trust, or unincorporated association, organizations that directly operate programs (rather than limiting their activities to grantmaking) typically prefer the corporate form.[22]

## What If There Is No Income Tax Treaty?

If the United States has not entered into an income tax treaty with the country in which your organization is operating (or if the treaty does not apply to you), then that country's internal laws will determine whether and under what circumstances your organization is subject to tax there. Unfortunately, many of the developing countries in which U.S.-based nonprofit organizations conduct activities do not have income tax treaties with the United States. For example, among African countries, only four (South Africa, Morocco, Tunisia, and Egypt) have entered into income tax treaties with the United States. Appendix C lists the countries with which the United States has an income tax treaty in force at the time of this book's publication.

Keep in mind that, even if a treaty does apply, the treaty may not protect you from imposition of taxes other than income taxes, discussed in section 9.4.

If you are sending employees, independent contractors, or volunteers for extended periods, you would be well advised to seek local legal assistance to be sure you know whether your organization may become subject to tax in that country. Note that your nonprofit corporation may become subject to local tax liabilities as a result of sending multiple people to work on a project over a period of time, even if no single individual stays for a very long time.

If you find out that your operations, or intended operations, may trigger local tax liabilities for your organization, you may want to structure your operations differently, for example by forming a separate foreign nonprofit corporation (or something similar under the laws of the foreign country). This is discussed in Chapter 5.

## What If an Income Tax Treaty Exists?

If there is an income tax treaty in effect between the United States and the country in which your organization is operating, the next steps are to determine whether that treaty applies to your organization and, if so, whether the treaty will protect the organization from income tax in the foreign country.

RECIPROCAL TAX-EXEMPT STATUS UNDER A TREATY   Only a small number of the income tax treaties the United States has entered into with other countries afford U.S. tax-exempt organizations with reciprocal tax-exempt status in the foreign country. This type of reciprocity is provided under the income tax treaties between the United States and Germany, the Netherlands, Canada, and Mexico, but each treaty contains its own limitations.[23]

For example, under the U.S. treaties with Germany and the Netherlands, a U.S. 501(c)(3) organization is afforded tax-exempt status in the other country, but only if it meets the requirements for tax-exempt status under the other country's laws. By contrast, the U.S. treaties with Mexico and Canada do not require that the organization qualify for exemption under the laws of the other country. Nevertheless, each of these four treaties contains special conditions, and it is critical to consult an advisor in the relevant country if you intend to rely on these treaty provisions.

Note that we are not addressing the question of whether a foreign country's residents can claim tax deductions for contributions to a U.S. organization that has a presence in that country. A few treaties (those with Canada, Mexico, and Israel) do contain a provision to this effect, subject to significant limitations. This is discussed in Chapter 7.

IF NO RECIPROCITY, DOES THE TREATY APPLY TO 501(C)(3) CORPORATIONS?   One of the features common to all of the U.S. income tax treaties is a section that sets forth rules for determining when a U.S. organization has a permanent establishment and, therefore, may be subject to income tax in the foreign country. Often, a treaty will provide more flexibility than would the local country's internal law, allowing a U.S.-based corporation to conduct more activities in the foreign country without being subject to income tax.

Before looking at specific permanent establishment provisions of a treaty, however, it is necessary to determine whether the particular treaty applies to 501(c)(3) corporations. Assuming your organization is formed as a nonprofit corporation under the laws of a U.S. state or the District of Columbia, the answer, in most cases, is *yes*.[24] There are, however, some older treaties that require, as a condition to eligibility for treaty benefits, that a 501(c)(3) organization devote a substantial portion (typically more than half) of its resources to residents of one or both of the countries that are parties to the treaty; and/or raise a substantial portion of its funds from one or both of those countries. In addition, a few older treaties are ambiguous as to whether a 501(c)(3) organization falls within the definition of a U.S. resident that is eligible to take advantage of the treaty.

You should also be aware that, even if an income tax treaty applies, it typically does not apply to taxes other than income taxes and capital gains taxes. In the United States, state and local income taxes, as well as sales taxes, are not affected by income tax treaties. Most foreign countries impose taxes in addition to income taxes, and those other taxes typically are not covered under a treaty.[25] Other types of foreign taxes are discussed in sections 9.14 and 9.15.

**IF A TREATY APPLIES, HOW DO YOU KNOW WHETHER YOU WILL BE TAXED?**  Each bilateral income tax treaty between the United States and another country contains some general guidelines for determining when a permanent establishment exists, such that the foreign country may impose its income tax on the organization. The U.S. Treasury Department has created a Model Treaty containing the terms that the United States aims for when negotiating with foreign countries. The U.S. Model Treaty sets forth the following list of activities as examples of activities that create a permanent establishment:

- A place of management.
- A branch.
- An office.
- A factory.
- A workshop.
- A mine, an oil or gas well, a quarry, or any other place of extraction of natural resources.[26]

This list is typical of many U.S. treaties, although variations exist. This means, for example, that if your organization is provided with office space for regular use within a foreign NGO's facility, your organization could be treated as having a permanent establishment in that country.

A construction project is another typical kind of permanent establishment. The U.S. Model Treaty provides that the maintenance of a construction site creates a permanent establishment, but only if the construction project lasts for more than 12 months.[27] This situation could arise, for example, if your organization is engaged in building schools or libraries in a foreign country.

Some treaties shorten the length of time it takes before you create a permanent establishment. Under the U.S.-India treaty, any building or construction project that lasts more than 120 days triggers a permanent establishment, and time spent on more than one project will be combined for purposes of determining whether the 120-day threshold is met.[28] Under the U.S.-Philippines treaty, a building site or construction project will trigger a permanent establishment if continued for more than 183 days.[29]

Another way of triggering a permanent establishment is through certain activities of an *agent* (such as an employee) in a foreign country. Most income tax treaties between the United States and other countries provide that a permanent establishment exists if, under specified circumstances, an agent (including an employee) in the foreign country has and regularly exercises authority to enter into contracts on behalf of the U.S. organization.[30]

Your organization can also create a permanent establishment merely by sending people to a foreign country for extended periods. For example, the U.S.-India Treaty[35] provides that a U.S. organization creates a permanent establishment by providing services (including consulting services) in India through employees or other personnel if the activities continue for more than 90 days within a 12-month period.[31] It is not clear whether the reference to *other personnel* includes volunteers. In any event, this is a very broad provision that could be used to impose income tax liability on a U.S. nonprofit organization that operates in India by sending people to provide services, even if no single individual is present for the threshold six months.

There are many other treaties that contain variations on the provisions cited above, and it is often not clear whether a permanent establishment exists. It is important to consult a lawyer in the country in which you want to operate so as to understand whether income and/or other taxes will apply to your operations and, if so, whether and how you can legally avoid them.

## What If Your Organization Will, or Might Be, Taxed in a Foreign Country?

If your organization is found to have a permanent establishment (or if no treaty exists, a taxable presence) in a foreign country, that country's taxing authorities may impose tax by attributing some portion of your organization's revenues to the operations in that country. In most (but not all) countries, grants and contributions will be tax-exempt, but any earned revenue may be subject to income tax. It is often difficult to anticipate how much, if any, revenue will be attributed and how much tax will be imposed.

For that reason, you may want to consider alternative ways of structuring your foreign operations so as to avoid subjecting your organization to the risk of foreign income tax.

You may want to consider these three alternatives:

1. *Applying for tax-exempt status in the foreign country.* In many countries, a branch of a foreign (such as a U.S.) organization can qualify for tax-exempt status.
2. *Having employees or volunteers work directly for an NGO in the country in which you are working.* If you are providing services for extended periods in collaboration with a foreign-based organization, they may be able to employ or sponsor those individuals. This is the model used by Friends of the Orphans (*see* Chapter 1), which refers individuals to work for extended periods as volunteers for a non-U.S. organization that operates orphanages in Mexico, Haiti, and a number of countries throughout Central and South America.

   If you are sending employees for extended periods of time, you might consider having a local country organization employ those individuals directly. You may be able to contribute funds to the organization to offset the costs of compensating employees. Of course, you may have to address visa issues. In addition, individuals employed by a local country organization will likely be subject to income tax in that country (*see* section 4.6).
3. *Forming a separate local nonprofit organization.* Finally, if your organization intends to maintain a long-term presence in a foreign country, for example, by maintaining an office and sending employees or volunteers for extended periods of time, you may consider creating a separate nonprofit corporation (or something similar under the laws of the foreign country). You will need to hire a lawyer in the foreign country to determine what type of organization you should form, how to achieve tax-exempt status, and to understand the applicable rules, operating restrictions, and registration and reporting requirements. In addition, you will need to consider how best to structure the relationship between the foreign country organization and your U.S.-based organization. These issues are discussed further in Chapter 5.

## 4.9   What Happens If Your Organization Conducts Business Activities in a Foreign Country?

While your U.S. organization is pursuing its mission in a foreign country, you may want to seek out sources of revenue to supplement grants, contributions, and, perhaps, fees you charge for performing charitable or educational services. In general, nonprofit organizations in the United States and abroad are becoming increasingly creative about finding revenue-generating opportunities. For example, an organization might use its particular expertise to provide consulting or other services to for-profit businesses, or it might engage in the sale of goods.

Under U.S. tax laws, if your U.S. 501(c)(3) organization earns income from business activities that are considered unrelated to its tax-exempt purposes, that income may be subject to U.S. federal (and possibly state) income tax. That income may also be taxed in the country in which the business activity is conducted. In some countries, the consequence of conducting business activities can be revocation of tax-exempt status, so be sure to investigate the foreign country's laws before you embark on a business venture.

## U.S. Tax on Unrelated Business Income

As a U.S. nonprofit corporation, your organization is subject to U.S. federal (and possibly state) income tax on its worldwide income. This means that the same rules apply to the U.S. taxation of so-called *unrelated business taxable income (UBTI)* regardless of whether the income is earned within or outside the United States.

### What Is Unrelated Business Taxable Income (UBTI)?

Even though a 501(c)(3) organization is exempt from federal (and in many cases state) income taxes, that exemption is not absolute. A 501(c)(3) organization is subject to income tax on its so-called unrelated business taxable income. UBTI is income that meets all three of the following criteria:

1. Attributable to a business.
2. Not substantially related to the organization's tax-exempt purpose.
3. Regularly carried on.[a]

Certain types of passive income, including dividends, interest, royalties, and certain rents, are not treated as UBTI.[b]

A common example of UBTI is income earned from selling goods as a way of raising funds for the organization. The sales might be through a physical location, or they might be made online, or both. They will not, however, be taxed as UBTI unless the goods sold are substantially unrelated to the organization's exempt purpose. In general, this means that to avoid UBTI, the goods themselves must serve a purpose of educating people about your mission, or promote awareness of your organization's activities. So, for example, the sale of a book about the social problem your organization is trying to solve should not generate UBTI. In addition, even if the item is unrelated to your tax-exempt purpose, the income earned will not be UBTI unless the sales are ongoing. A typical annual fundraising auction will not generate UBTI because it is not an ongoing event. There are some additional exceptions that may apply.

A detailed discussion of UBTI is beyond the scope of this book, but there are many resources available if you want to learn more.[c]

---

[a] I.R.C. § 513; Treas. Reg. § 1.513-1.

[b] I.R.C. § 512(b). Under an exception, interest, royalties and rents (but not dividends) are, under certain circumstances, treated as UBTI when received from a corporation (or other organization), whether or not tax-exempt, over which the recipient organization has voting control if the payor can deduct the payment to reduce its own U.S. taxable income.

[c] *See* IRS Publication 598, *Tax On Unrelated Business Income of Exempt Organizations* (March 2012), available at www.irs.gov/publications/p598/index.html.

---

### Foreign Consequences of Earning Business Income

If you plan to earn revenue by conducting any business activity, make sure you understand how the foreign country treats that activity. Be aware that foreign countries differ with respect to whether and the extent to which they allow tax-exempt organizations to earn revenue from business activities. In some countries, this kind of activity not only triggers tax, but it may also cause a loss of tax-exempt status. For example, in India some types of organizations may lose tax-exempt status if they earn revenue from activities unrelated to their tax-exempt purposes.[32]

If your organization is taxed in the United States on UBTI earned in a foreign country, and is also required to pay tax on that income in a foreign country, it may be able to claim a foreign tax credit to reduce the U.S. tax liability.[33] While the mechanics of the foreign tax credit can be rather complex, the underlying concept is simply that a U.S. taxpayer should not be taxed more than once on the same income.

### Consider Forming a For-Profit Subsidiary

If your U.S. 501(c)(3) organization is planning to engage in foreign income-generating activities that are treated, under U.S. or foreign law, as unrelated to your tax-exempt purposes, you may want to form a separate, for-profit subsidiary. That way, you avoid having to report taxable income in the United States and/or the foreign country in which you are operating. More important, this may be necessary to preserve your tax-exempt status in the foreign country. Of course, you will need to explore the foreign law consequences of operating through a separate business corporation (or the equivalent under foreign law), including whether the foreign subsidiary can distribute profits to your organization without any additional tax. This is discussed further in section 5.14.

## 4.10   Foreign Reporting Requirements

We saw, in section 4.5, that the requirements for registration, and sometimes registration renewal, of a foreign branch vary greatly among countries, and can be quite burdensome.

Even in countries that don't impose burdensome registration requirements, you may be required to make periodic filings of financial or other information. In many countries, branches are not required to file and report as much information as are legal entities, but that is not always the case. In some countries, such as Ethiopia, a branch may be subject to virtually the same level of regulation and reporting as a separate legal entity. In others, the regulatory burden is significantly lower.

## 4.11   U.S. Reporting Requirements

If your U.S. organization conducts activities in a foreign country, you will need to be aware of a number of U.S. laws and reporting requirements that apply specifically to U.S. organizations and individuals that conduct activities outside the United States. Some of these are specific to tax-exempt organizations, and some apply more generally to U.S. citizens and residents. At the same time, U.S. organizations that hire foreign individuals (those without U.S. citizenship or permanent resident status) to work in the United States, as employees or independent contractors, need to know about U.S. immigration and visa requirements. Chapter 8 provides an overview of additional U.S. laws and reporting requirements that apply to 501(c)(3) organizations engaged in foreign activities.

## 4.12   Review and Further Considerations

This chapter has explored a number of important legal and practical considerations that come into play once an organization decides to operate directly in a foreign country. To avoid subjecting your U.S. organization to the legal requirements, and potential liabilities, of a foreign country, you may want to consider forming a separate legal entity (a nonprofit corporation or something similar under a foreign country's laws) in the foreign country or countries where you want to conduct programs. The following chapter explores the formation and operation of separate foreign legal entities, as well as alternatives for structuring relationships among entities to achieve your purposes.

## Notes

1. Rev. Rul. 71-460, 1971-2 C.B. 231. See also *Bilingual Montessori School of Paris, Inc. v. Comm'r*, 75 T.C. 480 (1980), in which it was held that contributions to a 501(c)(3) organization incorporated in Delaware were deductible for U.S. federal income tax purposes, even though the organization conducted all of its activities outside the United States.

2. For example, in *Regan v. Taxation With Representation of Washington*, 461 U.S. 540 (1983), the United States Supreme Court rejected arguments that the imposition of lobbying restrictions on 501(c)(3) organizations violated the free speech or equal protection provisions of the U.S. Constitution. The Court noted that a 501(c)(3) organization can form a separate 501(c)(4) organization to conduct lobbying activities that are not funded with tax-deductible contributions.

3. For an overview of this trend, *see* "Global Philanthropy in a Time of Crisis," *Global Trends in NGO Law* 1, no. 2 (May 2009) ("Global Philanthropy in a Time of Crisis"), available at www.icnl.org/research/trends/trends1-2.html); *see also*, "Wave of Constraint: Recent Developments in Venezuela, Ecuador, Honduras, Iran, Bahrain, and Cambodia," *Global Trends in NGO Law* 2, no. 2 (Special Edition, December 2010), available at www.icnl.org/research/trends/trends2-2.html; and Douglas Rutzen, "Practice Note: Egypt and the Catalyst Constraint," *International Journal of Not-for-Profit Law* 14, no. 1–2 (April 2012), 49–51, available at www.icnl.org/research/journal/vol14iss1/index.html.

4. For an in-depth exploration of legal restrictions on global philanthropy, *see* "Defending Civil Society," co-authored by International Center for Not-for-Profit Law and World Movement for Democracy Secretariat at the National Endowment for Democracy, *International Journal of Not-for-Profit Law*, 14, no. 3 (September 2012) ("Defending Civil Society Report") available at www.icnl.org/research/journal/vol14iss3/art1.html. *See also* David Moore and Douglas Rutzen, "Legal Framework for Global Philanthropy: Barriers and Opportunities," *International Journal for Not-for-Profit Law* 13, no. 1–2 (April 2011), available at www.icnl.org/research/journal/vol13iss1/special_1.htm.

5. *See* International Center for Not-For-Profit Law NGO Monitor, available at www.icnl.org/knowledge/ngolawmonitor/jordan.

6. *See* David Moore and Douglas Rutzen, "Legal Framework for Global Philanthropy: Barriers and Opportunities," *supra* note 4, at 18.

7. *Id.* at 20; "Defending Civil Society Report," *supra* note 4, at 29.

8. *See* International Center for Not-For-Profit Law NGO Monitor, *supra* note 5.

9. *Id.*

10. As reported by David D. Kirkpatrick, "Egypt Rejects Bids From 8 U.S. Nonprofit Groups," *The New York Times*, April 23, 2012, available at www .nytimes.com/2012/04/24/world/middleeast/egypt-rejects-registration-bids-from-8-us-nonprofits.html?_r=1.

11. This is a form of what is commonly referred to as *fiscal sponsorship*, in which an existing 501(c)(3) organization agrees to assume financial management for a program or project which typically (but not always), does not have its own 501(c)(3) status. A fiscal sponsorship arrangement must be carefully structured to ensure that the sponsoring organization continues to qualify as a 501(c)(3) organization and that donors are eligible for U.S. federal income tax deductions. To learn more about structuring a fiscal sponsorship arrangement, *see* Gregory L. Colvin, *Fiscal Sponsorship: 6 Ways To Do It Right* (San Francisco, CA: Study Center Press, 2005).

12. "NGO Laws in Sub-Saharan Africa," *Global Trends in NGO Law* 3, no. 3 (June 2011) at 3, available at www.icnl.org/research/trends/trends3-3 .html; "Survey of Arab NGO Laws," *Global Trends in NGO Law* 1, no. 4 (March 2010), 4, available at www.icnl.org/research/trends/trends1-4.html.

13. *See* Country Information, United States International Grantmaking, available at www.usig.org/countryinfo/southafrica.asp.

14. *See* "Enabling Reform: Lessons Learned from Progressive NGO Initiatives," *Global Trends in NGO Law* 2, no. 3 (December 2010), 2, available at www .icnl.org/research/trends/trends2-3.html.

15. As reported in "Jimmy Wales's Wikipedia Balancing Act," *Bloomberg Businessweek*, June 6–12, 2011 at 92, available at www.businessweek .com/magazine/content/11_24/b4232092058415.htm?chan=magazine+ channel_etc.

16. Rev. Rul. 71-460 and *Bilingual Montessori School of Paris, Inc. v. Comm'r*, *supra* note 1.

17. Treas. Reg. § 1.501(c)(3)-1(d)(1)(ii).

18. In many cases, the organization's tax-exempt status will not be revoked, but harsh penalties, referred to as *intermediate sanctions*, will be imposed on the individual or organization that was in a position of influence over the organization, and penalties may also be imposed on individual officers, directors, and trustees of the organization. Treas. Reg. § 1.501 (c)(3)-1(f); I.R.C. § 4958.

19. It is outside the scope of this book to discuss U.S. tax-exempt organizations that are not 501(c)(3) organizations, such as trade associations that qualify for tax exemption under section 501(c)(6) of the internal Revenue Code. It is, however, worth noting that many countries do not have categories of tax-exempt status that correspond to these other (non-501 (c)(3)) types of tax-exempt status under U.S. law.

20. *See* David Moore and Douglas Rutzen, "Legal Framework for Global Philanthropy: Barriers and Opportunities," *supra* note 4, at 24.
21. This list is complete as of the time this book went to print. It is important to check for updates on the U.S. Department of Treasury website at www .treasury.gov/resource-center/tax-policy/treaties/Pages/default.aspx.
22. *See* section 5.3 for a summary of the differences between the corporation, trust, and nonprofit association.
23. Convention Between the United States of America and The Federal Republic of Germany for the Avoidance of Double Taxation (1989) ("U.S.-Germany Income Tax Treaty"), Article 27, available at www.irs.gov/Businesses/ International-Businesses/Germany----Tax-Treaty-Documents. Convention Between The United States and Canada With Respect to Taxes on Income and Capital (1983) ("U.S.-Canada Income Tax Treaty"), Article XXI, available at www.irs.gov/Businesses/International-Businesses/Canada--- Tax-Treaty-Documents.; Convention Between The United States of America and The Kingdom of The Netherlands for the Avoidance of Double Taxation (1992) ("U.S.-Netherlands Income Tax Treaty"), Article 36, available at www.irs.gov/Businesses/International-Businesses/ Canada---Tax-Treaty-Documents.; Convention Between The Government of The United States of America and The Government of The United Mexican States for the Avoidance of Double Taxation (1992) ("U.S.-Mexico Income Tax Treaty"), Article 22, available at www.irs .gov/Businesses/International-Businesses/Mexico---Tax-Treaty-Documents.
24. Most treaty benefits are limited to residents of one of the two countries that are parties to the treaty. Some newer treaties make direct reference to tax-exempt organizations. For example, the treaty with Bangladesh (which went into effect in 2006) directly states that tax-exempt corporations qualify for the treaty's benefits as long as they are established for *religious, charitable, educational, scientific, or similar purposes* (generally the kinds of purposes required to qualify under 501(c)(3)). Another group of treaties defines a resident eligible for treaty benefits to include a corporation that is subject to U.S. tax. In most cases, this language has been interpreted to include tax-exempt corporations, and official U.S. Treasury Department explanations clarify that. This is true, for example, with the U.S. Treaty with Indonesia, which went into effect in 1990.
25. Some U.S. treaties do cover certain foreign income taxes imposed at the local level. Examples of such treaties are those with Switzerland and China.
26. *See*, *e.g.*, United States Model Income Tax Convention of November 15, 2006 ("U.S. Model Income Tax Treaty"), Article 5, available at www.irs .gov/Businesses/International-Businesses/United-States-Model---Tax-Treaty-Documents.
27. *Id.*

28. Convention Between The Government of The United States of America and The Government of The Republic of India for the Avoidance of Double Taxation ("U.S.-India Income Tax Treaty") (1989), Article 5, available at www.irs.gov/Businesses/International-Businesses/India---Tax-Treaty-Documents.

29. Convention Between The Government of The United States of America and The Government of The Republic of The Philippines with Respect to Taxes on Income ("U.S.-Philippines Income Tax Treaty") (1976), Article 5, available at www.irs.gov/Businesses/International-Businesses/Philippines---Tax-Treaty-Documents.

30. *See, e.g.*, U.S. Model Income Tax Treaty, *supra* note 25, Article 5.

31. U.S.-India Income Tax Treaty, *supra* note 27, Article 5.

32. Noshir Dadrawala, "Income of Trusts in India Comes Under Scrutiny," January 10, 2012, available at www.icnl.org/news/index.html.

33. I.R.C. §§ 515, 901.

# Forming and Operating through a Foreign Legal Entity

O nce you have decided to operate a program in a foreign country, there are a number of reasons you may need or want to have more than just a branch or office. You may end up establishing a separate organization, or so-called *legal entity*, in that country rather than operating through a foreign registered office or branch.

## 5.1 Establishing a Foreign Legal Entity

This chapter explains the concept of a legal entity and the reasons you may need or want to form one. We also explore possible ways to structure the relationship between a U.S. organization and one or more separate foreign legal entities so as to achieve an appropriate balance between central control and local autonomy.

### What Is a Legal Entity?

When we refer to a legal entity, we mean a local country nonprofit corporation or trust, or something roughly similar, established under a particular country's law. Unlike a branch or registered office, a foreign legal entity has its own organizational documents (such as articles or a charter), board of directors or other governing body, and members if it's a membership organization.

If you form a legal entity to provide services or conduct other activities in a foreign country, it is likely that you will want to maintain a separate 501(c)(3) organization, formed under U.S. laws, so that your U.S. donors can receive a tax deduction. That U.S. organization becomes a grantmaker when it contributes funds to a separate foreign legal entity, and it must comply with the U.S. cross-border grantmaking rules discussed in Chapter 2 or 3, depending on whether the U.S. organization is a public charity or private foundation. By contrast, if your U.S. organization operates in a foreign country through an office or branch (discussed in Chapter 4), it is treated for U.S. tax and legal purposes as operating the foreign program directly, and therefore it is not treated as a grantmaker.

If your U.S. organization is creating a foreign legal entity to help carry out its mission in a foreign country, the U.S. organization may want to maintain a certain degree of control over the foreign entity to ensure that the latter's purposes and policies are consistent with those of the U.S. organization. At the same time, there may be practical reasons, or even legal requirements, for vesting a foreign entity with local control. Later in this chapter we consider ways to achieve the relationship that's right for your organization.

## Why Form a Separate Legal Entity?

Here are some reasons to form a separate legal entity:

- You are required to do so. This may be a condition to hiring local residents, or to their eligibility for social benefits, or it may be a condition to engaging in particular activities.
- You want to allow for local governance.
- Operating through a local entity may facilitate relationships with government officials, or make it possible to obtain funding from local country sources. For example, in the European Union (EU), some funding is available only for organizations incorporated in an EU country.
- Forming a separate legal entity may avoid subjecting the U.S. nonprofit organization to liabilities, including taxes, in the foreign country.
- Forming a separate legal entity may avoid disclosing the financial statements of your U.S. operations to foreign authorities.
- If you want to solicit contributions in a foreign country, it is likely that you'll be required to form a separate legal entity in that country.
- You may want to engage in substantial foreign business activity, or in lobbying or political activity, or in other activities that are not in furtherance of the U.S. 501(c)(3) organization's tax-exempt purposes.

- If your foreign operations are likely to grow significantly, you may need a separate legal entity down the road. It may be more efficient to structure the foreign operation through a separate legal entity from the outset.

Here, on the other hand, are some reasons to operate through a foreign office or branch, rather than forming a separate legal entity:

- You want the U.S. 501(c)(3) organization to have maximum control over the foreign operations.
- You want to solicit funds for your foreign projects without having to comply with the *discretion and control* requirement (see section 2.3). Note that if you choose to operate a foreign program through a foreign legal entity, while funding that program through a U.S. 501(c)(3) organization, you may be creating a *friends of* structure, discussed in Chapter 2.
- You want to avoid the administrative burdens of maintaining a separate legal entity.
- You want to facilitate government relations. In some countries, a U.S. organization operating through a local branch may find it easier to work with local government officials than would a locally incorporated entity.
- You want to minimize the burden of financial and other reporting requirements, which may be less cumbersome for branches or registered offices than for legal entities.

In determining whether and how to form a foreign legal entity, you will need to consult with a lawyer in the foreign country, and that lawyer should be physically in, or knowledgeable about, the locality in which you are operating. In addition, it is important to talk with other international NGOs to better understand the practical issues you will face. For example, you may want to consult other NGOs and question them about whether government interference is greater for a legal entity or for a branch, and whether one is preferable for purposes of government relationships.

## Converting a Foreign Branch into a Legal Entity

As foreign operations expand or become more complex, it becomes more likely that a separate legal entity will become necessary and/or useful. It is often more cumbersome and expensive to transfer operations into a separate legal entity after you have been operating for some time as a branch. To do so, you will need to identify all assets, employees, and contracts so that you can transfer legal ownership, most likely with the help of a local attorney. In addition, transferring employees can create traps for the unwary. For example, in some countries this type of transfer triggers employees' rights to severance payments.

If you anticipate maintaining a presence, such as an office and staff, in a foreign country on a long-term basis, you may be better off creating a separate legal entity from the outset. While this may take more effort up-front, you will avoid the cost of having to transfer your operations down the road. This is a question to raise with your attorney in the foreign country.

## Case Study: Ashesi University (Ashesi)

The following case study illustrates the reasons one organization decided to form a separate legal entity in a foreign country and the challenges it faced in getting its program up and running.

Ashesi University (www.ashesi.edu.gh), based in Ghana, is an independent college that describes its missions as "to educate a new generation of ethical, entrepreneurial leaders in Africa; to cultivate within our students the skills, ethical foresight and courage it will take to transform their continent."

Patrick Awuah, Ashesi's founder and President, grew up in Ghana and saw a need for a fresh approach to educating Ghana's future leaders. Patrick obtained a liberal arts degree in the United States, and he wanted to bring that model to Ghana while blending it with fundamental training in computer science, management information systems, and business management. In this way, Ashesi would equip its graduates with the tools to think critically and creatively as professional, business, and government leaders. Most importantly, ethical behavior would be an overarching theme for Ashesi.

Patrick began working on a business plan for Ashesi while he was studying for his master's degree in business administration. He sought and received helpful advice from fellow students, professors, and former coworkers at Microsoft, where he had worked as a software engineer. Although the school would charge only modest tuition, Patrick believed scholarships were essential to providing opportunities for students who demonstrated the ability and desire to thrive in Ashesi's culture. While some funding could be raised within Ghana, significant funds would have to be raised from U.S. donors to supplement tuition.

At the time Patrick completed his initial business plan and began recruiting people to work on the project, there were many pieces yet to be addressed. These included developing a detailed curriculum, determining the legal structure for U.S. and Ghanaian operations, and designing the campus that the college would eventually build and occupy some 12 years later.

All of these pieces, large and small, would be guided by a strong vision that pervaded every aspect of Ashesi from the very beginning. Patrick's vision of a community, built around strong leadership and solid ethical practices, influenced the way he and the institution's trustees, volunteers, consultants, staff, and ultimately students, would interact with Ashesi and with each other. Patrick's strong vision and core values helped to attract the right people.

## Initial Legal Structure

Patrick identified some initial funding sources for the project. These were friends, former coworkers, and family members, all U.S. residents. To afford tax deductions for his donors, Patrick needed to form a U.S. nonprofit organization and apply for 501(c)(3) status. In 1999, he formed Ashesi University Foundation (the *Foundation*) as a nonprofit corporation in Washington state.

Once the Foundation received its IRS determination of 501(c)(3) status in 2000, a wider fundraising net could be cast. Meanwhile, the hard work would begin—to plan and start the school in Ghana.

Initially, Patrick and the trustees envisioned that the Foundation, a Washington state nonprofit corporation, would both conduct fundraising in the United States and operate the school in Ghana. Patrick had recruited trustees who, having attended U.S. colleges and universities, understood the rationale for introducing liberal arts education in Ghana.

## Why Form a Separate Legal Entity?

As the planning in Ghana proceeded, Patrick learned that it would be necessary to operate the school through a Ghanaian legal entity in order to receive accreditation, a condition to recruiting students. At the same time, there were additional reasons to operate the college through a separate legal entity. Because the college was dependent upon funding from the Foundation, the Foundation was in a position to prohibit the college from engaging in, or participating in, any unethical practices such as bribery. Of course, it had always been Patrick's intention to operate the college in this way, but when government officials and others tried to exert pressure, the school could simply respond that it was the Foundation that imposed those requirements.

In addition, Patrick and the initial Foundation trustees learned quickly that operating in Ghana through a branch of a U.S. nonprofit corporation would mean that a single legal entity would have to comply separately with both U.S. and Ghanaian laws. That would mean, for example, having to maintain two separate sets of employment policies within a single legal entity. It would also mean that the entire legal entity's financial statements would be subject to government inspection in Ghana, as well as being provided to the Internal Revenue Service in the United States. Without separate legal entities, funds held in the United States could potentially be at risk for liabilities incurred in Ghana because the United States and Ghanaian operations would be part of a single legal entity.

For all of these reasons, Patrick and the Foundation trustees decided to create a dual-entity structure. They created a Ghanaian nonprofit legal entity in the form of a *company limited by guarantee*, a form of nonprofit membership corporation.

To form a Ghanaian legal entity, Ashesi needed a Ghanaian lawyer. Indeed, finding and working with a competent lawyer in Ghana proved to be well worth the investment. Ashesi discovered that in Ghana, as in many developing countries, the official requirements for establishing a nonprofit legal entity were not easy to find, and were not always available in writing. Patrick and the trustees saw other NGOs wasting valuable time and resources while their applications were rejected, repeatedly, for failure to meet minor requirements that were disclosed only one step at a time. The process could indeed be very frustrating and fraught with bureaucracy.

## Relationship between Legal Entities

The Ghanaian entity was formed with the name *Ashesi University College* (the *College*) for the purpose of operating the school in Ghana. The relationship between the two entities was influenced by operational considerations, and also by U.S. and Ghanaian laws. Ghanaian law required local representation on the board of trustees. This was also considered important from an operational perspective. At the same time, Patrick and the Foundation believed it was important that the Foundation have ultimate control, primarily because the U.S. trustees shared his understanding of the U.S. liberal arts model.

The Ghanaian entity that would operate the College was structured as a membership organization (a so-called *company limited by guarantee*), with the Foundation as the sole member. This gave the Foundation ultimate control, as it had the ability to appoint (and if necessary, replace) the entire board. To satisfy Ghanaian law, the College's board was comprised of Ghanaian nationals. The Foundation made the decision that only Ghanaian nationals who sat on the Foundation's board would be eligible to sit on the College's board. This helped provide the Foundation with strong oversight. At the same time, the trustees of the College never comprised a majority of the Foundation's board of trustees.

The Foundation and the College also recruited advisory boards. The Foundation's advisory board is comprised of advisors from highly esteemed U.S. academic institutions, while the College's advisory board is comprised of academic and business leaders in Ghana.

## Tax Status in Ghana

Obtaining tax-exempt status in Ghana has been an ongoing challenge for the College. At the time it was formed as a separate legal entity, the College did not have tax-exempt status for Ghanaian income tax or VAT purposes. While educational institutions are eligible for tax-exempt status under Ghanaian tax law, the Ghanaian tax authorities have refused to afford tax-exempt status to private institutions of higher education. Such institutions did not exist, and in fact were not legally permitted, in Ghana at the time the tax law was enacted. Even a Ghanaian Supreme Court ruling in favor of tax-exemption for a private high school did not persuade the tax authorities to grant tax-exempt status to Ashesi. This means that the College is subject to corporate income tax and VAT, just as any business enterprise would be, although contributions and grants are not taxed. As of the time of this book's publication, the College was continuing its efforts to persuade the tax authorities that a private college, such as Ashesi, is entitled to exemption from tax under Ghanaian law.

Consistent with its policies, the school's tuition is low and many of its students receive full or partial scholarships. Contributions, including grants from the Foundation, are not treated as taxable income. As a result, the College has not, to date, been liable for income tax. VAT, however, is a burden. The College, like so many nonprofit organizations in so many countries, is required to pay VAT on purchases but, unlike a for-profit business, it cannot recover the VAT because it does not sell products to end consumers and therefore has no way to recover the VAT it pays. *See* section 9.14.

Ghanaian donors do not receive any income tax benefits. In fact, Ghanaian law does not provide any tax benefits to individuals who donate to nonprofit organizations, whether or not the organization has received public benefit status. Notwithstanding the unavailability of tax benefits, alumni and others have been willing to contribute to the College, and it is hoped that the base of local support will grow as the College's alumni continue to pursue successful careers.

## Obtaining Accreditation for the College

The College could not begin recruiting students before receiving accreditation. The accrediting body was unaccustomed to, and rather skeptical of, the liberal arts model on which Ashesi was built. *Why should students majoring in computer programming study literature,* they asked? The accreditation process dragged on with a seemingly endless stream of inquiries and demands. Meanwhile, the initial funds that had been raised were running out.

Patrick and the Foundation trustees realized that they would need to take a proactive approach to accreditation. Rather than merely responding to the endless stream of questions, they decided to bring the accreditation board to the campus, give them a tour, and explain their approach to education. They also made clear that funding from the United States was limited. There would not be an unlimited flow of funds, and the College needed accreditation within a tight timeframe if it was ever to open its doors to students.

The proactive approach worked. The College received accreditation and was able to open its doors to students before funds ran out.

## Operating Ethically in Ghana

Ashesi's code of ethics has been a fundamental pillar from the outset. The College operates with an honor code, and students and faculty are held to the highest standards of ethical behavior in all facets of college life. Administratively, the College (as well as the Foundation) maintains a strict ethics policy that prohibits engaging in or cooperating with any unethical practices when dealing with outsiders such as vendors and government officials.

In Ghana (as in many other developing countries), bribery is a way of life, and it is not easy to buck the trend. Of course, all U.S.-based organizations are subject to strict U.S. legal prohibitions against engaging in bribery (*see* section 8.4).

To establish and reinforce its culture of ethical behavior, the College adopted a written policy that prohibits employees from engaging in or cooperating with any unethical behaviors, including agreeing to pay bribes or accept kickbacks. The College found that a written policy not only established expectations for employees, but was helpful to the employees when they needed to make difficult decisions to walk away from transactions.

The College's policies go even further, creating procurement procedures that require obtaining multiple bids for projects, and establishing a procurement committee that reviews bids in a committee format. This removes the opportunity for one employee to succumb to the pressure to pay bribes or accept kickbacks.

Initially, the College found that it was very difficult to operate in this way in a country where engaging in bribery is considered a normal way of conducting business. As a matter of policy, the staff and trustees had to be willing to walk away from important transactions rather than meet demands for unethical behavior. Over time, however, this way of operating has proven to be an asset. The College has developed a set of trustworthy vendors. In the long run, the organization has no doubt that operating in this way has paid off.

Meanwhile, by the end of the 2010–2011 academic year, the College had graduated 269 students, of whom 95 percent remained in Africa, working to improve the lives of fellow citizens and to help Africa grow.

## 5.2   How Hard Will It Be to Form a Foreign Legal Entity?

If you conclude that you want or need to operate through a separate foreign legal entity, here are two initial questions you should explore:

1. Is it possible to form an organization in the particular country for your intended purposes?
2. Are there any restrictions on the founding of organizations by organizations or individuals who are not nationals of that country?

Some countries prohibit foreign organizations or individuals from forming nonprofit organizations. These include Malaysia, Thailand, and Qatar.[1] Others restrict the purposes for which foreigners can form nonprofits, for example by prohibiting foreign organizations and individuals from involvement in human rights issues. Under Ethiopian law, any organization that receives more than 10 percent of its funding from outside Ethiopia is prohibited from advancing human rights among other issue areas.[2]

In some countries, procedural barriers make it impossible, as a practical matter, for foreign organizations or individuals to establish an organization. Procedural barriers can also take the form of periodic, even annual, reregistration requirements that add to the cost, burden, and uncertainty of operating. These kinds of procedural barriers may be written into the law (national or local), or they may exist only as a matter of practice.

In Angola, the registration process requires going back and forth among several governmental bodies at various levels (national and local) such that the process can drag on for years.[3] Mexico, among other countries, requires that a majority of members be Mexican citizens, and imposes additional procedural hurdles when an organization has non-Mexican members.[4]

Other countries make formation of a nonprofit organization difficult by requiring large numbers of founders or members. For example, Turkmenistan requires a minimum of 500 founding members, while Yemen requires 41, and Sudan requires 30.[5]

Some countries, including Egypt, effectively exclude or limit foreign participation in their nonprofit sector by prohibiting or restricting local country nonprofit organizations from collaborating with foreign organizations.[6] Many countries throughout the Middle East and Northern Africa (the so-called *MENA region*) require prior government approval of an NGO's affiliation with any foreign organization.[7]

Still other countries vest government officials with broad, or even complete, discretion to approve or reject the establishment of nonprofit organizations. This kind of discretion can be used to preclude nonprofit organizations with noncitizen founders or members, as well as to bar organizations that have purposes the government does not sanction. China, Bahrain, Russia, Egypt, and Malaysia are examples of countries with laws that afford this kind of broad administrative discretion. In Uganda, the process of registering an organization requires the submission of many letters of recommendation from government officials and others, while the law provides no objective criteria for government officials to approve or deny registration.[8]

As a matter of local country law, once you create a legal entity you may be required to have local representation among your membership and/or board. Or, government officials may have the right to involve themselves in the internal affairs of the organization, as in Russia and China. In Senegal, the government has the right to appoint voting representatives to an organization's governing body.[9]

The foregoing are examples of the wide range of restrictive laws and practices that may impede or inhibit your ability to form and operate a legal entity in a foreign country. Do consult a lawyer, but also talk to organizations that have established operations where you want to operate to find out about their experiences. Finally, keep in mind that laws are continually changing.

The mere fact that you can get permission to establish and operate an entity in a country today doesn't guarantee that you'll be able to stay, or to continue pursuing your purposes tomorrow. Of course, some countries' political and legal regimes are more stable than others, and some kinds of nonprofit activities are more likely to be targeted when there is hostility to foreigners. The key point is, do your homework and assess the risks before investing resources.

# 5.3  What Kind of Legal Entity Should You Create, and Why Should You Care?

## Isn't This Something Just the Lawyers Should Care About?

There are a number of reasons that you need to care about the kind of legal entity you are creating in a foreign country. The form of legal entity you choose may determine any or all of the following:

- The nature of permitted activities.
- Whether or not there are members.
- Whether there is a required minimum number of members.
- Whether, and the extent to which, members and/or board members may be foreign (including U.S.) nationals.
- Whether the entity is permitted to engage in fundraising.

The form of legal entity may affect the degree to which members and/or directors or trustees could be held liable for the organization's actions; for example, if someone is injured due to an employee's or volunteer's negligence while providing services.

In addition, you need to be concerned about the relationship between the foreign entity you are creating and other entities you have created, or will create in the United States and perhaps other countries. For example, if you are raising funds in the United States through a U.S.-based 501(c)(3) organization (remembering from Chapter 1 that U.S. taxpayers can only deduct contributions to U.S. 501(c)(3) organizations), and providing services through a foreign entity, you need to consider whether, and the extent to which, the U.S. organization should control or influence the activities of the foreign service provider. The alternatives for achieving the relationship you desire, or getting as close as possible given the legal constraints, will depend on the kind of foreign legal entity you form.

## Review of U.S. Legal Entities That Can Qualify For 501(c)(3) Status

Before we look at some basic types of nonprofit entities that are commonly found under foreign country laws, it is helpful to have a frame of reference based on U.S. law. Let's take a step back to review the types of legal entities that can qualify as 501(c)(3) organizations. Keep in mind that in the United States legal entities are defined and formed under state laws, while 501(c)(3) status (affording federal income tax exemption and tax deductions for donors) is conferred under federal tax law.[a]

A 501(c)(3) organization, whether classified for federal income tax purposes as a public charity or private foundation, may be organized as a nonprofit corporation, a trust, or even an unincorporated association. An organization that is operating programs internationally will, in most cases, be organized as a nonprofit corporation, although in some cases the trust form may be appropriate.[b] A nonprofit corporation may be formed solely to receive contributions and make grants, or it may be a service provider, or it may do a combination of both. The trust form is less commonly used for providing services, although it generally can do so.

This book will not delve into all of the distinctions between nonprofit corporations and other legal entities. Rather, the descriptions of U.S. legal entities below are intended to provide a frame of reference as we move on to explore some possible ways to structure nonprofit organizations in foreign countries.

### Nonprofit Corporation

A *nonprofit corporation* may be created under the laws of any state or the District of Columbia, and while state law requirements vary, nonprofit corporations have certain common characteristics, notably:

- *No distribution of profits to members.* A key feature distinguishing nonprofit corporations from for-profit corporations is that the former are prohibited from distributing profits (such as dividends) to their members. Nonprofit corporations typically are not permitted to issue stock.[c] Many people prefer the term *not-for-profit* over *nonprofit* because the defining characteristic of the not-for-profit corporation is the purpose for which the corporation exists. While a for-profit, or business, corporation exists to make money for its shareholders, a nonprofit, or not-for-profit corporation exists for a purpose other than to make money for its members. As such, it is typically not prohibited from earning a profit, but is required to devote any profit toward the pursuit of its purposes.
- *May choose whether or not to have members.* A nonprofit corporation typically may choose to be a membership corporation or a non-membership corporation. If it has members, the members may have the right to vote on certain matters, such as the selection of officers, but members typically do not have the right or responsibility to oversee the corporation's affairs. State laws vary as to whether, and the extent to which, they grant rights to members. Some states' laws provide for different categories of nonprofit corporations, some of which are membership corporations.
- *Limited liability for members.* This means that members, if any, are generally not liable for the debts of the corporation, although they can be held liable under certain circumstances for their own acts or negligence. For example, if your organization is operating a childcare center and a child is injured, generally the individual members cannot be held personally liable.[d]
- *Centralized management through directors and officers.* A board of directors (sometimes referred to as a board of trustees, although these are not the same as trustees of a trust, described below) is responsible for overseeing the affairs of the corporation, and ensuring that the organization serves its mission and uses its funds appropriately. The board may be *self-perpetuating* (that is, the board elects successor members), elected by members, appointed by designated parties, or some combination of these. Officers of the corporation, paid or volunteer, may have responsibility for day-to-day management, reporting to the board.
- *Perpetual existence.* A corporation typically continues to exist indefinitely until it is dissolved by action of the board or members; dissolved by the government if the organization fails to maintain its legal registration; or until it is merged out of existence.

A nonprofit corporation's organizational documents typically consist of articles of incorporation and bylaws, which set forth the general rules for governance of the organization, such as procedures for electing directors and holding board and, if applicable, membership meetings. Either or both of these documents are typically filed with a state government office, such as a secretary of state's office, in order to establish the corporation.

A nonprofit corporation does not automatically qualify as a 501(c)(3) organization and, in fact, it may choose not to be tax-exempt for federal or state income tax purposes. If it does choose to qualify under section 501(c)(3), allowing it to attract tax-deductible contributions, it will be subject to additional restrictions.

The corporate form is normally the preferred form for organizations that directly provide services or engage in other activities beyond grantmaking. Even organizations that engage only in grantmaking should use the corporate form if they hope to attract any contributions from U.S.-based corporations. Due to a historical quirk in the U.S. tax law, corporations cannot take charitable deductions for contributions that are ultimately used outside the United States, unless the contributions are made to a 501(c)(3) corporation and not to a trust.[e]

## Charitable Trust

A trust is used to hold funds or other property for the benefit of a designated person or persons, called *beneficiaries*.[f] Trustees hold legal title to the trust assets. They are responsible for managing the trust's funds, and for making sure trust funds are used for the trust's purposes. Like nonprofit corporations, trusts are governed by state law. Unlike a nonprofit corporation, however, a trust can typically be created without registering any documents with the state.

A *charitable trust* is a special type of trust created to hold funds or other property to be used for charitable (501(c)(3)) purposes. In this case, the beneficiaries typically consist of a broad category of undefined individuals, or even the public at large. A charitable trust can generally exist in perpetuity, although it can be created for a limited term. Like a nonprofit corporation, a charitable trust does not automatically qualify for 501(c)(3) status. It must apply to the IRS, demonstrating that it meets all 501(c)(3) requirements, and must have a formal written organizing document even though this may not be required under state law. A charitable trust may have state law reporting requirements to allow for government oversight of the use of funds designated for charitable purposes.

Charitable trusts are used most commonly as grantmaking organizations, rather than organizations that operate programs directly. Because they typically have a small number of contributors (*grantors*), they are frequently classified as private foundations for federal tax purposes (*see* Chapter 3).

One of the reasons a grantor might choose to create a trust rather than a nonprofit corporation is to ensure adherence to the grantor's purposes. Terminating a trust or changing its purposes typically requires a court's approval.

## Unincorporated Association

An *unincorporated association* is a group of people who come together informally for a purpose. Unincorporated associations can obtain 501(c)(3) status, although in order to do so they must have formal organizing documents. Unincorporated associations do not afford protection from liability for their members and managers, although a few states have enacted laws that provide limited protection. This form is generally not advisable for organizations engaged in international activities.

---

[a] For U.S. federal income tax purposes, legal entities can be classified differently from their state (or foreign) law designations and, in some cases, entities can elect their tax classification. This has limited relevance for tax-exempt organizations and is beyond the scope of this book. *See* Treas. Reg. § 301.7701.

[b] Most operating organizations, as distinguished from those that are exclusively grant-makers, are formed as nonprofit corporations.

[c] A few states do permit nonprofit corporations to issue stock. Like other nonprofit corporations, these nonprofit corporations are not permitted to make dividend distributions to their owners.

[d] In addition, many states have enacted laws that protect directors from liability for negligence. The extent of protection varies by individual state. Many of these state laws provide that a director can be held liable for monetary damages only if the director was grossly negligent or acted in bad faith.

[e] I.R.C. § 170(c).

[f] A trust may technically be considered not a legal entity because the assets of the trust are legally owned by the trustee or trustees.

---

## Some Common Forms of Foreign Nonprofit Organizations

The number of different types of foreign legal entities is too numerous to describe here, and foreign laws are constantly changing. We will look at a few categories of legal entities, each of which is used in a number of countries. This will allow us to explore how you might structure the relationship between a U.S. and a foreign legal entity, or even among multiple legal entities, to achieve the optimal balance for your organization between central control and local autonomy.

While there are numerous variations in legal entity forms among countries, here are some notable themes:

- Many countries have laws that provide for something similar to a U.S. nonprofit corporation, and something akin to a trust.
- Membership and nonmembership organizations are, in some legal regimes, distinct types of legal entities.

- In some countries, the form of entity is dictated by whether the nonprofit organization is a grantmaking organization or a direct service provider.
- In some countries, national laws govern the formation and registration of legal entities, while in others local laws apply.
- The form of legal entity dictates its tax status in some countries, while in others, obtaining tax-exempt status involves a separate process.

In the United States, state laws determine the form of legal entity, while federal (and sometimes state) tax law imposes additional requirements for tax-exempt status. Many countries, including England and Wales, Canada, and India have a similar two-step process whereby a legal entity, once formed, must apply for a particular status, often called *charity* or *public benefit* status.[10] This affords the organization an income tax exemption, and in some cases exemption from VAT and other taxes. Yet, an additional step may be required to obtain permission to solicit contributions from the public, and/or to qualify for the receipt of tax-deductible contributions. In addition, the governmental body that confers this special status may or may not be the tax office. For example, a charitable organization established under the laws of England or Wales must register with the Charity Commission of England and Wales, an entity separate from the taxing authority. The organization then must apply to the tax authorities to obtain tax-exempt status and authorization to attract tax-favored contributions.

A word of caution is in order regarding terms used to designate legal entities. It is critical to look behind the term used in any country, and to understand the characteristics of that entity. For example, the term *foundation* is used in many countries, throughout Europe and elsewhere, to designate a form of legal entity that bears some similarities to a nonmembership nonprofit corporation. In China, the term *foundation* designates a form of legal entity that is rather unique (*see* section 10.2). In the United States this term does not designate a form of legal entity, but rather the term *private foundation* is used in federal tax law to designate a type of 501(c)(3) organization (*see* Chapters 2 and 3). To add further confusion, many U.S. organizations that qualify as public charities, rather than private foundations, have names that include the term *foundation*.

**MEMBERSHIP NONPROFIT COMPANY OR ASSOCIATION**   Many countries have laws that provide for a form of legal entity that has certain key features in common with a U.S. nonprofit membership corporation, such as:

- Limited liability for members.
- Prohibition against distributions of profits to members.
- Centralized management through a board of directors or trustees.

Some terms commonly used to designate this type of entity are *company limited by guarantee* and *association*.

Among other individual country variations, the minimum required membership can vary from one to many. This can be an important factor when you are considering how to structure the relationship between the U.S. and foreign (and perhaps multiple) entities. For example, if you want your U.S. entity to have control over setting the strategies of the foreign entity, you can achieve that by designating the U.S. entity as the sole member, assuming the organization is permitted to have a single member. If many members are required, that can be more challenging. If there is a requirement that all or a certain number of members must be nationals of the foreign organization's country, you will need to find other ways of achieving control, such as through contractual arrangements.

Members may have legal rights that cannot be altered, such as the right to elect and remove directors. It's important to know what those rights are before you form a membership organization.

The *company limited by guarantee* is commonly used by charitable organizations in England and Wales, and in other Commonwealth countries (whose laws were influenced by the British legal system), such as Ghana, Kenya, and Uganda, to name just a few. In a company limited by guarantee, typically members cannot be held liable for obligations of the company in excess of a nominal amount. A newer form of organization, the *charitable incorporated organization (CIO)*, became available in Scotland as of 2011, and as of this book's publication, it was pending in England and Wales. This form is similar to the company limited by guarantee, but with streamlined registration and reporting requirements.

*Associations* are another common form of legal entity that also have key features in common with a U.S. membership nonprofit corporation. Associations exist throughout much of Europe, including most of the Central and Eastern European (*CEE*) countries.[11]

In Mexico the most commonly used form of nonprofit organization is the *associación civil (A.C.)*, which is a membership organization bearing similarities to a U.S. nonprofit corporation.[12]

In South Africa, the so-called *section 21 company* bears similarity to the company limited by guarantee. It is required to have a minimum of seven members.[13]

As another example, in India the *section 25 company* has similarities to a nonprofit corporation formed under state law in the United States, and is eligible for Indian tax benefits when formed for charitable purposes, assuming additional requirements are satisfied.[14]

It is important to note that countries vary widely in the degree to which they restrict nonprofit activity. The formation and operation of a company limited by guarantee may look very different between one country and another, and it may not be possible in a particular country to achieve the kinds of control discussed further on.

**NONMEMBERSHIP NONPROFIT ORGANIZATION**   In a number of countries, a nonmembership organization is a distinct form of legal entity. For example, the *foundation* is a form of nonmembership nonprofit legal entity found throughout much of Europe, including most CEE countries.

In many countries, a *foundation* has the following features:

- It is formed for public benefit (charitable) purposes.
- It has no members.
- It does not raise funds from the public, but rather receives funds from one or a small number of individuals or entities.

In some countries, foundations are limited to grantmaking, and they may be required to have significant endowments. The Czech Republic and Slovenia are examples. In other countries, foundations may function either as grantmakers or as operating organizations, and the lack of members distinguishes them from associations. Bulgaria and Estonia are examples.[15]

Some notable exceptions to the above are Germany, China, and the United States. Germany does not require that a foundation be formed solely for public benefit purposes. China permits certain foundations to raise funds from the public and, in fact, the public foundation is the only type of Chinese entity that is permitted to do so (*see* Chapter 10). In addition, Chinese foundations can, and often are, formed with government funding.

In the United States, state laws, which define and govern forms of legal entities, do not define a separate type of entity known as a foundation. Rather, the term *private foundation* is a tax law construct that triggers certain tax consequences (*see* Chapters 2 and 3).

**CHARITABLE TRUST**   Many countries (including, for example, India) afford tax-favored status to charitable trusts, similar in form to the charitable trusts that exist in the United States. Trusts are more commonly used to hold and grant funds, or to hold other property, and are generally considered less suitable for directly conducting programs, although there are exceptions.

**UNINCORPORATED OR VOLUNTARY (INFORMAL) ASSOCIATION**   In many countries, as in the United States, a group of individuals may come together to pursue a charitable or other purpose without creating a legal entity that is registered or otherwise recognized under the law. Not all countries permit this kind of informal association. Equally important, if your organization is operating in a foreign country on a long-term basis, hiring employees and/or owning assets, you will most likely need to register a legal office or form a legal entity.

Again, terminology can be misleading. Before you decide what kind of legal entity to form, look behind the labels to understand the characteristics of the forms of legal entity available to you in a particular country.

## Form of Legal Entity: Factors to Consider

Once you decide to form a separate legal entity in a foreign country, you may have the opportunity to choose among two or more forms of legal entity. While it is always critical to seek legal advice in a foreign country, the following factors may influence your decision and should be explored with an attorney:

- Which, if any, types of legal entities afford limited liability for members and directors?
- What kinds of tax benefits are available for a particular type of entity and its donors? What additional conditions must be satisfied to obtain those benefits?
- How difficult, and how expensive, is it to establish a particular type of entity?
- What are the ongoing reporting requirements?
- Do government officials have the right to examine internal documents?
- If a membership structure is available, can all, or at least some, membership interests be held by a U.S. (or other foreign) organization or citizen?
- How many founders and/or members are required in order to form and maintain a particular type of entity?
- What kind of governance structure (such as a board of directors) is required or permitted? Is there a requirement of local control?

## 5.4   Do You Want a Model of Control or Collaboration, or Both?

If your U.S. 501(c)(3) organization finds that it wants or has to form a separate legal entity in a foreign country to carry out its programs, you may want to be sure that the foreign legal entity will adhere to the U.S. organization's policies and strategies. Of course, you can always attach conditions to grants from the United States. Indeed, as seen in Chapters 2 and 3, you will need to do just that in order that U.S. donors can take income tax deductions for their contributions.

You may, however, want to take further steps to ensure that the foreign legal entity conducts itself in accordance with the policies of the U.S. organization. There are a variety of ways to do that. In deciding what is right for your organization, you should consider the following:

- What forms of legal entity are available in the foreign country?
- How much (if any) foreign control is permitted?
- Do you want to adopt a model of centralized control, collaboration that involves the foreign country entity in the creation of policy, or local country autonomy?

You will need to weigh the pros and cons of centralized control against those of a collaborative model or one that affords local autonomy, and then decide what works best for your organization. The following sections describe a variety of formal structures for achieving control and collaboration. You can mix and match these models as appropriate, subject to whatever legal constraints may be imposed by the foreign country or countries in which you operate.

## 5.5   Control

Nonprofit organizations, in the Unites States and elsewhere, typically are not permitted to have shareholders in the same way that business corporations do.[16] This is because the nonprofit receives special treatment, such as tax exemption and possibly the ability to attract tax-deductible contributions, in exchange for permanently dedicating funds in furtherance of its mission. As a result, you typically cannot achieve control through stock ownership as you could with a for-profit business.

There are, however, some other ways to achieve control over the foreign operations.

### Control through Membership

If you can structure the foreign nonprofit legal entity as a membership corporation, such as an association or company limited by guarantee, then you may be able to designate your U.S. 501(c)(3) organization as the sole member. Or, you may be able to designate one or more individuals, such as the board members of the U.S. organization, as sole or controlling members. You will need to understand what the foreign country allows. You will also want to understand the legal limits on member liability, particularly if members must be individuals.

The key point here is, if your U.S. organization or its board members can control the membership of the foreign organization, then it will be able to ensure that the foreign organization operates consistently with the purposes for which it was formed. The U.S. organization will do this either by acting as the governing body of the foreign entity, or by electing the foreign entity's board of directors and replacing those directors as necessary. While the board of directors of the foreign organization must act independently of the U.S. organization, the U.S. organization has the ability to replace the board, thereby ensuring that the foreign organization acts in accordance with the general policies of the U.S. organization.

Of course, there are many variations on foreign country laws. Not all countries allow foreign organizations to hold membership interests. Some country laws require more than one member, some prohibit organizations from serving as members, and some prohibit foreign individuals and/or organizations from serving as members or as sole member.

As examples, Ghana permits a U.S. nonprofit organization to act as the sole member of a company limited by guarantee, while most CEE countries require that an association have more than one member. Most of the CEE countries permit foreign individuals to join as members, although not all permit organizations to be members, and some require that the founders be citizens.[17]

## Control through Appointment of Directors

It may not be possible for your U.S. organization to control the foreign entity through membership, either because the foreign entity cannot be structured as a membership organization or because the foreign law requires local members. In this case, your U.S. organization may be able to achieve a degree of control by providing, in the foreign entity's organizational documents, that the U.S. entity's board has the right to appoint directors to the foreign entity's board or other governing body.

Alternatively, the foreign entity's governing documents might provide that its board consists of, or includes, a specified number of board members and/or officers of the U.S. entity. The use of overlapping directors is a common way to achieve some control. At the same time, it's important to keep in mind that a director who serves on the boards of both a funding organization and the recipient of its funds has a conflict of interest, and may have to abstain from voting on funding decisions. For this reason, and in order to satisfy the IRS that the U.S. 501(c)(3) organization is not controlled by the foreign entity, at least a majority of the U.S. entity's directors should not also be directors, officers, or employees of the foreign entity.

Of course, you will have to determine whether any of these strategies is permissible under the laws of the particular foreign country.

Some countries require that all or a majority of board members be local nationals. For example, in the case of an organization formed in the Netherlands, the majority of board members must be Dutch nationals.

You may also want to have representatives of the foreign entity's board on the U.S. entity's board to facilitate communication and collaboration. Under

U.S. state laws, a nonprofit corporation typically is permitted to designate board members in this way.

Boards that have members residing in multiple countries encounter logistical issues in holding meetings. Most U.S. state laws permit meetings to be held by teleconference or video, but laws have not always kept up with technology. You may be surprised to find that you can't conduct formal board business across the globe using the technology of your choice. You may also find it difficult to communicate in real time with board members in remote parts of developing countries. The key point here is, before you decide to have a board that looks like the United Nations, think about how the board is going to operate and communicate, and be sure it is realistic and feasible.

## Control through Contractual Arrangements

Even without direct control of the membership or board of a foreign organization, your U.S. organization can control aspects of a foreign entity's operations through contracts. Assuming your U.S. organization is the sole, or even a significant, funder of the foreign organization's operations, you should be in a good position to maintain some control through contractual provisions. Of course, you will need to comply with applicable foreign law requirements.

Your contract might include provisions addressing any or all of the following:

- Mission of the organization.
- Values.
- Code of ethics.
- Governance structure.
- Scope of operations.
- Compliance with 501(c)(3) requirements, including conditions related to the use of funds granted by a U.S. organization.[18]
- Use of name and other intellectual property (discussed next).
- Requirements that the U.S. organization approve new programs and other major changes.
- Certain commitments that the U.S. organization may make, such as agreeing to provide support services to the foreign organization.
- Other matters of importance to your organization.

## Control through Licensing of Name, Logo, and Other Intellectual Property

One way to maintain some control over foreign legal entities is by licensing a name and/or logo. The U.S. organization may also have copyrighted written materials that it wants to license. These kinds of intangible assets are referred to as *intellectual property*, and they have value to your organization. You can license these assets subject to conditions that allow your organization to maintain a consistent image and message worldwide. For example, you may enter into a written license agreement that gives the U.S. entity the right to review and approve, or refuse to approve, any use of your trademark. That way, you can be sure that the message associated with your trademark is consistent worldwide. In fact, you need to exercise this kind of control over the use of your trademarks in order to maintain protection in the United States (*see* section 9.7).

**ALWAYS HAVE WRITTEN LICENSE AGREEMENTS**   The legal entities should execute a written license agreement, which should be prepared in consultation with lawyers in both countries. The agreement should set forth the conditions of use, and should also make clear that the licensed intellectual property will be used to further the U.S. organization's 501(c)(3) purposes, if that is the case.

A lawyer in the foreign country can also advise you as to how to protect your intellectual property in that country. For example, it may be necessary to register a trademark in order to be able to enforce your rights against copycats.

**SHOULD YOU CHARGE ROYALTIES?**   Assuming that your organization is licensing intellectual property to a foreign organization for use in activities that further your organization's 501(c)(3) purposes, you should not have to charge a royalty. However, if the foreign licensee is not using your intellectual property exclusively for purposes that meet section 501(c)(3) requirements, you may need to charge a royalty in order to avoid jeopardizing your organization's 501(c)(3) status.[19]

If your U.S.-based 501(c)(3) organization does receive royalties from licensing trademarks and other intellectual property, in most cases your organization won't be taxed on that revenue in the U.S., even if the license does not further your tax-exempt purposes. That is because royalties fall under an exception from unrelated business taxable income (*see* section 4.9).

Service fees do not fall under this exception, however, and therefore can be taxed as unrelated business taxable income if a service is not performed in furtherance of your tax-exempt purposes. This could be the case, for example, if your organization decides to license copyrighted materials to a business entity, and you also agree to provide printing and distribution of the materials. If you are providing a service in connection with a license, it may be a good idea to enter into a separate service agreement so that the service fee is isolated from the royalty. You should consult a lawyer to help structure this type of arrangement.

Keep in mind that some countries may impose a tax on payments of royalties to a U.S. organization. This would typically be in the form of a *withholding tax*, which requires the payor to withhold the amount of the tax from the royalty payment and remit it to the government. Some countries may even prohibit the payment of royalties to a foreign (such as a U.S.) organization.

## A Word of Caution for Private Foundations

The discussion above assumes that your U.S. organization qualifies as a 501(c)(3) public charity (*see* Chapter 2). If your organization is, instead, classified as a private foundation, structuring relationships with foreign organizations can be a bit more tricky.

A private foundation is well advised to consult an attorney in order to understand whether, and how, the self-dealing rules (described in section 3.1) may restrict its ability to make grants and enter into transactions with other organizations and individuals. In addition, a U.S. private foundation that controls a foreign (or domestic) organization, must meet additional requirements if it wants to make grants to the organization it controls, and to include those grants in computing its annual minimum distribution requirement.[20] *See* Chapter 3 for a summary of additional restrictions on cross-border grantmaking by private foundations.

## 5.6 Collaboration

Rather than seeking control over a foreign entity, you may want a model of collaboration in which the U.S. organization and one or more foreign entities jointly set strategy and policy. As your organization grows and evolves, you may find that it is beneficial, if not essential, to set organizational policies collaboratively with those people who are closest to the provision of services.

Nonprofit corporations formed in the United States (under the laws of a particular state or the District of Columbia) typically are permitted to have board members who are not U.S. citizens or residents. You may want to provide in your bylaws that one or more board members will be appointed by a foreign service organization, or that one or more of its board members will be members of the U.S. organization's board of directors. Be mindful, however, that your 501(c)(3) organization must be able to satisfy the IRS that it is not controlled by the foreign entity.

Alternatively, you might adopt an informal mode of collaboration, for example by designating an advisory council comprised of representatives from the foreign entity or entities, as well as from the U.S. organization. If you use this approach, be sure that each entity's board of directors, or other governing body, has and exercises the right to make final decisions regarding any recommendations by the advisory council. This is critical to maintaining the separate legal status of the entities (*see* section 5.12).

These forms of collaboration can be combined with any of the control models described earlier in this chapter. For example, your U.S. organization may be the sole member of a foreign membership entity, such as an association or company limited by guarantee, and have the power to control policy and strategy by appointing, and if necessary removing, the foreign entity's board. At the same time, you may recognize that the leaders of the foreign entity understand the environment in which it is operating, and for that reason you want their participation in setting policy. To achieve that balance, you might provide in the U.S. organization's bylaws that the foreign entity will designate one representative to the U.S. organization's board. If more than one foreign entity is involved, each one might designate a representative, while the U.S. entity continues to have ultimate control over the foreign entities.

As you consider structuring relationships among your U.S. and foreign entities, you should also think about whether you are concerned about public disclosure of the identities of foreign affiliates, and transactions among foreign and U.S. entities. These kinds of disclosures are required by the IRS (through Form 990, which is available to the public) when a U.S. tax-exempt organization is treated as controlling a foreign entity, whether or not tax-exempt, in certain ways. This is discussed further in section 8.10.

## 5.7   Two Case Studies: One Very Large and One Very Small Organization

This section presents two case studies, showing how two very different organizations chose to structure the relationships among U.S. and foreign entities, and the considerations that influenced their decisions. The first case study provides an overview of how one very large, mature, global organization is structured, and some of the major considerations that drive the legal structure. The second case study provides a glimpse into the way one very small start-up organization is structured. Each of these organizations worked to find the right balance between central control and local autonomy to best achieve its objectives, while taking into account the organization's size and complexity.

### Case Study: World Vision

World Vision (www.wvi.org) is a very large, multinational Christian organization dedicated to assisting the world's most vulnerable children, families, and communities. Since its founding in 1950, World Vision has adjusted relationships among the various local country offices to ensure that the governance structure, within each country and for the worldwide organization as a whole, helps rather than hinders the organization in achieving its objectives.

In particular, World Vision recognizes that each country office needs a degree of autonomy to effectively address the unique needs of the local population. At the same time, some centralized control is essential to maintaining a consistent set of global values and strategic goals. World Vision strives to achieve an optimal balance between the needs for local autonomy and central control.

World Vision works in approximately 90 countries, and has two kinds of operations: *field offices* and *support offices*. Field offices engage in a wide range of services in the developing world, including helping communities to address poverty and responding to disasters. Support offices engage in fundraising, principally in the developed world, primarily to support field office activities, including raising funds for child sponsorships. In most countries, World Vision's activities consist of either a field office or a support office, but not both. Nevertheless, some support offices engage in poverty or disaster response projects within their own country. Some field offices raise substantial funds within their own country for their own projects (Brazil and India). And still other country offices have transitioned over time from primarily *field* to primarily *support* (South Korea and Taiwan).

## Legal and Governance Structure

*Field Offices*. Historically, field offices have been operated as branches of World Vision International (*WVI*), a California-based 501(c)(3) corporation, rather than through separate foreign country legal entities. In contrast, because fundraising offices often must be locally incorporated entities in order to solicit donations and give tax benefits, most support offices historically have been established as local entities with their own boards of directors. In addition, global governance structures originally were heavily weighted towards support offices. In the mid-late 1990s, World Vision made a decision that in any country where it would operate in a long-term stable environment (whether through a field or support office), it preferred to operate through a separate local legal entity with its own board of directors. As a result of this decision, there has been a long process of gradually replacing many branches with separate legal entities. During this same period, global governance structures were revised, allowing field offices to participate along with support offices in global decision-making.

With respect to self-governance, the branches typically have local advisory councils, but are managed by national directors employed by WVI, and ultimately are governed by WVI's board of directors. When a separate entity is formed, the entity will have its own governing board, with local country nationals comprising 75 percent of board members. To ensure a degree of central oversight and coordination, WVI's president (or a delegate) always has a seat on the board.

In addition, when WVI forms a legal entity to function as a field office, the organization strives to have some representation but usually does not retain formal control, even when that is legally possible. For example, if WVI forms a company limited by guarantee, WVI will hold a membership interest, but will not be the sole member.

*Support Offices.* Each support office is typically formed as a separate legal entity in the country in which it conducts fundraising. In the United States, fundraising is conducted by World Vision U.S., a separate 501(c)(3) corporation. The formation of most support entities as legal entities reflects legal constraints, as noted previously. As with field offices which are separate legal entities, each support office separate entity is governed by an external board, comprised predominantly of local country nationals.

Support offices are required to send funds to WVI, which pools the funds and uses them to support the various field offices. Some exceptions are made in order to comply with individual country laws. For example, the German support office often funds field offices directly, rather than sending funds to WVI.

## Partnership Structure and Centralized Governance

World Vision's global operations are structured as what is colloquially called a *partnership* (not a true partnership in the legal sense) among the many separate country legal entities. In addition, several field offices that continue to be operated as branches of WVI also participate in global governance through their advisory councils.

Centralized oversight is achieved through two governing bodies: the WVI board of directors, and the WVI Council. World Vision further centralizes a degree of control by placing ownership of the World Vision name and logo into WVI, which in turn authorizes each separate legal entity to use the name and logo in its country through a formal license agreement. WVI is responsible for registering and protecting its trademarks in each country in which World Vision operates.

WVI's board of directors has authority to admit new member offices, both field and support, and to issue global policies. Twenty-two members of the 24-person board are elected on a regional geographic basis from pools of candidates consisting of the members of the boards of the national legal entities and the advisory councils of the remaining field office branches. The remaining 2 members of the board are WVI's president, and a "founder's chair" appointed by World Vision U.S. (the original World Vision entity).

The WVI Council is the only body with authority to amend the partnership's core documents, including its Core Values, Mission Statement, Vision Statement, and Statement of Faith. The Council is comprised of WVI's board of directors, plus a representative from the board or advisory council of each member country office. This ensures that each member country office, whether operated as a separate entity or a branch of WVI, has a voice in decisions that are fundamentally linked to the values and policies of the worldwide organization.

## Case Study: Lumana

Lumana (www.lumana.org) was founded in 2008 for dual purposes:

- Providing microfinance services in rural African communities.
- Developing young leaders for the microfinance sector by providing opportunities for young people to gain hands-on volunteer experience.

Lumana seeks to help rural African communities develop financial self-sufficiency by combining its microlending with financial and business education, referred to as *business development services*, and by developing strong relationships within the communities it serves. Lumana chose to launch its first microfinance programs in Ghana.

In the United States, Lumana operates through a nonprofit corporation that has 501(c)(3) status. Lumana formed a separate legal entity, under Ghanaian law, to hire local staff and to operate programs in Ghana. From the outset, Lumana's vision was that the U.S. and Ghanaian entities would operate independently, while coordinating on strategy.

The purposes of the U.S. entity are threefold: to raise funds to be used directly for lending to clients in rural communities; to provide hands-on experience in microfinance for young people through volunteer internships; and, to work in concert with the Ghanaian entity to develop the overall strategy for serving rural African communities through microfinance services.

The purpose of the Ghanaian entity is to assist rural communities in Ghana to become financially self-sufficient. This is accomplished by providing microfinance services and financial education, and by coordinating with existing community-based organizations to help develop and improve the social infrastructure.

The U.S. entity has the right to appoint board members of the Ghanaian entity. The board is composed entirely of Ghanaian residents. Lumana believes that the Ghanaian entity must be governed separately by Ghanaian individuals who understand the needs of the rural communities served, and who can build on existing relationships with local organizations and governmental entities. Lumana has also found that employees who work directly with rural community members are most effective if they have existing ties to the community served.

The separateness of the two entities is also important to Lumana's U.S. strategy, particularly with regard to funders. Lumana is able to demonstrate to funders that the Ghanaian organization is self-sustaining, with employee compensation and administrative costs funded entirely by the interest earned on loans. As a result, funding received from the United States can be used exclusively to fund new loans to clients in rural communities.

To help coordinate the strategies and policies of the two entities, Lumana relies on the liaison efforts of a Ghanaian chief who has strong ties to the rural communities Lumana serves.

Lumana's longer-term vision is to replicate its microfinance programs in order to help create financially self-sufficient rural communities throughout Ghana and elsewhere in Africa. To realize that vision, Lumana believes it is critical that the operations are conducted in rural communities by self-sustaining, locally governed legal entities. Lumana's U.S. nonprofit corporation will continue to provide support, will help set high-level strategies, and will continue to develop future leaders for the microfinance sector by providing hands-on volunteer opportunities for young people with a passion for Lumana's work.

## 5.8  Headquarters Offices: Centralized versus Decentralized Services

You may be able to operate two or more legal entities more efficiently by centralizing some administrative services in one of the entities. For example, you might have a U.S. 501(c)(3) organization provide accounting, website, information technology, treasury, human resources, and/or other support services for one or more foreign entities. Or, you may decide to centralize administrative services in another country entity, perhaps somewhere in Europe.

## How Much Centralization Do You Want?

If you are operating in multiple countries, you should think about the advantages and disadvantages of centralizing services, and then decide whether, and to what extent, centralization is right for your organization.

Here are some reasons to centralize services:

- You may save money by avoiding redundant functions in multiple countries.
- You may end up with more consistency, for example, in adherence to policies.
- You may be better able to hire experts in a headquarters location for some functions, like treasury and information technology, whereas it may be difficult to find and hire qualified experts in the countries where you are operating.

Here are some reasons to opt for decentralization:

- Some functions may require an understanding of local laws and sensitivity to local culture. This may be true, for example, in human resources.
- You may need some local administrative staff to maintain adequate internal controls, or to oversee the management of financial resources.
- Decentralization may avoid some of the costs of travel for headquarters personnel.

## How Will the Headquarters Office Be Funded?

Once you decide to centralize some functions in a headquarters office, you need to determine how you will fund those functions. If the headquarters office is also a fundraising office, this may be as simple as retaining sufficient funds to cover expenses, before funding foreign operations. Be aware, however, that funders, particularly institutional funders (foundations, corporations, and government bodies) often prefer to fund programs, and many place strict limitations on the extent to which grant funds can be used for administrative (overhead) expenses.

DO YOU WANT TO CHARGE FEES?    As a practical matter, it may be quite difficult to fund headquarters costs by charging fees to the foreign entities that benefit from centralized functions. Particularly in developing countries, it can be extremely difficult to raise enough funds through any combination of contributions and grants, earned revenue, and investment income (assuming all of those are permitted) to fund the local operations while maintaining adequate cash reserves. Even when a foreign entity has its own revenue stream, such as through fees or foreign government grants, it may have trouble collecting those funds. In addition, it can be highly inefficient, if it is even possible, to transfer funds out of some developing countries, due to the costs of transferring funds and converting currencies.

**DO YOU HAVE TO CHARGE FEES?**   In some circumstances, you will have to charge fees for headquarters services. If the foreign entity is engaged in any activities that do not further your U.S. organization's 501(c)(3) purposes, you need to be sure that either you are not assisting those activities, or that you are charging a fair price for the benefit you are providing. Failing to do so could jeopardize your organization's tax-exempt status, as the IRS could find that you are providing a so-called *private benefit*.

**WILL FEES BE TAXED BY THE UNITED STATES?**   Moreover, if you do charge fees for providing management and administrative services, that revenue may be treated as unrelated business taxable income (UBTI), and taxed in the United States, if there is profit after deducting allocable expenses.[21] This is an evolving area of U.S. tax law. Even if your organization is providing management and administrative services to an organization that furthers your exempt purposes, it is possible the IRS may treat fees for management services as unrelated business income.[22]

The key point here is that, if your 501(c)(3) organization is providing management and administrative support services to foreign entities, you are entering into a highly technical and evolving area of U.S. tax law. Careful drafting of an agreement for the provision of services can help ensure that the services you are providing are treated as furthering your organization's exempt purposes, and that any fees are treated as exempt purpose revenue. You should engage a lawyer to help draft this type of agreement, and to advise you whether your organization will be subject to any U.S. or foreign taxes.

Of course, if you are using a non-U.S. entity to provide headquarters functions, you will need to determine what is required under the laws of the country in which that entity is established.

## Always Have a Written Service Agreement

In Chapter 2, we explored the need to document and monitor the use of funds you provide to a foreign grantee to be sure that those funds are used exclusively for 501(c)(3) purposes. Similarly, when your U.S. organization provides services to a foreign entity, you are providing something of value, and if you don't charge a fee you need to be sure that the services are furthering your organization's own tax-exempt purposes. You should have a written agreement between the two (or more) entities that describes the services to be provided. The agreement should make clear that the support provided by your organization will be used by the foreign recipient solely to further your organization's tax-exempt purposes, if that is the case. If you are providing services for non-501(c)(3) purposes, you also need a written agreement, describing the services and fees to be paid. Particularly if you are charging fees, you are well advised to consult a lawyer in each country.

## Case Study: Social Venture Partners International (SVPI)

The following case study shows how one organization created a unique, community-based model of philanthropy, then introduced that model to other U.S. cities, and eventually across the globe. As a result, there is now an international network of autonomous legal entities that are connected by a common mission, vision, and values. A separate U.S.-based organization provides services to the autonomous entities.

SVPI (www.svpi.org) is a U.S.-based 501(c)(3) organization that supports a network of separate legal entities, called *Affiliates*, each of which is comprised of members, called *partners*, who make a minimum financial contribution, and pool their funds for purposes of making grants to nonprofit organizations based in the particular community.

Each SVPI Affiliate shares a commitment to catalyzing significant, long-term positive social change in its community by serving a dual mission.

- *Individual philanthropy development.* Creating communities of lifelong informed, and inspired philanthropists. SVPI partners are individuals who make meaningful contributions to nonprofit organizations by sharing their skills, time, and financial resources.
- *Nonprofit capacity building.* Making strategic investments that build long-term capacity for nonprofits so they can better fill their missions. SVPI grant recipients are nonprofit organizations that seek new resources and innovative approaches for addressing a variety of issues, including education, environmental protection, and youth development. Capacity building grants focus on increasing the ability of each grantee to achieve its mission, and include cash grants, skilled volunteers, professional consultants, leadership development, and management training opportunities.

## The Beginning: SVP Seattle

SVP began in the late 1990s with a single 501(c)(3) organization based in Seattle, Washington. The early partners came primarily from the high-tech sector, and the organization grew rapidly as the word spread among business executives and professionals who were looking for ways to give back to their community. Seeking to do more than donate money, the founding partners developed a model of venture philanthropy that pools funding, and also provides opportunities for partners to serve the needs of nonprofit organizations by contributing their professional skills.

## Expanding into New Cities and Creating the Network

As the word about SVP spread among colleagues across the United States, groups of individuals based in other cities began showing interest in forming their own local SVP entities. By 2001, several separate SVP organizations had been formed in cities across the United States. Each was established as a separate 501(c)(3) organization. To help support the separate SVPs, and to facilitate sharing of best practices among them, the partners decided to create SVPI as a separate 501(c)(3) organization with its own staff.

Each separate SVP that chooses to become an Affiliate by participating in the SVPI network is required to sign a membership agreement and pay dues to SVPI. Dues are used to provide support to the Affiliates in the form of branding and communication materials, regular conference calls and webinars related to venture philanthropy, and live conferences that offer educational and networking opportunities.

As a condition to participating in the SVPI network, each SVP Affiliate also commits to adhere to certain shared principles.

- *Engaged Venture Philanthropy.* Partners invest time, expertise, and money in nonprofits. They seek collaborative relationships with nonprofits that last for at least three years.
- *Entrepreneurial Spirit.* Partners use innovative approaches to achieve leveraged results in their nonprofit partnerships and communities. They delegate decisions, resources, and authority to those closest to the work.
- *Philanthropic Education.* Partners educate themselves and become informed, effective lifetime philanthropists. Ongoing individual philanthropy is catalyzed through hands-on experience and education.
- *Community and Collaborative Action.* Partners believe in the power of collective, self-organized effort. They encourage and maintain highly participatory, partner-driven organizations that use non-hierarchical communications and operating practices. SVPs

support an open exchange of knowledge and lessons learned, and avoid partisan, religious, or political activities.

- *Mutual Respect*. Partners respect the expertise of community non-profit organizations. They form close working relationships with organizations.
- *Accountability and Results*. Partners are mutually accountable to each other, their grant recipients, and their community. They achieve and document measurable results, both in their own work and through their nonprofit partnerships.

At the same time, each Affiliate retains autonomy to:

- Determine its own grantmaking focus.
- Construct appropriate philanthropy promotion vehicles.
- Choose organizational governance structure.
- Determine appropriate levels of corporate or foundation support.
- Seek local sponsorship or strategic alliances.
- Evaluate its own organizational development needs.
- Choose its grantees.
- Determine the best ways to support grantees with capacity building support.
- Determine appropriate methods of providing administrative support.
- Hire and fire its own staff and contractors.

The board of SVPI is comprised of partners from the various Affiliates. Board members do not directly represent their separate Affiliates, although they are expected to bring to bear the diverse perspectives of the separate Affiliates. Each Affiliate in good standing is entitled to one vote (cast by the Affiliate's board chair) for each SVPI director position.

As of this book's publication, there are 21 SVPs throughout the United States and several more in the process of forming. New SVP Affiliates in U.S. cities typically begin and grow through grass roots interest. SVP partners tend to be outgoing and enthusiastic about the work they are doing. They love to spread the word among their friends and colleagues. When a few individuals in a particular location become interested, they invite others to get involved. As a group reaches critical mass of 20 to 25 prospective partners, it typically forms a separate nonprofit corporation, applies for 501(c)(3) status, and hires a part-time director. SVPI provides support throughout this process.

## Expanding into Foreign Countries

As of this book's publication, SVP Affiliates have been established in Canada and Japan. An Indian SVP is well under way, and discussions have begun with a group of philanthropists in China. SVP partners believe that the SVP model of venture philanthropy can be adapted and used in many cultures throughout the world to have a positive impact on local communities. In some countries, such as Canada, the model developed in the United States works well, with little need for adaptation. In others, such as China, SVP's model may be a mere starting point for creating a uniquely Chinese model of venture philanthropy. SVPI is open to working with interested groups throughout the world by sharing the SVP model and, where appropriate, bringing new SVP organizations into the network.

SVP's experiences to date in Canada, Japan, India, and China illustrate a range of possibilities for adapting the SVP model across the globe, and for structuring relationships among separate legal entities.

### Canada

SVP Calgary, founded in 2000, was one of the first SVP organizations established outside of Seattle. Since then, three additional SVP Affiliates have been established in Canada. These are situated in Vancouver, Waterloo, and Toronto. Like the various U.S. SVP Affiliates, each Canadian SVP was founded by individuals who had business or professional connections to partners in other SVPs.

It has been relatively easy to adapt the SVP model for use in Canada, given similarities between Canada and the United States in nonprofit culture, the prevailing use of English, and the proximity of time zones within U.S. cities. Similarly, the Canadian SVP Affiliates are able to pay dues and fully participate in the SVPI network.

Branding and communications materials provided by SVPI, always in English, are useful to the Canadian SVP Affiliates. Canadian partners can also readily participate in network-wide conference calls, and they even attend live conferences.

### Japan

The origin of SVP Japan is somewhat different from that of the U.S. and Canadian SVPs. During the early 2000s, a young man named Hideyuki Inoue was involved with social innovation in Tokyo, where he was living. Having become interested in the SVP model, he obtained a fellowship to work for SVPI for several months during 2005. Following his return to Tokyo, Hideyuki was able to garner interest in forming an SVP Affiliate among young, socially-minded people like himself. As of the time of this book's publication, SVP Japan is one of the largest SVP Affiliates, with approximately 150 partners.

SVP Japan has adopted the SVP model with only a few minor variations. For example, while the U.S. and Canadian SVPs delegate the selection of nonprofit grantees to grantmaking committees, SVP Japan involves the entire partnership in such decisions. The partners typically meet for an entire day to review grant proposals and agree on the awarding of grants.

While SVP Japan is able to meet its dues obligations, participation in the network is challenging. Branding and communications materials provided by SVPI are of little use to the Japanese Affiliate due to language differences. Similarly, language and time differences are obstacles to Japanese partners' participation in conference calls.

Despite the challenges to full participation in the network, SVP Japan appears committed to continuing the relationship, and SVPI remains committed to working to enhance SVP Japan's ability to benefit from the relationship. At the same time, SVP Japan's leaders have been instrumental in promoting the SVP model throughout Asia, for example by providing ongoing support and advice to a group in Hong Kong. While neither the Hong Kong group, nor others like it throughout the region, will become members of the SVPI network, SVPI believes that its mission is advanced when SVP Affiliates and their partners promote the SVP model with venture philanthropists throughout the world.

## India

In 2012, SVPI began working to support the establishment of an SVP organization in India. The concept of an SVP in Bangalore, India came about through contacts that U.S. partners had with high-tech industry executives in India there. A Seattle-based SVP partner with connections to India suggested that Bangalore could be a logical place to establish an SVP organization, given that many U.S. high-tech companies have a presence there. A few U.S.-based SVP partners followed up on the idea, working through their tech industry contacts in Bangalore to determine whether there was sufficient interest.

SVPI decided to support the hiring of a part-time consultant in Bangalore to help garner interest. This was a departure from the typical SVP start-up process. Other SVPs had hired staff or consultants only after a sufficient number of prospective partners were identified. However, in the case of Bangalore, SVPI realized that it would be too difficult for its Seattle-based staff to support the start-up process.

As of the time of this book's publication, the process of identifying prospective partners in Bangalore is moving along well, and SVPI is optimistic that the Bangalore organization will fully participate in the SVPI network as an Affiliate. The use of English in Bangalore makes participation in the network easier than it is for SVP Japan. Geographical remoteness will, however, continue to be an obstacle to individual partners' participation in conference calls and live conferences. Once again, as SVPI expands its network internationally, it is committed to finding new ways to engage with partners in remote locations.

### China

During 2012, a few members of SVPI's board developed some contacts with a group of philanthropists in China who were interested in learning about SVP's model. As of the time of this book's publication, discussions are continuing. While it is not expected that an SVP Affiliate will be established in China, at least not in the near future, SVPI sees value in sharing its model, and possibly structuring some form of information sharing and collaboration.

### Further Global Expansion and Need for Flexibility

SVPI's leadership remains enthusiastic about expanding the SVP model into new locations, including foreign countries where widespread individual philanthropy is a relatively new concept. At the same time, SVPI recognizes that in some countries, due to significant cultural and language differences, a particular foreign organization may not be able to fully participate in the network. For example, language differences may prevent an organization from using SVPI's branding and communication materials, while both time and language differences may be an obstacle to participating in conference calls. It may be impossible, as a practical and/or legal matter, for some foreign organizations to pay dues to SVPI.

While establishing SVP Affiliates may be impractical or impossible in many countries, SVPI's leadership recognizes that there are many untapped opportunities to support the development of venture philanthropy, internationally as well as in the United States. To that end, SVPI remains open to pursuing flexible and mutually satisfactory relationships with venture philanthropists around the globe.

## 5.9  Shared Employees

Similar to the centralized services situation, you may have employees that split their time between your U.S. 501(c)(3) organization and a foreign legal entity. If U.S.-based employees are traveling outside the United States to monitor the use of funds provided by the U.S. organization, they are working on behalf of the U.S. organization. However, if they are providing services directly for the benefit of the foreign entity, for example, by managing staff in the foreign country, then they are working for the foreign legal entity. If an employee is working for two separate legal entities, then that employee should have two separate employment contracts, and should be compensated separately by the two organizations. This is commonly referred to as a *dual employment* arrangement.

Each of the respective employment contracts should comply with applicable labor laws of the relevant country. The contracts should also take local tax considerations into account. For example, in some countries it is legal, and efficient from a tax perspective to provide significant fringe benefits, such as use of a car, while reducing cash compensation. In the United States, and some other countries, many forms of fringe benefits are subject to tax and require burdensome recordkeeping on the part of the employer and employee.[23] You should always seek legal advice in each country when crafting employment agreements.

## 5.10  Will a Foreign Legal Entity Be Tax-Exempt in Its Local Country?

In section 4.8, we looked at whether, and when, a U.S. organization might be taxed by a particular foreign country when operating through a local office or branch, or even sending employees for extended periods. In contrast, once you create a separate legal entity in a foreign country, that entity falls under the taxing jurisdiction of that country. In this case, the question is not whether the activities reach a threshold that makes them taxable, but rather, whether the nature of the entity or its activities makes it eligible for exemption from tax.

### Do Not Assume a Foreign Legal Entity Will Be Tax-Exempt

Do not assume that an organization will be tax-exempt in a foreign country, even if it would qualify for 501(c)(3) status in the U.S. The criteria for tax-exempt status vary widely from country to country. When exploring the question of tax-exemption, make sure you understand which taxes apply, and from which you can claim exemption. For example, VAT can be a greater burden than income tax for nonprofit organizations. *See* section 9.14.

In some countries, the form of legal entity you create may determine its tax status. In others, you may need to apply separately for tax-exempt status, which may be available to organizations that serve certain purposes.

In many countries, tax-exempt status is linked to the concept of *public benefit*, which generally requires that an organization serve a broad class of people, and that it does not merely benefit private interests. Beyond that basic requirement, there is wide variation among countries. Some counties interpret the concept of public benefit quite broadly, while in others it is narrowly defined. And, in some countries the criteria are quite specific, while in others the determination is left to the discretion of government officials.

Tax-exempt status may also be limited to certain sources of revenue. Your organization may receive funding through some combination of contributions and grants from individuals, foundations, and governmental bodies, and also from investments, and even business activities. An exemption from taxes may be available for some but not all of these types of income.

## Earned Revenue

Special considerations come into play if a foreign tax-exempt entity intends to generate *earned revenue*, or revenue from the sale of goods, the provision of services, or even from the rental of property or licensing of trademarks and copyrights. In the United States, a 501(c)(3) organization is exempt from tax on all revenue as long as it is substantially related to the organization's exempt purposes. On the other hand, a U.S. organization that conducts business activities unrelated to its 501(c)(3) purposes may be taxed on its unrelated business taxable income (*UBTI*). *See* section 4.9.

In the foreign context, some countries prohibit a tax-exempt organization from earning the kinds of revenue that would be taxable as UBTI in the United States. Other countries permit unrelated activities, but impose a tax on business revenue.

There are countries, however, that simply do not recognize the earning of revenue as consistent with the concept of a tax-exempt organization, whether or not the revenue-generating activity is related to the exempt purpose. In India, some organizations have been surprised to learn that their tax-exempt status was revoked because they were earning some of their revenue in the form of consulting fees or proceeds from the sale of products.[24]

Restrictions on earned revenue can even extend to the point of prohibiting or taxing investment income, making it difficult to accumulate needed cash reserves in a country where an organization provides services. If your organization finds itself earning business income in a foreign country, you may want to explore creating a separate for-profit subsidiary. *See* section 5.14.

Innovative approaches to social entrepreneurship can present great challenges in developing countries. It is beyond the scope of this book to describe the ways in which cutting-edge organizations are blending charitable and business activities.[25] It is simply worth noting that organizations hoping to go down that path are well advised to hire local counsel early on to determine whether there is a legal structure that fits their business model.[26]

## 5.11   Will a Foreign Legal Entity Be Taxed in the United States?

In general, income earned by a foreign legal entity through operations outside the Unites States is not subject to U.S. federal income tax, whether or not the foreign entity is tax-exempt in its home country.[27]

### What Kinds of Activities Trigger U.S. Tax for a Foreign Legal Entity?

There are three exceptions to the rule that a foreign legal entity is not subject to U.S. federal income tax, as follows:

1. *Income earned from regular operations in the United States.* If a foreign entity conducts activities in the United States and does not qualify for tax-exempt status under U.S. law, it may have to pay U.S. federal (and possibly state) income tax on income it earns through its U.S. activities. The nature and extent of U.S. activity that triggers U.S. tax depends on whether there is a treaty between the United States and the foreign entity's home country, and if so, the terms of the treaty.

   If no treaty applies, then a foreign corporation is subject to U.S. tax on income that is considered to be *effectively connected with the conduct of a trade or business* in the United States.[28] If a treaty applies, then the question will be whether the foreign corporation maintains a so-called *permanent establishment* in the United States. A treaty's permanent establishment provision typically allows a corporation to conduct more activity in the United States before it becomes subject to U.S. tax than does the U.S. law (non-treaty) standard. The concept of *permanent establishment* is explained in section 4.8.

2. *Unrelated business taxable income.* A foreign entity that is treated as a 501(c)(3) organization for U.S. tax purposes (or that qualifies for some other type of U.S. tax-exempt status) is taxed on certain income earned through U.S. activities to the extent that the income is attributable to the operation of an unrelated business in the United States. *See* section 4.9.

3. *U.S. withholding tax on certain income earned from U.S. sources.* A foreign legal entity may be taxed in the United States on certain types of income, including interest, dividends and royalties, if attributable to U.S. sources. The mechanism for collecting U.S. tax on this type of income is a withholding tax, meaning that the payor deducts the tax and remits it to the IRS. This is explained in section 8.11.

### How Can a Foreign Legal Entity Claim Exemption from U.S. Tax?

A foreign legal entity that meets certain requirements may be able to claim a full or partial exemption from U.S. tax under one or more of the alternatives

described next. In order to rely on any of these alternatives, a foreign entity
will generally have to obtain a U.S. federal tax identification number, and it
may be required to file annual tax returns with the IRS. *See* section 8.11. Many
foreign organizations prefer not to get into the U.S. tax system because it is
cumbersome and it can be difficult to get out of the system at a later time, even
if the organization ceases to earn income from U.S. sources.

For these reasons, a foreign entity is often well advised to avoid earning
revenue from U.S. sources, if at all possible. And, if there is a related U.S.
entity, you should try to structure operations and investments so that the U.S.
activities and investments are conducted by the United States, not the
foreign, entity.

**RECIPROCAL TAX-EXEMPT STATUS UNDER A TREATY**   Some foreign legal entities
formed under the laws of Germany, the Netherlands, Canada, or Mexico are
eligible for U.S. tax-exempt status under the reciprocal provisions of a bilateral
tax treaty. Each of these reciprocity provisions (described in section 4.9)
contains limitations. It is important to consult a lawyer, and you may need a
formal written legal opinion if you intend to rely on one of these provisions.

**CLAIMING TAX-EXEMPT STATUS AS A FOREIGN TAX-EXEMPT ORGANIZATION WITH
LIMITED U.S. SOURCE INCOME**   A foreign entity that satisfies the requirements of
section 501(c)(3) may qualify for tax-exempt status without filing an application with the IRS, if the organization receives less than 15 percent of its support from U.S. sources.[29] An organization that qualifies for U.S. tax-exempt
status in this way may nevertheless have to file annual tax returns with the IRS.

**CLAIMING EXEMPTION FROM U.S. WITHHOLDING TAX AS A FOREIGN ORGANIZATION
THAT QUALIFIES UNDER SECTION 501(C)(3)**   The U.S. income tax regulations
provide a procedure by which a foreign organization can claim exemption
from U.S. withholding tax if it meets the requirements of section 501(c)(3).
In many cases, withholding is the sole mechanism for collection of the tax,
so that elimination of withholding is equivalent to an exemption from the
tax. To qualify for this withholding exemption, the organization must either
apply for and obtain an IRS determination of 501(c)(3) status, or obtain a
formal written opinion from an attorney licensed to practice in the U.S.[30]

**CLAIMING ELIGIBILITY FOR ZERO OR REDUCED WITHHOLDING UNDER A TREATY**
If a tax treaty exists between the United States and the foreign legal entity's
home country, it is likely that the treaty provides for a reduction of the
withholding rate, or even total exemption from withholding. A foreign
organization can rely on these treaty provisions regardless of whether it meets
the requirements of 501(c)(3). Certain procedural requirements apply.
*See* section 8.11.

APPLYING FOR 501(C)(3) STATUS   It is possible for a nonprofit organization formed in a foreign country to apply for and obtain U.S. section 501(c)(3) status, although this has limited use. A foreign organization that has obtained 501(c)(3) status can earn revenue in the United States through activities related to its exempt purposes, and it can receive investment income from U.S. sources, without being subject to U.S. tax. Note, also, that some U.S. private foundations will make grants directly to a foreign entity only if it has qualified as a section 501(c)(3) public charity.

U.S. taxpayers (individuals and corporations), however, will not be eligible for income tax deductions for contributions they make directly to a foreign organization, even if it has 501(c)(3) status.[31] Moreover, the burdens of qualifying as a U.S. 501(c)(3) organization will, in many if not most cases, outweigh the benefits. It may be easier to segregate U.S. activities and investments into a U.S. entity, while avoiding U.S. activities and investments for a foreign entity.

It is important to weigh the burdens against the benefits of obtaining 501(c)(3) status. A foreign entity that obtains 501(c)(3) status must comply with all of the requirements applicable to 501(c)(3) organizations. Once a foreign organization has obtained 501(c)(3) status, it will be required to file annual reports with the IRS, subject to limited exceptions. *See* section 8.10.

In short, a foreign entity should not file an application for tax-exempt status under section 501(c)(3) without carefully weighing the pros and cons.[32]

## 5.12   The Importance of Keeping U.S. and Foreign Activities Separate

Once you have established two or more separate country legal entities, it is important to be meticulous about keeping track of which employees, activities, revenue, and expenses belong to each of the entities. This requires maintaining separate financial and employment records, and making sure contracts are entered into by the right entities. In general, it is advisable to keep all U.S. activities in the U.S. entity and all foreign activities in the foreign entity. This doesn't mean that staff cannot travel between countries to oversee, monitor, learn, or otherwise do their jobs. What it does mean is that you need to look at the activities that are conducted in each country, and make sure that the employees, expenses, and revenues associated with those activities are in the right legal entity.

Here's a simple example: U.S. NGO conducts fundraising from U.S. donors to support a school in Africa. U.S. NGO formed a legal entity, Africa NGO, to operate the school. Africa NGO is a separate legal entity. It has its own board of directors and employs a staff to run the school. The school president is responsible for all of the school's operations including managing staff, and he or she reports to Africa NGO's board.

Under this scenario, the school president and other staff are formally employees of Africa NGO. All of the expenses of operating the school, including salaries and benefits for the president and staff, belong in Africa NGO's financial statements. Tuition revenue, funds received from U.S. NGO, as well as revenue from any other non-U.S. sources (such as other African NGOs) also belong to Africa NGO and must be reflected on its separate financial statements.

U.S. NGO employs all of the staff responsible for fundraising in the United States, along with an executive director and some administrative staff. The expenses related to U.S. NGO's staff belong on the financial statements of the U.S. entity. Importantly, funds raised by U.S. NGO belong to it. When U.S. NGO makes a grant to Africa NGO, that is a transaction that is reflected on the financial statements of both organizations.

If the president of Africa NGO spends significant time in the United States to engage in U.S. fundraising, she may need to enter into a dual employment arrangement. This way, she is employed by and paid by U.S. NGO when she is engaged in fundraising in the U.S. If she were to engage in U.S. fundraising as an employee of Africa NGO (rather than entering into a dual employment arrangement), she might risk subjecting Africa NGO to U.S. taxation and/or cause Africa NGO to run afoul of state laws that require registration by any entity that engages in solicitation.

By contrast, if the president of Africa NGO travels to the U.S. for, say a week or two, for purposes of reporting on Africa NGO's activities to U.S. NGO's staff and board, that is an activity that belongs to Africa NGO because part of the president's job is to communicate with the U.S. funding entity. Africa NGO can send the president to the United States for a short period of time, to represent Africa NGO, without running into tax-related trouble.

## 5.13  Consider the Burdens of Maintaining Two or More Separate Legal Entities

Maintaining separate legal entities will almost always be more burdensome and costly than operating in foreign countries through branches. A foreign legal entity must have its own governing body that holds regular meetings, makes decisions on behalf of the entity, and keeps minutes.[33] A separate legal entity will almost always require at least one paid employee. In addition, a legal entity often, although not always, is subject to more burdensome governmental reporting requirements than a branch.

Financial reporting may or may not be more burdensome when you operate in a foreign country through a separate legal entity rather than a branch. You should consult with a lawyer or accountant in the particular country to under-stand financial reporting requirements. You should also explore how the choice of a branch or separate entity structure affects financial disclosure requirements in each country. For example, operating through a branch may trigger a foreign country obligation to disclose the financial results of the organization's U.S. activities because the foreign branch is part of the same legal entity. This will not be the case in all countries, but you should know what the requirements are before you decide how to structure your operations.

If one entity provides any services or licenses its name or logo to the other, you will need formal written agreements. It may become necessary to implement charges between the entities, and to research and document what is a reasonable market rate. Separate legal entities must also maintain their own websites, although they may link to each other.

Of course, the requirements for maintaining a separate legal entity vary widely by country, and some countries impose greater burdens than others.

## 5.14 For-Profit Subsidiaries

If your organization intends to operate a significant foreign revenue-generating business that is not related to your organization's tax-exempt purposes, you might consider forming a separate foreign entity to conduct that business. Operating a taxable business through a separate legal entity avoids any risk that the business could jeopardize your organization's tax-exempt status, as might be the case if the business were operated directly by the tax-exempt entity.

If the foreign for-profit business entity issues stock, it is permissible for the U.S. 501(c)(3) organization to own 100 percent of that stock.[34] Alternatively, if you have formed a tax-exempt entity in the particular foreign country, you may want that entity to own the stock of a for-profit entity you establish in the same country to help generate revenue for the foreign tax-exempt activities.

You will, of course, need to explore the foreign law implications of operating a taxable subsidiary, including whether dividends or other pay-ments from the foreign entity to a U.S. or foreign parent will be subject to additional foreign taxes.

## 5.15 Soliciting Funds from U.S. Donors

When a U.S. fundraising entity and a foreign operating entity are closely related, it is tempting to treat them as a single organization for fundraising purposes. In raising funds, the U.S. organization must be careful to comply with the discretion and control requirements described in section 2.3.

You need to make sure donors know they are contributing to the U.S. organization, not directly to the foreign organization. Donors must also be advised that, while they may suggest that contributions support a specific foreign entity's project, the U.S. organization has the discretion to withhold or redirect funds if necessary to ensure compliance with section 501(c)(3) requirements.

In addition, the U.S. organization must maintain its own website, separate from the foreign entity's website. The U.S. organization's website may include a link to the website of the foreign organization, but be careful that visitors can clearly see which organization's website they are visiting.

## 5.16  Review and Further Considerations

Once you decide to operate a program directly in one or more foreign countries, you need to decide whether to operate through a branch or office, or alternatively, to form a separate legal entity. It's important to weigh the pros and cons of each, given your particular situation. If you decide to create one or more separate foreign legal entities, the next step is to determine what kind of relationship those entities should have, and to figure out how you can achieve that relationship under the laws of the countries involved.

Regardless of whether you operate in a foreign country through an office or a separate legal entity, you will need staff or volunteers in that country to carry out the program. A number of legal and practical considerations come into play as you make decisions about how to staff your foreign operations. For example, should you send U.S. employees or hire locally? These considerations are addressed in the following chapter.

In addition, even if you have segregated your foreign activities into one or more separate, non-U.S. legal entities, you need to know about various U.S. laws that pertain to international operations. Some of these, such as U.S. tax-withholding requirements, apply to transactions between U.S. and foreign legal entities or individuals. Others, such as anti-bribery laws, reach the activities of foreign legal entities under certain conditions. Chapter 8 provides an overview of additional U.S. laws that apply to a U.S. organization's international activities, while Chapter 9 provides an overview of legal and practical considerations commonly encountered by nonprofit organizations operating in foreign countries.

## Notes

1. *See* "Defending Civil Society," co-authored by International Center for Not-for-Profit Law and World Movement for Democracy Secretariat at the National Endowment for Democracy *International Journal of Not-for-Profit*

*Law*, 14, no. 3 (September 2012) ("Defending Civil Society Report"), 16, available at www.icnl.org/research/journal/vol14iss3/art1.html.

2. *See* David Moore and Douglas Rutzen, "Legal Framework for Global Philanthropy: Barriers and Opportunities," *International Journal of Not-for-Profit Law* 13, no. 1–2 (April 2011), 21, available at www.icnl.org/research/journal/vol13iss1/index.htm.

3. *See* David Moore and Douglas Rutzen, "NGO Laws in Sub-Saharan Africa," *Global Trends in NGO Law* 3, no. 3 (June 2011), 4, available at www.icnl.org/research/trends/trends3-3.html.

4. *See* International Center for Not-For-Profit Law NGO Monitor, available at www.icnl.org/research/monitor/mexico.html.

5. *See* David Moore and Douglas Rutzen, "Legal Framework for Global Philanthropy: Barriers and Opportunities," *supra* note 2, at 25; "Survey of Arab NGO Laws," *Global Trends in NGO Law* 1, no. 4 (March 2010), 5, available at www.icnl.org/research/trends/trends1-4.html; David Moore and Douglas Rutzen, "NGO Laws in Sub-Saharan Africa," *supra* note 3, at 6.

6. Legislation pending in Egypt in 2012 will, if enacted, impose additional restrictions on the nonprofit sector and on foreign participation in the Egyptian nonprofit sector, including providing the government with very broad discretion to reject or revoke a nonprofit's operating license, and to interfere with a nonprofit organization's activities. *See* Nick Gallus, "Protection of U.S. Nongovernmental Organizations in Egypt Under the U.S.-Egypt Bilateral Investment Treaty," *International Center for Not-For-Profit Law, International Journal of Not-for-Profit Law*, 14, no. 3 (September 2012), 63-64, available at www.icnl.org/research/journal/vol14iss3/index.html.

7. "Survey of Arab NGO Laws," *supra* note 5, at 6.

8. *See* "NGO Laws in Sub-Saharan Africa," *supra* note 3, at 6.

9. *See* David Moore and Douglas Rutzen, "Legal Framework for Global Philanthropy: Barriers and Opportunities," *supra* note 2, at 26.

10. Among U.K. countries, only England and Wales share a body of law and a government commission that govern so-called *charities*. Scotland and Northern Ireland, which belong to the United Kingdom, have their own regimes for the governance of charitable organizations.

11. For detailed information about the legal framework for NGOs in Central and Eastern European countries, *see* Douglas Rutzen, David Moore, and Michael Durham, "The Legal Framework for Not-for-Profit Organizations in Central and Eastern Europe," *International Journal of Not-for-Profit Law* 11, no. 2 (February 2009), available at www.icnl.org/research/journal/vol11iss2/index.htm.

12. For a detailed explanation of how to form a Mexican *asociación civil*, *see* "Beyond Borders: Observations for U.S. organizations considering

nonprofit incorporation in Mexico," by U.S.-Mexico Border Philanthropy Partnership (February 2010), available at www.borderpartnership.org/membership/publications.html.

13. *See* United States International Grantmaking Project, Country Information, South Africa (August 2011), available at www.usig.org/countryinfo/south-africa.asp.

14. *See* United States International Grantmaking Project, Country Information, India (March 2012), available at www.usig.org/countryinfo/india.asp.

15. *See* Douglas Rutzen, David Moore, and Michael Durham, "The Legal Framework for Not-For-Profit Organizations in Central and Eastern Europe," *supra* note 11, at 29.

16. There are a few states that allow nonprofit corporations to issue stock. This form of nonprofit corporation is typically not used to operate a 501(c)(3) organization.

17. *See* Douglas Rutzen, David Moore, and Michael Durham, "The Legal Framework for Not-for-Profit Organizations in Central and Eastern Europe," note 11, at 28–29.

18. *See* Chapters 2 and 3 regarding the procedures required for a U.S. 501(c)(3) organization to make grants to a foreign organization.

19. If you are making intellectual property, such as a logo or copyrighted material, available to another entity and that entity's use does not further your organization's 501(c)(3) purposes, then the IRS could conclude that you are providing a so-called *private benefit* to the other organization. This could jeopardize your tax-exempt status if the value is considered more than merely incidental. *See* 4.8 regarding the 501(c)(3) prohibition against providing more-than-incidental private benefits.

20. I.R.C. § 4942(g).

21. *See, e.g.,* IRS Tech. Adv. Mem. 9608003 (Jun. 28, 1996); IRS Priv. Ltr. Rul. 9641011 (Oct. 19, 1995). For a more detailed explanation of this issue, *see* Bruce R. Hopkins *The Tax Law of Unrelated Business for Nonprofit Organizations* (John Wiley & Sons, 2005). In addition, if your organization charges fees to an organization over which it has voting control (for example, as the sole member of a membership entity), then you may need to comply with technical U.S. tax rules for determining the appropriate fees. The IRS allows you to charge back your costs, without a markup, for some common headquarters-type functions. This means there is no profit for your 501(c)(3) that could be subject to tax. Other kinds of services may have to be charged back with a markup over costs, thereby generating a profit.

22. In 2011, the IRS denied 501(c)(3) status to a U.S. health care organization that primarily provided management and consulting services to fee-paying foreign hospitals and governments, for the purposes of assisting with the design, development, and operation of health care facilities in

certain foreign countries. *See* IRS Priv. Ltr. Rul. 201128012 (Apr. 19, 2011). For a discussion of this IRS ruling, *see* Lawrence M. Brauer and Howard A. Levenson, "Health Care Related Services to Foreign Entity Ruled to Not Qualify for Section 501(c)(3)," *Taxation of Exempts* (WGL) Preview, April 2012.

23. *See* IRS Publication 15-B, *Employer's Tax Guide To Fringe Benefits* (December 2011), available at www.irs.gov/app/picklist/list/publica tionsNoticesPdf.html.

24. This is a recent development, occurring in 2011 and 2012. *See* Noshir Dadrawala, "Income of Trusts in India Comes Under Scrutiny," January 10, 2012, available at www.icnl.org/news/2012/10-Jan.html.

25. Outside of the United States, one of the few countries that has attempted to create a legal structure to accommodate the concept of social enterprise is the UK. In the UK, a special form of entity called a Community Interest Company (CIC) is intended for businesses conducted primarily for community benefit, rather than for private advantage. Further information is available on the website of the Office of the Regulator of Community Interest Companies, at www.bis.gov.uk/cicregulator.

26. For a description of the variety of business models and legal forms found in the realm of social entrepreneurship, *see* Robert A. Wexler, "Effective Social Enterprise—A Menu of Legal Structures," *Exempt Org. Tax Review* 63, no. 565 (June 2009).

27. In addition, while U.S. business corporations can be subject to U.S. tax on certain types of income earned by their foreign subsidiaries, a U.S. tax-exempt organization should not be taxed on income earned by a foreign subsidiary unless the U.S. organization actually receives payments that are treated as unrelated business taxable income (UBTI). Under the so-called *Subpart F regime* of the Internal Revenue Code (I.R.C. §§ 951–965), certain types of income, when earned by a foreign corporation, are treated as taxable income to certain U.S. residents that have voting control over the foreign corporation (a so-called *foreign controlled corporation*, or CFC). While not entirely free from doubt, IRS Private Letter Ruling 9024086 (March 22, 1990) (although not an official legal authority) may be interpreted to say that a U.S. tax-exempt organization will not be taxed, under the Subpart F regime, on income of a foreign entity controlled by the U.S. tax-exempt organization.

28. I.R.C. § 882.

29. I.R.C. § 4948(b). Churches and certain organizations related to churches, whether domestic or foreign, are also exempt from the need to apply for 501(c)(3) status.

30. Treas. Reg. § 1.1441-9.

31. I.R.C. § 170(c). Estate tax deductions are, however, allowed for bequests to foreign organizations, subject to certain conditions. I.R.C. § 2055.

32. For a detailed analysis of the advantages and disadvantages of a foreign entity's claiming U.S. tax-exempt status, see Paul D. Carman, "Structuring and Operating an International Exempt Organization in the United States," *Journal of Taxation of Exempt Organizations (WG&L)* 15, no. 1 (July/August 2003).

33. While a U.S. organization may have the right, for example, as sole member, to appoint the board of the foreign entity, the foreign entity's board must act independently. If the U.S. organization, through its staff or board, manages the day-to-day affairs of the foreign legal entity, one consequence could be that the foreign legal entity is treated for U.S. tax purposes as a branch. That could be disastrous to the U.S. organization, for example by jeopardizing its 501(c)(3) status if the foreign entity does not in all respects comply with 501(c)(3) requirements. In addition, the U.S. organization could become subject to liabilities in the foreign country.

34. This assumes that the U.S. 501(c)(3) entity is a public charity and not a private foundation for U.S. federal income tax purposes (*see* Chapters 2 and 3). Private foundations are subject to certain restrictions on the ownership of for-profit businesses. I.R.C. § 4943.

# CHAPTER 6

# Staffing Foreign Operations: Employees and Volunteers

In Chapters 4 and 5, we explored a variety of alternatives for structuring foreign operations, and relationships among legal entities in multiple countries. Once you have decided to operate programs in one or more foreign countries, whether through branches or separate legal entities, you will need to consider how to staff those operations. Will you send U.S. staff to work for short, medium, or long-term assignments in a foreign country? Will you hire locally? Will you rely on volunteers, either U.S. or foreign?

The answers to these questions have consequences for your organization and the individuals who work for you. This chapter delves into some rather complex legal issues in an effort to help guide you in making decisions that will facilitate the most efficient use of your resources. If you find yourself getting lost in the weeds, keep in mind that the paramount concern in staffing foreign operations is that there be sufficient oversight to ensure that your scarce resources are being used for the intended purposes.

## 6.1 Staffing Foreign Operations: Will You Send U.S. Staff or Hire Locally?

If your organization is operating programs directly in a foreign country, you may need or want to have staff or volunteers who are based there, rather than trying to manage programs remotely. If you have decided to form a separate legal entity in a foreign country you will most likely need at least one employee. The next question will be whether to send U.S. staff, hire locally, or combine U.S. and local personnel.

Some factors to consider in deciding whether to send U.S. staff or hire locally are:

- U.S. staff may have a better understanding of your organization's culture.
- Local staff may have a better understanding of the local culture.
- If you are operating in a country where corruption is a way of life, it may be difficult to find people who operate ethically.
- It can be very expensive to send U.S. staff to work in a foreign country.
- Some countries require that you hire locally, or make it very difficult to obtain visas.

The case study of SightLife, in Chapter 1, shows how one organization balanced these considerations by hiring an India country manager who was an Indian national with education and work experience from the United States.

Some organizations opt to send U.S. staff to a foreign country for an initial period in order to establish a program while finding and training the right people. This can be a practical way of starting up a foreign program, and it may also satisfy certain legal requirements. For example, in order to register in Uganda, an organization must submit a plan to replace non-Ugandan employees with Ugandans.[1]

## 6.2 Sending People Overseas: Initial Considerations

### Work Permits and Visas

The first question you need to ask is whether the country in which you intend to operate admits U.S. individuals to work and, if so, under what conditions. The answer may vary depending on the nature of the job and the length of time they will stay. Obtaining work visas can be costly and time-consuming, so start looking into this early.

### Do Foreign Labor Laws Apply?

Once you've determined that you can send employees to work in a particular country, you will need to know whether local labor laws apply to them and, if that is the case, you must then understand the applicable requirements and restrictions. For example, are there restrictions on working hours, required paid or unpaid leave, and/or required employer-funded benefits? Will you be required to pay severance if you lay people off? Is it even possible to lay people off? The answers to these questions may differ depending on whether you are operating through a branch or a separate legal entity.

If you are going to hire from within a foreign country as well as sending staff who are U.S. citizens, you should consider whether disparities in pay and benefits will create workplace friction and/or legal violations.

### Minimize Culture Shock (or Worse)

Americans who go to work in foreign countries are not always prepared for major differences in cultural norms and legal regimes. These differences can be vast when people go to work in developing countries. The consequences of sending people unprepared can include embarrassment to your organization and loss of credibility that undermines all of the good work you are trying to do. Even worse, your staff could find themselves in trouble with the law, or even in jail, without realizing they have committed crimes. Some transgressions that would not be serious in the United States are very serious in other countries.

In addition, Americans tend to have an expectation that their individual rights will be respected in ways that do not necessarily hold up in foreign countries. We have all seen *Miranda* warnings on TV, and Americans are sometimes unpleasantly surprised when a foreign country does not afford them the rights they expect. For example, in some countries, if government authorities merely suspect wrongdoing, employees may be subjected to questioning, and office files may be confiscated.

The message here is, you can avoid a host of problems, small and large, by making sure that before you send staff or volunteers to a foreign country they are trained in basic cultural and legal norms. Once in that country, they must be well supervised.

## 6.3 If You Send U.S. Employees to Work in a Foreign Country, Will They Be Taxed There?

Individuals who spend extended periods working in a foreign country can become subject to individual income tax in that country. The first question to ask is whether there is an income tax treaty between the United States and the country in which your employees are working.[2] If there is no treaty, the laws of that country will determine whether your employees are subject to tax.

## Does a Tax Treaty Apply?

If a treaty is in effect between the United States and the foreign country in which an employee is working, the specific provisions of the treaty will determine what your employees can do without becoming subject to individual income tax in that country, assuming that the treaty applies to a particular individual. Many treaties allow an individual to work in a foreign country for up to six months before being taxed in that country.

In most cases, an individual will be able to take advantage of a treaty only if all of the following conditions are met:

- The individual is working for a U.S. entity and not a legal entity formed in the foreign country.
- The individual is not working for a branch of a U.S. entity that is registered in the foreign country. In some countries, however, the treaty may apply if the individual is paid by the U.S. headquarters office, even though a foreign branch has been registered.[3]
- The individual meets the definition of a U.S. resident under the applicable treaty. An individual who is a U.S. citizen or resident alien (described in section 6.4) is generally eligible to take advantage of a treaty when working in a foreign country. Note, however, that a U.S. citizen who establishes residency in a foreign country may not necessarily be eligible for treaty benefits that apply to U.S. tax residents. Many treaties do not automatically apply benefits to all U.S. citizens, but rather, an individual must also be considered to have closer ties to the United States, determined by various factors such as whether the individual maintains a permanent home in the United States while living in a foreign country. It's important to understand the specific terms of the applicable treaty.

Some treaties allow a foreign country to tax U.S. employees even though they are spending less than six months working in the foreign country. For example, the U.S.-Philippines Treaty allows the Philippines to impose individual income tax on your employees if they spend a mere 90 days working for your U.S. organization in the Philippines.[4] Under the U.S.-Indonesia Treaty, an individual employed by a U.S. organization may become subject to Indonesian income tax if he or she spends 120 days or more in Indonesia during a 12-month period.[5]

Note that, when you send U.S. resident employees to work overseas, you can generally avoid subjecting your U.S. organization to foreign tax by having them employed directly by a separate foreign entity. However, in that case the employee will most likely become subject to the foreign country's individual income tax.

There may be times, when your employees are working in another country, that the easiest way to provide them with foreign currency is to make compensation payments or advances through an organization established in that country. It may be possible to do this without subjecting the employees to tax in that country, but careful documentation is needed to ensure that they are not viewed as employees of the foreign country organization.

If your organization pays a U.S. resident as an independent contractor to work in a foreign country, the contractor may be required to pay income tax in the foreign country. Many treaties provide exemptions for U.S. individuals working in a foreign country temporarily as independent contractors, even if they are paid directly by a local country organization.[6] These treaties often provide, however, that if the contractor has a base of operation in the foreign country, the contractor will be subject to that country's income tax. This could occur, for example, where you collaborate with a local country NGO and that organization provides an office for the contractor you have engaged.

### Special Treatment of Teachers, Researchers, and Students

Many treaties provide special tax treatment for U.S. residents visiting a foreign country for certain purposes such as teaching in a school or university, or for conducting research in the public interest. These exemptions typically apply even if the individual is employed directly by an institution established in the foreign country. These treaties, which include the U.S. treaties with China and India, among others, typically provide an exemption from the foreign country's tax for up to two or three years.[7] Many treaties also provide a limited tax exemption for U.S. residents visiting a foreign country as students or technical trainees.

### Claiming Beneficial Treatment Under a Treaty

In order to claim the benefits of any treaty provision, it will be necessary to obtain and file the necessary forms. If your U.S. employees are relying on a treaty provision to avoid or reduce individual tax liability in a foreign country, you should consult an attorney in that country.

## 6.4  If Your Employees Are Taxed in a Foreign Country, Will They Still Be Taxed in the United States?

Living and working in a foreign country does not relieve a U.S. citizen or so-called *resident alien* from U.S. tax filing requirements. For these individuals, any income earned outside the United States is subject to U.S. individual income tax, even if the individual is employed by a foreign entity. If your organization employs U.S. citizens or resident aliens outside the United States, you will still be required to withhold federal income tax, unless your organization is also required to withhold income tax in the foreign country.[8]

There are, however, some mechanisms for individuals to eliminate or reduce U.S. taxes on income earned abroad, including the so-called *foreign earned income exclusion*, housing exclusion or deduction, the foreign tax credit, and deduction of foreign taxes. These are discussed further on.

On the other hand, a so-called *nonresident alien* is not subject to U.S. tax on income earned while working outside the United States, and is taxed on income earned while working in the United States only if he or she is present in the United States for a specified period of time. Nonresident aliens are also subject to U.S. tax on income connected to a business they regularly conduct in the United States, and certain other types of income, such as dividends, interest, and royalties, if they are treated as earned from U.S. sources.[9]

## Who Is a Resident Alien?

A non-U.S. citizen is treated as a resident alien, and is therefore subject to U.S. tax on his or her worldwide income, if he or she meets any one of the following tests for a particular year:[a]

- Has U.S. permanent resident status (green card holder).
- Is physically present in the United States for at least 183 days during a calendar year.
- Satisfies a *substantial presence test* and does not have a *tax home* in and *closer connection* to a foreign country.

The *substantial presence* test means the individual is physically present in the United States at least 31 days during the current year. In addition, the individual's presence over three years (including the current year) must meet a 183-day threshold, calculated by adding 100 percent of days present in the current year, plus one-third of the days present in the immediately preceding year, plus one-sixth of days present in the second preceding year.

An individual has no *tax home* in a foreign country if he or she does not have a regular place of work in the foreign country to which the individual intends to return within a finite period of time. Whether an individual is treated as having a closer connection to a foreign country is based on multiple factors that consider whether the individual maintains personal, professional, and community ties to the foreign country.

---

[a] I.R.C. § 7701(b).

## U.S. Foreign-Earned Income Exclusion

A U.S. citizen or resident alien who is working outside the United States, as an employee or independent contractor, may be able to exclude the income earned outside the United States from U.S. income tax, up to a fixed amount of income.[10] To be eligible for this exclusion, an individual must be a U.S. citizen or resident alien, and in most cases the foreign assignment must be expected to last at least one year. Additional requirements apply. If your organization has employees or independent contractors who might benefit from this exclusion, they should be referred to a U.S.-based tax advisor to work through the specific requirements before heading out of the country.

If an individual employee or independent contractor does not meet the foreign residency requirement, he or she may still be able to deduct, as business expenses, some or all of the costs of travels, meals and lodging in a foreign country, assuming those expenses are not reimbursed by the organization. The individual must maintain receipts and records demonstrating that the expenses were reasonable and necessary to the performance of services as an employee or independent contractor of the organization.

## Foreign Housing Exclusion or Deduction

If your organization pays for an employee's housing, the rental value of that housing is normally treated as taxable income to the employee, subject to limited exceptions. However, an employee who is working outside the U.S., and qualifies for the earned income exclusion described earlier, may be eligible to exclude a portion of an employer-provided housing allowance. Even if the employer does not provide housing or separately reimburse housing costs, an employee who incurs foreign housing costs, and otherwise qualifies, can exclude an additional portion of compensation from income that is otherwise subject to U.S. federal income tax. If the individual is an independent contractor, rather than an employee, he or she may be eligible to deduct a portion of the cost of foreign housing. Both the exclusion and deduction are limited in amount.[11]

## U.S. Foreign Tax Credit or Deduction

An employee or independent contractor who has to pay income tax in a foreign country may be able to claim a foreign tax credit, which reduces the individual's U.S. federal (and possibly state) tax on the income earned abroad.[12] Unlike a deduction or exclusion, which reduces taxable income, a tax credit reduces the tax itself. While the mechanics of the foreign tax credit can be rather complex, the underlying concept is simply that a U.S. citizen or resident alien should not be taxed more than once on the same income. In concept, each dollar of foreign income tax paid reduces an individual's U.S. federal income tax by one dollar, but various limitations can reduce the value of the credit. Foreign taxes that are not income taxes, such as value added taxes, do not generate U.S. foreign tax credits and therefore do not reduce U.S. taxes.

As an alternative to taking a foreign tax credit, an individual may deduct foreign taxes. This means reducing U.S. taxable income by the amount of foreign income taxes paid. A deduction, unlike a credit, does not directly reduce U.S. tax dollar for dollar. However, due to the complex mechanics of the foreign tax credit, it is sometimes more advantageous to claim a deduction rather than a credit. Individuals who pay foreign taxes should work with a tax advisor to determine how best to minimize U.S. tax liability.

## Social Security Taxes

For U.S. employees working in a foreign country, the combination of U.S. Social Security and Medicare (FICA) taxes, and local country social taxes can be more burdensome than income taxes. These taxes, in turn, can become a significant burden for your U.S. organization when sending people to work overseas. Most foreign countries impose social taxes when individuals work within their borders for more than a short period. If your organization pays the local country social taxes for the employee, that payment may itself be taxed in the foreign country, compounding the tax bill for the employee and/or the organization.

**EMPLOYEES WORKING FOR A FOREIGN BRANCH**   Individuals who work outside the United States for a branch office of a U.S. organization (rather than for a separate foreign legal entity), frequently have to pay both U.S. FICA taxes and foreign social taxes. The individual's income earned outside the United States will be included in the FICA wage base even if the income is eligible for the income tax exclusion discussed above. In addition, unlike income taxes, FICA tax cannot be reduced by a foreign tax credit. Note, also, that paying into a foreign country's social security system does not by any means guarantee that the employee will be eligible to receive any social benefits in that country.

The double social tax problem can be avoided for individuals who are working for a branch of a U.S. organization in any of the countries with which the United States has entered into so-called *totalization agreements*. As of the time of this book's publication, the U.S. has totalization agreements in effect with 24 countries.[13] Most of these agreements provide that an individual who is working in a foreign country for five years or less pays only U.S. FICA taxes, and continues to accrue U.S. benefits, without having to pay social taxes in the foreign country. If the individual works in the foreign country for more than five years, he or she pays foreign social tax and ceases to pay U.S. FICA tax.[14] Note that this has no effect on an individual's U.S. income tax liability.

**EMPLOYEES WORKING FOR A FOREIGN LEGAL ENTITY** If a U.S. individual is working for a foreign legal entity rather than a branch, there is a limited opportunity to avoid the double social tax problem. The foreign entity must have a certain relationship with a U.S. entity, and the U.S. entity must enter into an agreement with the U.S. Treasury Department.

**INDEPENDENT CONTRACTORS** U.S. citizens and resident aliens who work outside the United States as independent contractors also face the double social tax problem. Like employees, contractors often have to pay social taxes when working in a foreign country, while U.S. self-employment tax applies to income earned outside the United States. Totalization agreements, where in effect, can eliminate this problem for independent contractors as well as employees.

It is critical to consult with a legal advisor in the United States, and possibly in the foreign country, to understand the required procedures for taking advantage of any mechanisms for avoiding double social taxes.

## 6.5  Making Payments to People Working in Foreign Countries

Sending funds across international borders can be surprisingly difficult and expensive. If your organization has employees in a foreign country, you will probably need a local bank account. If you are paying independent contractors on a sporadic or short-term basis, it may be easier to wire funds from the organization's U.S. bank account directly to the individual's foreign account. In either case, wire transfers across borders can be costly, and at times frustrating. Not all U.S. banks have the ability to wire funds to all foreign locations.

In some countries, funding from outside the country is required to flow through designated bank accounts, or even government-owned bank accounts. For example, effective 2010, China mandated that most Chinese NGOs receiving foreign funding establish separate bank accounts to hold foreign funds, submit various documents, and report the purpose for all withdrawals of those funds.[15]

Beware of unwittingly facilitating tax evasion. If an employee or independent contractor requests that you make payments in an unusual way, this could be a sign that the individual is seeking to evade taxes. Such unusual requests might include being asked to make payments into a bank account in another country, or into an account owned by another individual or corporate entity. You should be wary of these types of requests.

## 6.6  Hiring Locally

If you plan to hire foreign country nationals to work in their own country, you need to explore whether this requires forming a separate legal entity. Even if not legally required, this may be a condition for your employees to be eligible for social benefits. If you hire people from within a foreign country, your organization may be required to withhold income and/or social taxes, and you will need to set up systems to do this.

If you are operating through a foreign branch, rather than a separate legal entity, you should determine whether your employees will be eligible for social benefits. This can be a critical factor, affecting your ability to recruit qualified employees.

### Hire the Right People the First Time

Hiring employees who fit an organization's culture and values is always important, but it can be a greater challenge when hiring in a foreign country. Organizations that venture into a new country sometimes make the mistake of looking for the most experienced people, believing experience is needed to navigate territory unfamiliar to the organization. While experience can certainly be helpful, it can be a hindrance in places where unethical business practices are the norm. You may be better off hiring and training a young, less experienced person who conforms to your values.

Hiring the wrong person can be a costly mistake. In many countries, it's difficult to lay people off. Mandatory severance packages can be expensive, and legal disputes even more so. You will be better off for having taken the time to find the right people the first time.

### Research Local Compensation and Benefits

Setting compensation levels in a foreign country, particularly in a developing country, can be challenging. The importance of doing your homework to determine market rates cannot be overstated. In many developing countries, a U.S. organization is viewed as a cash cow. If you negotiate without doing research you run the risk of paying far more than the market commands. In addition, keep in mind that if you are a small organization, you probably do not need to, nor should you, set compensation comparable to the levels of large global NGOs. Explore the local market and benchmark against organizations that are of a similar type and size to yours.

You may also be legally required to provide certain fringe benefits. Even if not legally required, some benefits may be expected as a matter of custom, and you may be at a considerable disadvantage in hiring and retaining employees if you do not provide these. For example, benefits that are customary in some countries may include transportation subsidies or lunch vouchers.

Finally, you should know whether you will be subject to legal requirements regarding vacations, leave, and even mandatory severance in the event that you need to reduce staff or close the foreign office entirely.

### Always Have Written Employment Contracts

Too often, organizations hire employees in a foreign country only to be surprised by the rights their employees have. If you are hiring employees in a foreign country, the cost of hiring a local lawyer will be money well spent. It is generally advisable to work with a local attorney to draft detailed employment contracts that specify all of an employee's responsibilities, fringe benefits, and other rights including rights upon severance. Be sure to document the conditions under which you can lay people off, and understand what your liability will be and under what conditions.

Consider including a mediation clause in employment contracts if the applicable foreign law allows it. In many countries, particularly developing countries, a legal dispute can continue in the court system for years, and legal bills can be hefty.

## 6.7 Hiring or Sending Non-U.S. Citizens/Residents to Work in the United States

U.S. penalties for hiring illegal aliens are harsh! To establish that an employee is eligible to work in the United States, a U.S. employer is required to examine certain identity documents of an employee at the time of hire, and to record that on U.S. Citizen and Immigration Services (*USCIS*) Form I-9.

Your U.S.-based organization may wish to hire employees in a foreign country and have them work in the United States for a period of time to become familiar with the organization. Or, you may want to hire foreign individuals who have particular knowledge of and experience with the kinds of programs your organization conducts. Whatever the reason, if your organization wants to bring individuals who are not U.S. citizens or legal residents to work in the United States, either permanently or temporarily, you will need to consider visa requirements and U.S. tax consequences.

### U.S. Visa Requirements

Employees of a foreign legal entity who are not U.S. citizens or permanent residents may need visas to work temporarily in the United States. Under the U.S. Visa Waiver Program, individuals who come from any of 26 participating countries are eligible to enter the United States without a visa if they plan to stay for no more than 90 days and meet additional requirements. Most individuals who are planning to enter the United States for business purposes, and don't meet the Visa Waiver Program requirements, must obtain a visa. There are many categories of temporary business visas, with varying requirements according to the type of visa. Authority to issue visas rests with the U.S. embassy or consulate in each foreign country.[16]

As a general rule, it is advisable to plan visits in advance and have foreign employees apply for U.S. business visas early.

## U.S. Tax Considerations for Nonresident Aliens Working in the United States

Suppose your foreign affiliate sends a so-called *nonresident alien* (*see* section 6.4) employee to the United States to assist the U.S. organization for a period of time, or to undergo training by working in the U.S. operations. You will probably want to keep that employee on the foreign entity's payroll, at least for a period of time. If the U.S. entity becomes the employer, the individual will, in most cases, immediately become subject to U.S. federal income tax on the income earned in the United States.

The length of time a nonresident alien individual can spend working in the United States before having to pay U.S. tax depends on the status of the employer (U.S. or foreign organization), whether there is a tax treaty in effect between the United States and the individual's country of residence, and the specific provisions of any applicable treaty.

**WHO IS THE EMPLOYER?**   To determine whether non-U.S. employees are subject to U.S. federal income tax, you first need to ask: *who is the employer?* For this purpose, there are three possible types of employers:

1. A U.S. organization (such as a nonprofit corporation established in the United States).
2. A foreign branch of the U.S. organization.
3. A separate foreign legal entity.

It is always advisable to enter into written employment contracts. This protects the organization in a number of ways and also establishes which entity is the employer. It is possible, and common, for a single individual to be employed on a part-time basis by each of two related entities (for example, one U.S. and one foreign entity) under a so-called *dual employment* arrangement. *See* section 5.9.

**FOREIGN INDIVIDUALS EMPLOYED BY A U.S. ENTITY**   In most cases, a nonresident alien individual employed by a U.S. entity will be subject to U.S. federal income tax on all income earned while physically working in the United Sates and the U.S. employer will be required to withhold and remit the tax to the IRS.[17] A limited exception applies where the individual is working for a foreign branch of a U.S. entity. A foreign individual is also generally required to pay U.S. FICA (Social Security and Medicare) taxes while working for a U.S. employer, even if only temporarily.

**FOREIGN INDIVIDUALS EMPLOYED BY A FOREIGN BRANCH** If your foreign operations are conducted through a foreign branch office of a U.S. 501(c)(3) organization, rather than through a separate foreign legal entity, the branch office is treated for U.S. tax purposes as part of the 501(c)(3) organization. However, employees of the foreign branch are not subject to U.S. income taxes as long as they are not U.S. citizens or resident aliens and they are not physically working in the United States.

If a nonresident alien comes to work in the United States and is paid by a foreign branch of a U.S. entity, rather than being paid by the U.S. headquarters or office, the individual may be eligible for a limited exclusion of up to $3,000, if the individual is present in the United States for no more than 90 days during a given year.[18]

Treaty exemptions generally do not apply to a nonresident alien if the individual is working for a U.S. corporation as an employee, even if the individual is working for a foreign branch of a U.S. corporation.[19] Some treaties, however, provide a special tax exemption for certain categories of individuals, such as teachers and researchers.

**FOREIGN INDIVIDUALS EMPLOYED BY A FOREIGN LEGAL ENTITY** A nonresident alien who comes to work temporarily in the United States as an employee of a foreign legal entity is exempt from U.S. tax on the first $3,000 of income, if the individual is present in the United States for no more than 90 days during the year, as in the case of an employee working in the United States for a foreign branch described previously.

An employee of a foreign entity may also be eligible for a more generous exemption from U.S. federal income tax under an income tax treaty between the United States and the individual's country of residence. Many treaties allow a foreign individual to work in the United States for up to 183 days during a 12-month period without becoming subject to U.S. income tax.[20] There are, however, a number of treaties that shorten this period.[21]

**INDEPENDENT CONTRACTORS** If your U.S. organization hires nonresident alien independent contractors to work temporarily in the United States, unless a treaty applies they will generally become subject to U.S. tax, and your organization will be required to withhold taxes. Like employees, non-U.S. independent contractors are eligible for a limited income tax exemption of up to $ 3,000, but only if they are under contract with a foreign entity or a foreign branch of a U.S. entity. If there is a treaty in effect between the United States and the contractor's country of residence, a more generous exemption may apply. Many treaties will allow a contractor to work in the United States for up to 183 days before becoming subject to U.S. tax, although some provide for shorter periods.[22]

While the distinction between employees and independent contractors is beyond the scope of this book, it is critical to seek legal advice before you decide to treat an individual as an independent contractor rather than an employee for tax purposes.

## 6.8   Special Considerations for Volunteers

### Volunteers Traveling: The Cultural Safari

Many organizations provide opportunities for volunteers and/or donors to experience the organization's mission first-hand, by visiting foreign programs and even volunteering their services. This can be a great way of developing strong supporters who will spread the word about the great things your organization is doing. Often, volunteers combine service and vacation into one trip. In fact, some organizations will even help arrange some sightseeing. All of this helps to deepen appreciation for the organization, its mission, and the culture within which your organization works.

Volunteers often want to know whether they can take a federal income tax deduction for their travel expenses, including airfare and in-country lodging and meals. A volunteer can deduct out-of-pocket costs, but not the value of his or her time, as long as the volunteer is performing a service for the organization in a genuine and substantial sense. While the tax law says that there must be no significant element of personal pleasure, recreation, or vacation, the mere fact that these selfless individuals derive pleasure from helping others does not disqualify them from taking a tax deduction.[23]

Of course, individuals can only deduct expenses that they actually incur, so if your organization funds or reimburses any expenses, they are not deductible by the individual. On the other hand, a volunteer who pays his or her own expenses indirectly, by reimbursing the organization for travel expenses it pays on the volunteer's behalf, may still deduct the travel expenses. Beware, however, of the individual who offers to make an ear-marked contribution to your organization to fund another individual's travel. That may be an indirect gift to an individual, rather than a charitable contribution.

It is best to avoid giving any tax advice to your volunteers. Instead, you should tell them to consult their own tax advisors to determine which expenses they can deduct. You will, however, have to make a judgment about whether an individual provided services that benefited your organization. Volunteers who wish to deduct expenses of $250 or more must obtain a written acknowledgment from the organization setting forth the nature of the service that the volunteer provided, among other information.[24]

Most organizations do not fund the cost of foreign travel for volunteers, including board members and donors. There is good reason for this. If an organization uses its funds to pay for expenses that end up being personal in nature, that could trigger tax penalties for the organization. In the extreme case, this type of payment could even result in loss of tax-exempt status. In many cases it will be difficult to monitor whether an individual traveler is engaging in significant personal recreation or vacation while on a trip, so your organization is generally better off staying away from funding these kinds of expenses.

Of course, there are occasions where organizations recruit volunteers for foreign projects and agree to reimburse some or all expenses. This can be entirely appropriate when the individual is clearly traveling to perform a service that benefits the organization.

If your organization chooses to fund the cost of some travel for donors and volunteers, you should have a written policy that sets forth which expenses will be funded, and under what conditions. In addition, it is always advisable to enter into written agreements with volunteers that travel overseas, setting forth the respective responsibilities of the volunteer and the organization, as well as which expenses will be reimbursed. Consider also including a clause releasing the organization from liability in the event of sickness or harm.

## Sending Volunteers for Extended Periods

Some organizations recruit volunteers to assist with programs in a meaningful way, staying for extended periods of one year or longer. Sending volunteers for extended periods can raise immigration and visa issues similar to those applicable to employees. Some countries, including the Philippines and South Africa, have adopted legislation in recent years to make it easier for foreign volunteers to obtain visas.[25] It is important to understand the requirements of the particular country to which you wish to send volunteers. In addition, if volunteers are spending extended periods in a foreign country, you may want to investigate the visa requirements and restrictions applicable to their dependents.

Volunteers will also be concerned about whether they might be subject to civil liability in a foreign country in connection with their volunteer services. In the United States, legislation has been adopted at the federal and state levels to encourage volunteerism by removing legal pitfalls that discourage individuals from serving as volunteers. For example, the

Volunteer Protection Act of 1997 encourages volunteers to work for non-profit organizations, by sheltering them from individual civil liability for harm caused by their own negligence, as long as they do not intentionally cause harm or act with gross disregard for the risk of harm.[26] This U.S. law does not, however, protect volunteers from liability under foreign country laws, and many countries do not have laws that protect volunteers in this way.

Safety and security can also be an issue for volunteers. What happens if a volunteer is injured while in service? Many countries do not afford workplace protections to volunteers. At the least, your organization needs to advise volunteers of the need to be responsible for their own medical needs while working in a foreign country, and protect the organization by having volunteers sign well-crafted waivers of liability.

## Tapping into Foreign Volunteers

In the U.S., we take for granted that individuals can freely volunteer in a multitude of ways in furtherance of humanitarian, social, political, and a host of other causes. Volunteers also enjoy certain protections, discussed above. In many countries, the legal environment creates obstacles to volunteering. In the extreme, it may be illegal to engage volunteers, even for the benefit of a nonprofit organization. This is the case in the former Soviet States.[27]

Even if you are allowed to engage volunteers, in many countries the laws do not distinguish between volunteers and employees. The effect of this may be that your organization is required to pay into social programs for volunteers. In some countries, if you reimburse expenses of a volunteer you may become subject to a host of labor laws, and volunteers may be required to pay income tax on reimbursed expenses.

In addition, volunteers may be reluctant to serve for fear of legal liability. Few countries have enacted laws similar to the U.S. Volunteer Protection Act, previously described, to protect volunteers from liability.

The important point here is that it is not always easy, or even possible, to engage volunteers in a foreign country. While local volunteers may be a great asset to your organization, you will need legal advice in the relevant country to find out whether and how you can engage volunteers without undue costs, and risks, to your organization and your volunteers.

## 6.9   Review and Further Considerations

Chapters 4, 5, and 6 have addressed important legal and practical considerations for organizations that want to move beyond grantmaking so that they can conduct programs in one or more countries outside the United States. In these chapters, we have explored a variety of ways your organization can structure its foreign activities, and we've looked at factors that come into play in determining the optimal structure.

In Chapter 7, we turn to another kind of foreign activity, fundraising. Charitable organizations, particularly those that conduct programs in developing countries, can sometimes identify potential supporters in multiple countries. These organizations typically want to know whether and how prospective donors, outside the United States, can obtain tax deductions (or other tax benefits) in their own countries. While this is often possible, it requires careful structuring. This is the subject of Chapter 7.

## Notes

1. *See* "NGO Laws in Sub-Saharan Africa," *Global Trends in NGO Law* 3, no. 3 (June 2011), 10, available at www.icnl.org/research/trends/trends3-3 .html.
2. Appendix C lists the U.S. income tax treaties in force as of the time of this book's publication. An updated list, and the text of each treaty, can be found on the United States Treasury Department website at www .treasury.gov/resource-center/tax-policy/treaties/Pages/default.aspx. *See also* IRS Publication 901, U.S. Tax Treaties (April 2011), available at www.irs.gov/publications/p901/index.html.
3. *See*, e.g., United States Model Income Tax Convention of November 15, 2006 ("U.S. Model Income Tax Treaty"), Article 14, available at www.irs .gov/Businesses/International-Businesses/United-States-Model—Tax-Treaty- Documents. Article 14 provides treaty benefits to individuals employed by a U.S. corporation that has a permanent establishment in the foreign country, as long as the compensation is not borne by the foreign office.
4. Convention Between The Government of The United States of America and The Government of The Republic of The Philippines with Respect to Taxes on Income ("U.S.-Philippines Income Tax Treaty") (1976), Article 16, available at www.irs.gov/Businesses/International-Businesses/ Philippines—Tax-Treaty-Documents.
5. Convention Between The Government of The United States of America and The Government of The Republic of Indonesia for the Avoidance of Double Taxation ("U.S.-Indonesia Income Tax Treaty") (1988), Article 16, available at www.irs.gov/Businesses/International-Businesses/ Indonesia—Tax-Treaty-Documents.
6. In some treaties, this falls under an exemption for so-called *independent personal services*, while in others it falls under an exemption for business profits that are not connected with a permanent establishment in the particular country.

7. Convention Between The Government of The United States of America and The Government of The People's Republic of China for the Avoidance of Double Taxation (1984) ("U.S.-China Income Tax Treaty"), Article 19, available at www.irs.gov/Businesses/International-Businesses/China—Tax-Treaty-Documents.; Convention Between The Government of The United States of America and The Government of The Republic of India for the Avoidance of Double Taxation (1989) ("U.S.-India Income Tax Treaty"), Article 22, available at www.irs.gov/Businesses/International-Businesses/India—Tax-Treaty-Documents.

8. I.R.C. § 3401(a)(8). In addition, withholding is not required if the employer reasonably believes that the income will be eligible for the foreign earned income exclusion, discussed in section 6.4.

9. I.R.C. § 871. For more information about the U.S. taxation of nonresident aliens, *see* IRS Publication 519, *U.S. Tax Guide for Aliens* (February 2012), available at www.irs.gov/publications/p519/index.html.

10. I.R.C. § 911. *See* also IRS Publication 54, *Tax Guide for U.S. Citizens and Resident Aliens Abroad* (December 2011), available at www.irs.gov/publications/p54/index.html. The foreign earned income exclusion does not apply when an individual is working in a U.S. Territory or Possession. This means it does not apply to individuals working in Puerto Rico, Guam, the U.S. Virgin Islands, American Samoa, or the Northern Mariana Islands. Separate exclusions, with their own requirements, apply to individuals working in any of these U.S. Territories or Possessions.

11. I.R.C. § 911. The housing exclusion reduces total income on an individual's U.S. federal tax return, while the deduction is taken into account in computing adjusted gross income. The housing exclusion and deduction, along with the earned income exclusion, are computed and reported using IRS Form 2555.

12. I.R.C. § 901. For detailed information about the individual foreign tax credit, *see* IRS Publication 514, *Foreign Tax Credit for Individuals* (April 2012), available at www.irs.gov/publications/p514/index.html.

13. Totalization agreements are in effect, as of the time of this book's publication, with: Italy, Germany, Switzerland, Belgium, Norway, Canada, the UK, Sweden, Spain, France, Portugal, The Netherlands, Austria, Finland, Ireland, Luxembourg, Greece, South Korea, Chile, Australia, Japan, Denmark, Czech Republic, and Poland.

14. Detailed information about Social Security taxes for individuals working outside the United States and the effect of specific country totalization agreements can be found on the U.S. Social Security Administration website at www.socialsecurity.gov/international.

15. *Circular of the State Administration of Foreign Exchange (SAFE) on Relevant Issues Concerning the Administration of Donations in Foreign Exchange by Domestic Institutions*, issued December 30, 2009. An English

language version is available at www.safe.gov.cn/model_safe_en/news_en/new_detail_en.jsp?ID=30100000000000000,221&type=&id=2. A summary is available at hrichina.org/content/403.

16. Detailed information about the types of visas and requirements for obtaining a visa, is available on the U.S. Department of State website at http://travel.state.gov/visa.

17. I.R.C. §§ 871, 861(a)(3).

18. *Id.*

19. *See,* for example, U.S. Model Income Tax Treaty, *supra* note 3, Article 14.

20. *Id.*

21. *See,* e.g., U.S.-Indonesia Income Tax Treaty, *supra* note 5, Article 16, which allows the United States to tax a nonresident alien once that individual has been working in the United States for a foreign employer for at least 120 days during a 12-month period. Treaty provisions are reciprocal so, for example, under the U.S.-Indonesia Treaty, a non-U.S. resident becomes subject to tax after spending 120 days working in the United States, just as a U.S. citizen or resident becomes subject to Indonesian tax once he or she has spent 120 days working in Indonesia.

22. For example, the U.S.-India Income Tax Treaty, *supra* note 7, provides for a 90-day period of exemption.

23. I.R.C. § 170(j).

24. *See* IRS Publication 526, *Charitable Contributions* (February 2012), 4, available at www.irs.gov/publications/p526/index.html.

25. *See* United Nations Volunteers Programme, "Drafting and Implementing Volunteerism Laws and Policies: A Guidance Note" (2011), available at www.icnl.org/research/resources/volunteerism/index.html.

26. 42 U.S.C. § 14503.

27. *See* United Nations Volunteers Programme, "Drafting and Implementing Volunteerism Laws and Policies: A Guidance Note," *supra* note 25, at 11.

# CHAPTER 7

# Raising Funds Globally

## 7.1 Why Do You Want to Raise Funds in a Foreign Country?

As your organization grows in size and complexity, you may want to tap into a donor base outside the United States. However, before you decide to move forward with fundraising in any foreign country, you need to assess whether the potential benefit to your organization justifies the resources you will need to invest, initially and on an ongoing basis. Take a hard look at the reasons your organization might engage in fundraising in a particular country. Who are the donors you intend to target, and why do you believe they will be attracted to your organization? Will the funds support programs within or outside that country?

If you have done your homework and determined that potential supporters in a foreign country are waiting to take out their checkbooks and contribute to your cause, then you are ready to learn whether and how your organization can raise funds in that country. The basic questions you need to ask are:

- Is it permissible to solicit funds for your organization's purposes, and under what conditions?
- Are tax benefits afforded to donors in the particular country, and are they important to your prospective donors?
- Do you need to establish or find a legal entity in the country in which you intend to raise funds?

- If you raise funds in a particular country, are there any restrictions on using those funds outside of that country?[1]

In many countries, conducting fundraising is even more challenging than operating programs. A 2010 report by *Worldwide Initiatives for Grantmaker Support* (WINGS) and *The Philanthropic Initiative* (TPI) found that many countries' legal structures were designed without contemplating private philanthropy. As a result, the scope of permissible philanthropic activities, and of tax treatment for donors, is often unclear.[2]

Finally, you should be aware that there are vast differences in attitudes and approaches toward philanthropy among countries.[3] Tax incentives may play a role, but equally if not more important are cultural norms. Looking at charitable giving as a percentage of a country's GDP tells only part of the story. For example, in some countries much of the giving is religious in nature, while in some others, much of the charitable giving is done informally (for example, to beggars on the street), and is not reflected in charitable giving data.

The important point here is to make sure you have identified a donor base for your organization before you devote scarce resources to establishing a fundraising presence in any particular country.

## 7.2   Will You Be Permitted to Solicit Contributions in a Foreign Country?

Previous chapters have touched upon a variety of constraints on the operation of charitable activities in various countries. Many countries impose yet another set of constraints on soliciting contributions.

In the United States, individual state laws regulate the solicitation of funds, while federal (and often state) laws dictate the conditions under which contributions are eligible for tax benefits. The majority of U.S. states require some form of registration and reporting by organizations that solicit contributions from the public. However, while states can enforce these requirements (and impose penalties for noncompliance) in the interest of protecting the public from fraud, the U.S. Supreme Court has repeatedly held that laws restricting charitable solicitation violate the First Amendment of the United States Constitution.[4]

In many foreign countries, the solicitation of funds is not a protected activity, and legal constraints may take a variety of forms. China has severely restricted public fundraising by prohibiting such activity to all but so-called *fundraising-oriented*, or *public*, foundations. As of this book's publication, very few organizations have succeeded in obtaining public foundation status, and no foreign (non-Chinese) organization has succeeded in doing so.[5]

To avoid violating laws, and possibly incurring penalties, you may need to obtain permission and/or satisfy registration and reporting requirements that are much more onerous than those imposed by any state in the United States. Some, but not all, countries permit only certain types of fundraising activities, such as annual events. Many of the countries throughout the Middle East and Northern Africa (the so-called *MENA* region) require obtaining a license or other form of approval before engaging in fundraising. The application process can be quite burdensome.

Some of the most restrictive countries in the MENA region include:

- Bahrain, where a license application must describe how the money will be collected and how it will be used, and must disclose the name of the bank account where funds will be deposited. A license is good only for two months.
- Kuwait, where organizations are permitted to raise funds only once each year.[6]

Keep in mind that your organization may need to comply with local as well as national laws of the country in which you wish to solicit funds.

## 7.3  Does the Foreign Country Provide Tax Benefits, and Are They Important to Your Donors?

Before deciding whether and how to structure your organization so that you can attract donations in any particular country, do your homework to determine what motivates your prospective donors. In particular, you should know what tax benefits are available to them, and the extent to which tax benefits are a motivating factor in their giving. Tax benefits can take a number of forms, such as income tax deductions, credits (where a portion of the donation directly offsets the tax owed), and estate tax deductions.[7]

Most, but not all countries provide some form of tax benefit for donors, although some make it very difficult for donors to claim the benefits. Some countries afford tax benefits only when funds are used for narrowly defined purposes. Kenya and the Slovak Republic are among the countries that provide no tax incentives for individual giving. In Turkey, it is very difficult for an organization to obtain public benefit status such that donors are eligible for tax benefits.[8]

Most countries impose a limitation or cap on the extent to which an individual can reduce taxes by making charitable contributions.[9] Those limits vary widely among countries, and the potential value of tax incentives may be relevant in assessing whether tax benefits are important to your donors.

While it is often assumed that donors are motivated by tax benefits when they are available, the issue attracts continuing debate in the United States and elsewhere.[10] In Singapore, a government investigation found that tax benefits had limited impact on donors' giving decisions.[11]

It may not be too difficult to find out whether tax benefits are important to your organization's major supporters in a particular country, even though economists disagree over the impact of tax incentives on large donor populations. Creating an international fundraising structure that affords tax benefits, particularly for cross-border giving, can be quite cumbersome and expensive, so before you go through all that effort, it is worthwhile finding out whether it matters to your donors.

## 7.4   Is a Separate Legal Entity Required?

Assuming tax benefits are important to prospective donors in a particular country, you will need to identify the legal structure that affords tax benefits for your donors. In many countries, as in the United States, donors cannot receive tax benefits for contributions they make directly to foreign legal entities. Some countries, including the UK, not only deny tax benefits to individuals who make contributions directly to foreign entities, but also impose additional taxes (such as gift taxes) on such contributions.

This means that you need to create a separate legal entity, or find one that can attract donations for your organization. At the same time, forming and maintaining a separate foreign legal entity can be quite burdensome and costly, as we saw in Chapter 5. For that reason, you may want to explore working with an organization that is already established and able to raise funds in the country you wish to target.

### Consider Working with an Existing Fundraising Organization

If you intend to raise and use funds within a single country, you may be able to find an existing organization, such as a community foundation, that can accept contributions for your program. Community foundations exist in many countries throughout the world for the purpose of raising funds to support projects within their own countries.[12]

By contrast, organizations that facilitate cross-border fundraising are relatively rare. There are, however, some international organizations that operate cross-border donor-advised funds, receiving tax-deductible contributions in one country and contributing them to NGOs in one or more other countries. One notable example is *Charities Aid Foundation* (CAF), which facilitates cross-border giving by individuals in the UK, Australia, and Singapore, as well as the United States.[13]

## Should You Create Your Own Fundraising Entity?

Before proceeding to form a separate fundraising entity in a foreign country, you should carefully weigh the pros and cons of forming your own fundraising entity, rather than partnering with an existing one.

Among the reasons to partner with an existing fundraising entity are these four:

1. *Maintaining a separate legal entity is burdensome.* The nature and degree of burden varies significantly by country, but in all cases you will need to understand and comply with local legal requirements, often including charitable solicitation regulations. A legal entity typically must have its own governing body, which in some countries must be comprised partially or entirely of individuals who are nationals of that country. *See* section 5.2. In all cases, you will need to engage a local attorney to create a separate set of governing documents.
2. *Avoid ongoing legal and financial reporting requirements.* Maintaining a separate legal entity typically requires maintaining and filing a separate set of financial statements. Many countries require additional ongoing reports at the national or local level.
3. *Avoid the need to create and comply with complex legal agreements between the fundraising and operating entities.* Some countries, including Canada and Australia, impose burdensome requirements on fundraising entities that contribute to organizations in other countries. *See* section 7.6.
4. *An existing organization may provide valuable local expertise.* If you work through an existing community foundation, a variety of advisory and support services may be available. You may find that you can benefit from valuable expertise that helps you raise funds in a particular country.

Among the reasons to form your own fundraising entity are these four:

1. *No alternative is available.* In many countries, you will find that there simply is no community foundation or NGO that can or will raise funds for your program. In that case, you will need to determine whether the potential benefit to your organization outweighs the expense and burden of creating and maintaining a separate entity.
2. *Retain control over communications with potential donors.* It may be important to your organization to control the use of your brand, and the nature and timing of communications, to existing and potential donors. Having a local entity with its own volunteers or staff can certainly be helpful in this regard. The strategies discussed in Chapter 5 can be used to maintain control over a fundraising entity's communications with donors.

There may, however, be ways to control communications without creating your own entity. If you are working with a local NGO that makes cross-border grants to your program, you may still be able to communicate independently with donors and potential donors. In this case, you need to make sure that your communications do not run afoul of any charitable solicitation laws. In addition, if a foreign organization is going to use your organization's name, logo, or other intellectual property in communicating with donors, you should enter into a written agreement that gives you approval authority over messaging related to your organization. *See* section 9.7.

3. *Avoid a conflict of interest with the organization that is raising funds for you.* If you are working with a local NGO that funds programs of its own, or of other organizations your organization may not be promoted, to the extent it would be if you had created your own fund raising entity.

4. *Avoid paying fees.* Of course, any NGO or community foundation that agrees to raise funds for your organization will require a fee for its services. It may be a fee your organization pays directly, or it may be a fee charged against the contributed funds. Either way, you don't receive all of the funds contributed. You will want to explore this carefully. You may find that the fee is no more, and possibly less than, the total costs you would incur in creating and maintaining a separate legal entity.

## 7.5  Tax Benefits for Cross-Border Philanthropy

The question of whether your donors are afforded tax benefits may be different depending on whether you intend to use the contributed funds within or outside of the country in which the donor resides. In addition, if you form an entity in one country to raise funds for programs in another, you need to be sure that the fundraising entity itself will be tax-exempt. In some countries, organizations that directly operate or fund foreign activities are subject to advance approval or burdensome procedural requirements, or may even be denied favorable tax treatment.[14] The all-too-common practice of imposing restrictions on cross-border philanthropy is sometimes referred to as the *landlock*.[15]

### Restrictions on Using Funds to Operate Foreign Programs

Many countries, such as the United States, allow a tax-exempt organization, formed under the county's own laws, to raise funds locally and use those funds to directly conduct programs in another country. For example, you might form a charitable organization in Canada to support a program in China. If the Canadian organization directly operates the program in China, it can raise funds from Canadian donors, and the donors are eligible for tax benefits.

However, not all countries permit organizations to raise funds locally and use those funds to conduct foreign programs. Brazil and India are two countries that deny tax exemption to organizations that use funds in foreign countries. Egypt, the United Arab Emirates (*UAE*), Malaysia, and Indonesia impose advance approval requirements on organizations that want to conduct foreign activities.[16] In addition, many countries have adopted anti-terrorism laws that impose restrictions on nonprofit organizations that send funds outside their borders. *See* section 9.2.

## Restrictions on Using Funds to Support Foreign Organizations

In many cases, the fundraising entity you establish in one country will not be the entity that operates the program in another country. This means funds will have to be contributed across borders, between entities. A number of countries distinguish between directly operating in a foreign country and acting as a cross-border grantmaker. As we saw in Chapters 2 and 3, the United States makes this distinction, requiring that a public charity exercise discretion and control over funds it sends to a foreign organization. U.S. private foundations are subject to even more stringent requirements when they fund foreign organizations.

A number of other countries draw this distinction, holding their own tax-exempt organizations accountable in various ways for the use of funds contributed to foreign entities. Canada and Australia represent one end of the spectrum, requiring that their tax-exempt organizations have a degree of direct control over the foreign projects they fund. Some other countries, such as the UK, take a more flexible approach to ensuring that funds are dedicated to charitable purposes when granted to foreign entities.

The following sections describe restrictions imposed by three countries that rank among the world's highest in charitable giving.[17] The case study of Half the Sky Foundation, in Chapter 10, illustrates how one organization structured a fundraising entity in each of these three countries to support programs in China.

CANADA Canadian registered charities (those that are eligible for tax-exempt status and to receive tax-creditable contributions from Canadian residents) are, in most cases, not permitted to act as intermediaries by funding the foreign operations of non-Canadian organizations. Rather, Canadian charities are required to use their resources to carry on their own activities, whether inside or outside Canada.[18] This is referred to as the *own activities* test. Organizations that fail to comply risk losing their tax-favored status and becoming subject to onerous penalties.

When a Canadian charity conducts operations outside Canada, the Canada Revenue Authority (*CRA*) considers the charity to be conducting its own activities if it does one of the following:

- Conducts operations in a foreign country directly through its own employees or volunteers.
- Hires an agent to conduct activities under the direction of the Canadian charity.
- Forms a joint venture or cooperative arrangement with a foreign organization by pooling resources for a specific project, or by allocating responsibility to the Canadian charity for a defined aspect of a project.

In all cases, the Canadian charity must maintain *direction and control* over the use of the resources it provides. When the charity operates through an agency or joint venture agreement, or cooperative arrangement, it is critical to have a written agreement to establish that the Canadian charity satisfies the direction and control requirement. Equally important, the parties must operate in accordance with their detailed agreement.

In addition, the CRA requires that a Canadian charity maintain extensive documentation to establish that it actually operates in a way that satisfies the direction and control requirement. The Canadian courts have upheld the CRA's revocation of charitable status where organizations failed to maintain extensive documentation establishing their direction and control over the use of funds outside Canada.[19]

A Canadian charity is also required to maintain its books and records, including all of the documentation needed to satisfy the requirements described previously, in Canada. It is not permissible to maintain books and records solely in electronic form on a foreign server.

The CRA's website provides extensive guidance on this topic, including detailed lists of recommended steps to establish direction and control, provisions that should be included in written agency, joint venture, or cooperation agreements, and documentation that must be maintained on an ongoing basis.[20]

**AUSTRALIA** In Australia, a donor is eligible for a tax benefit only if the Australian nonprofit recipient has obtained *Deductible Gift Recipient* (*DGR*) status. Similar to Canada, Australia prohibits an organization from acting as a mere intermediary by receiving tax-deductible funds and passing them on to a foreign organization. Rather, an organization that wants to have DGR status, for purposes of funding foreign projects, must demonstrate that it is directly engaged in a foreign project. It does this by acting in partnership with an organization based in the foreign country.[21]

Specifically, an Australian organization that wants to fund foreign projects must satisfy seven requirements under the so-called *Overseas Aid Gift Deduction Scheme* (*OAGDS*). Notable among those requirements are:

- The organization must have a number of members who are representative of the community in which the organization is based (i.e., must have Australian resident members).

- The organization must promote its Australian identity to its supporters and beneficiaries. For example, foreign projects supported by the organization might identify the organization's role, with a plaque or banner, so that the project is clearly identified as the work of the Australian organization.
- The organization must be engaged in development, and/or relief work, in a country that appears on a list of developing countries maintained by the Australian Minister for Foreign Affairs. Projects that are considered welfare, as distinguished from development work, are not approved. For example, donating food, clothing, and school supplies, and the provision of scholarships, are all considered ineligible welfare efforts. On the other hand, efforts that lead to sustainable benefits, such as training teachers, qualify as development activities. Projects that generate short-term benefits may qualify as relief measures when undertaken in emergency situations.
- The Australian organization must act in partnership with an organization based in the developing country, and must enter into a written partnership agreement setting forth the responsibilities of each party.

Australian organizations that want to engage in overseas development or relief activities must provide detailed documentation to the governmental authorities demonstrating that they satisfy these requirements, among others. Once qualified, an organization must maintain continuing documentation, establishing that each foreign project funded is carried out in a way that satisfies all of these requirements.

**THE UK**   The UK allows tax-exempt charities to fund the charitable activities of foreign organizations, subject to a requirement that a UK charity must take *reasonable steps* to ensure that funds are used for charitable purposes. The only exception to this requirement is where funds are transferred to a foreign supplier of goods or services in the charity's ordinary course of business.

In 2011, the UK tax authority, HM Revenue and Customs (*HMRC*) issued guidance (the *HMRC Guidance*) regarding the steps a charity must take to ensure that a payment to a foreign organization is applied for charitable purposes.[22] The HMRC Guidance also describes the information and documentation a charity must provide to tax authorities to establish that it took reasonable steps.

Rather than setting forth specific requirements for all cases, the HMRC Guidance takes an approach that looks at what is reasonable under any given set of facts and circumstances. In particular, circumstances to be taken into account are:

- The charity's knowledge of the overseas body.
- Previous relations with the overseas body.
- Past history of the overseas body.
- Amounts given, both in absolute and relative terms.

The HMRC Guidance provides several examples, and indicates how the minimum requirements may be satisfied in each case. On one end of the spectrum, a thank-you note and photograph showing how the funds were used are sufficient where the donation was a one-time event, the amount was small (£500), and the UK charity's pastor had a connection to the foreign organization.

Another example sets forth the required steps in the case of a long-term (18-month) school construction project that requires more significant funding (£250,000) from the UK charity. In this case, the charity is required to prepare, and be able to produce, comprehensive evidence of the trustees' considerations in deciding to fund the project. This evidence may include a detailed project plan, a formal funding application from the overseas body, and records of the trustees' evaluation of the project. In addition, the UK charity is expected to enter into a formal agreement with the foreign recipient, providing for staged grant payments based on specific project targets, reviews to monitor project delivery, and claw-back provisions in the event the project fails.

On the far end of the spectrum is a charity that wishes to provide an endowment of £1 million to a foreign organization, to be used at the discretion of the foreign organization. In this case, the charity must obtain detailed, legally binding assurances from the foreign recipient that the funds will be applied for charitable purposes. Alternatively, the UK charity may make its own determination that the foreign organization is legally required to use the funds for charitable purposes.

It is noteworthy that, in the final example, the UK charity is required to make a determination based on foreign law. It must determine either that an agreement between the parties is binding and enforceable in the recipient's country, or that the recipient is subject to certain legal constraints. This may be a difficult hurdle in some countries and for some smaller UK charities.

The HMRC Guidance leaves many questions unanswered. Undoubtedly, the rules will become clearer over time. It is worth noting, however, that the UK has taken a very different path from that of Canada and Australia, by recognizing that merely funding a foreign charitable organization can be a charitable activity. That is, unlike Canada and Australia, the UK does not require that a UK charity be directly involved in a foreign program.

## 7.6 Exceptions to the Separate Legal Entity Requirement for Fundraising in Foreign Countries

While most countries afford tax benefits only to donors who contribute to domestic legal entities, there are some limited circumstances in which tax benefits are available for cross-border contributions. A few of these are described in this section.

## Special U.S. Treaty Provisions

The income tax treaties between the United States and Canada, Mexico, and Israel have unusual provisions that allow U.S. taxpayers to claim U.S. income tax deductions for contributions to charitable organizations that are established in those other countries. Likewise, these treaties allow taxpayers of those other countries to claim tax deductions for contributions to U.S. 501(c)(3) organizations. In each case, there are significant limitations, described in the following paragraphs.

CANADA  The income tax treaty between the United States and Canada contains a special provision that allows U.S. residents to claim U.S. income tax deductions for contributions to a Canadian religious, scientific, literary, educational, or charitable organization that meets the requirements for U.S. 501(c)(3) status. A reciprocal provision allows Canadian residents to deduct contributions made to U.S. 501(c)(3) organizations.[23]

A U.S. donor's deduction is subject to the normal U.S. law limit on charitable deductions (as a percentage of income), with that percentage limitation applied only to the donor's income from Canadian sources. If the donor does not earn income in Canada, for example by performing services or owning rental property in Canada, no U.S. deduction is available. A similar limitation applies to Canadian donors. The limitation does not apply to contributions to a college or university in which the donor, or a member of his or her family, is or was enrolled.

In 1999, the IRS issued a notice clarifying that a religious, scientific, literary, educational, or charitable organization that is recognized as a registered charity in Canada will automatically qualify as a 501(c)(3) organization.[24] This means that U.S. donors can claim U.S. tax deductions for contributions to Canadian registered charities. Note, however, that under the IRS notice a Canadian charity is treated as a 501(c)(3) private foundation, not a public charity, unless it applies to the IRS for recognition as a public charity. As a result, individual U.S. donors may be subject to further limitations on their deductions, and U.S. private foundations that make grants to Canadian charities may have to satisfy additional requirements.[25]

MEXICO  In 1992, the United States agreed to a special income tax treaty provision with Mexico as a way to encourage U.S. donors to support Mexican charities. In doing so, the U.S. government recognized that many small Mexican charities seeking support from U.S. donors would not have the resources necessary to form a U.S. 501(c)(3) organization.[26]

This special treaty provision is somewhat different from the Canadian treaty. It allows a U.S. resident to claim a U.S. income tax deduction for contributions to a Mexican charity, but only if the two governments agree that Mexican law provides standards for Mexican charitable organizations similar to the U.S. law standards applicable to U.S. public charities. A reciprocal provision applies to Mexican residents who donate to U.S. 501(c)(3) organizations.[27]

Assuming the treaty provision is applicable to a particular contribution, the amount of the deduction is subject to a limitation similar to that under the U.S.-Canada treaty. That is, a U.S. donor's deduction is subject to the normal U.S. law limit on charitable deductions (as a percentage of income), with that limitation applied only to the donor's income from Mexican sources. If the U.S. donor does not earn income in Mexico, for example by performing services or owning rental property in Mexico, no U.S. deduction is available. A similar limitation applies to Mexican donors.

From the time the U.S.-Mexico treaty came into force, there were lingering questions about whether and how U.S. (or Mexican) donors could take advantage of this provision. In 2003, the IRS determined that Mexican charities that received Mexican government authorization would be treated as equivalent to U.S. 501(c)(3) organizations. However, subsequent changes in Mexican law have called into question whether U.S. donors can continue to rely on that determination.[28] In recent years, some major U.S. donors have been able to make qualifying donations.[29] Mexican organizations that want to attract contributions from U.S. donors must obtain authorization from Mexican authorities, and will be subject to additional restrictions.[30]

In light of these complexities, it is critical to consult U.S. and Mexican advisors before relying on this treaty provision.

**ISRAEL**  Under the U.S.-Israel income tax treaty, a U.S. resident may claim a deduction for a contribution to an Israeli charitable organization that meets the U.S. requirements for 501(c)(3) status. The deduction is limited to 25 percent of a U.S. individual's income earned from Israeli sources.[31] A reciprocal provision allows Israeli residents to claim Israeli tax deductions for contributions to U.S. 501(c)(3) organizations.

As with the Mexican treaty, it is critical to consult an attorney before relying on this provision.

**ESTATE TAX TREATIES**  U.S. citizens and resident aliens (*see* section 6.4) can receive U.S. estate and gift tax deductions for charitable gifts and bequests made directly to foreign organizations, even though they cannot take income tax deductions. However, individuals who are treated as nonresident aliens in the United States (and who are subject to U.S. estate and gift tax) are restricted in taking estate and gift tax deductions for gifts and bequests to foreign organizations, as well as to certain U.S. entities that use the gifts outside the U.S.[32]

A small number of U.S. estate tax treaties, along with the U.S.-Canada income tax treaty, provide limited estate tax benefits for U.S. nonresident aliens who make gifts or bequests to qualifying organizations in the other treaty country.[33]

## Intra-European Philanthropy

Within the European Union (*EU*) and the European Economic Area (*EEA*), individual country laws are evolving to facilitate cross-border giving. As of this book's publication, a single legal entity can raise funds and operate programs in multiple EU and EEA countries. At the same time, it is often a cumbersome process for an organization that is formed in one EU country (*Member State*), or EEA country, to qualify in another Member State or EEA country for tax-exempt status, and for the ability to attract tax-deductible contributions.

Some recent decisions by the European Court of Justice (*ECJ*) have resulted in changes of law in some countries, facilitating cross-border giving within the EU.[34] Notably, in 2009 the ECJ ruled that European law requires that a Member State afford the same tax benefits for contributions to a public benefit organization regardless of whether the organization is formed under its own laws or those of any other Member State. It is permissible, however, for the Member State to require that the foreign recipient organization meet its standards for public benefit status, and to impose procedures on the organization to establish that those standards are met.

Following the 2009 ECJ decision, a number of EU Member States and EEA countries enacted legislation permitting their residents to claim tax benefits for contributions to organizations formed in other Member States and EEA countries. As of this book's publication, these include Austria, Belgium, Bulgaria, the Czech Republic, Denmark, Estonia, Finland, France, Germany, Greece, Ireland, Latvia, Luxembourg, the Netherlands, Poland, Slovenia, and the UK.[35]

Even among those EU Member States that now afford tax benefits for cross-border contributions, the procedural hurdles can be quite burdensome. For example, a number of these countries require that a public benefit organization that is recognized in another Member State must nevertheless undergo a registration and approval process. The European Commission (*EC*) takes the position that these registration requirements contravene the EU rules on free movement of capital, and it has initiated proceedings against a number of countries, including the Netherlands, to challenge this practice.[36]

The UK responded to an EC challenge by enacting legislation that provides automatic UK charity tax status for any organization that is recognized in any other EU Member State, Norway, or Iceland, as long as the organization meets the English and Welsh definition of charity and has *fit and proper* management.[37] The legislation affords tax benefits for UK residents' contributions to non-UK organizations that obtain UK charity tax status in this way.

Within the UK, there are separate government bodies that regulate charities for England/Wales, Northern Ireland, and Scotland. Each of those countries has its own definition of charity. Once an organization is registered as a charity in one of those countries, it can then apply for tax-exempt status, and the ability to receive tax-favored contributions through the UK tax authority, HM Revenue and Customs.

German residents are eligible to deduct contributions to organizations formed in other EU Member States, or EEA countries, only if the recipient organization's activities could benefit Germany's reputation or support individuals who are permanent German residents.[38]

To further facilitate cross-border philanthropy in Europe, nonprofit organizations have been supporting the concept of a *European Foundation Statute* (EFS), which would allow organizations to create a single legal entity that would be recognized, based on uniform standards, in all EU Member States, without the need to comply with further procedures. The EFS would also facilitate transfers of an organization's registered branch or headquarters, and would eliminate intra-EU discrimination with respect to tax benefits for donors who contribute to organizations established outside their home countries.[39] As of this book's publication, the European Commission has adopted the EFS, and it is proceeding through the approval process.

### Additional Exceptions

There are some countries, notably within Europe, that afford tax benefits to residents who contribute to organizations established in other countries, even outside the EU or EEA. Many, if not most of the countries that afford deductions for contributions to foreign (and non-EU or EEA) organizations, require some form of registration or approval to ensure that foreign recipient organizations satisfy their standards.

The procedural difficulty of qualifying and maintaining qualification varies significantly among countries. In a number of European countries, such as the Netherlands, it is necessary to satisfy governmental officials that the organization meets the particular country's definition of a *charity* or *public benefit* organization, terms that have no universally accepted meanings. A single entity may find it difficult to satisfy the requirements of multiple jurisdictions, and may ultimately choose to form separate entities.

## 7.7  Structuring Relationships among Fundraising and Operating Entities

As we have seen in this chapter, once you decide to raise funds in multiple countries, you will probably need to create separate legal entities in all or most of those countries. Before proceeding, you will need to identify the most appropriate form of legal entity, taking into account the scope of activities you intend to conduct in the short and longer terms. Do you intend only to raise funds, or might you also operate programs in that country? In some countries, there is a form of legal entity used solely for fundraising and grantmaking. It is worthwhile thinking this through in order to avoid having to create a new entity should you change or expand your activities in the future.

It is also important to give careful thought to structuring relationships among various fundraising and operating entities. If you are forming an entity in one country to raise funds for programs in another, you may well be concerned about maintaining a consistent image, brand, and/or message with donors and others. In Chapter 5 we explored a variety of ways to maintain control over a separate legal entity, and that discussion is relevant here. You should be aware, however, that some countries impose more restrictions on fundraising entities than on operating entities, for example by requiring local control of the board, membership, or both. For this reason, you may have to rely on contractual arrangements to achieve the desired control over your brand in a foreign country. *See* section 5.5. Even in more restrictive environments, it should be possible to achieve your objectives through careful drafting of agreements.

## 7.8   Keep It as Simple as Possible

By the time you have decided to create one or more fundraising entities to support activities in other countries, you have traveled quite far down the road toward complexity. As we saw in Chapter 5, separate legal entities trigger ongoing legal compliance and reporting requirements, and these administrative burdens can be even greater for fundraising entities. If you choose to raise funds in countries that, like Canada and Australia, require that the fundraising entities conduct projects directly, you will have another layer of complexity to deal with.

At this point in the book, it goes without saying that you must evaluate whether the benefit to your mission warrants the burdens of maintaining multiple entities in multiple countries. Assuming they do, your mantra should be *simplicity*, wherever possible. For example, if you create a Canadian entity to raise funds in Canada, have that entity enter into a joint venture agreement with one single foreign entity for purposes of operating a discrete project. Avoid complex funding arrangements that involve multiple party agreements.

Finally, above all, be sure that you can comply with all of the terms of any written agreements between any of the separate country entities you create. You may hire lawyers in various countries to draft agreements that satisfy the government authorities, but those agreements will not help you if you can't implement them in accordance with their terms. Be sure to question anything that seems too complex or burdensome. There may be a simpler solution.

## 7.9   Review and Further Considerations

In this chapter, we have seen that if you want to raise funds from donors outside the United States, you may have to establish a separate legal entity in the country in which your donors reside. If you are raising funds in one country for use in another, you may have to comply with additional requirements and restrictions under the laws of the donor's country. Establishing and maintaining multiple fundraising entities adds another layer of administrative complexity for your organization. It's important that the benefit justify the burden.

In Chapters 8 and 9, we turn away from the subject of how to structure international activities, to focus on some additional U.S. and foreign legal and practical issues that international nonprofit organizations often encounter. Without going into depth on any particular topic, these chapters help identify the questions your organization may need to consider, and may serve as a starting point for discussions between the organization and its legal advisors.

## Notes

1. For a country-by-country summary of the legal, tax, and cultural environments for in-country and cross-border private philanthropy, *see* "Global Institutional Philanthropy: A Preliminary Status Report," A Report of WINGS: World Wide Initiatives for Grantmakers Support, and TPI: The Philanthropic Initiative (2010), Parts 1 and 2, available at www.wingsweb.org.
2. *Id.* at 8.
3. For an overview of giving patterns among 153 countries, *see* Charities Aid Foundation (CAF), "World Giving Index: A Global View of Giving Trends" (2011), available at https://www.cafonline.org/publications/2011-publications/world-giving-index-2011.aspx.
4. See *Village of Schaumburg v. Citizens for a Better Environment*, 444 U.S. 620 (1980); *Secretary of State of Md. v. Joseph H. Munson Co.*, 467 U.S. 947 (1984); *Riley v. National Federation of Blind of N.C., Inc.*, 487 U.S.781 (1988).
5. *See* section 10.2.
6. *See* "Survey of Arab NGO Laws," *Global Trends in NGO Law* 1, no. 4 (March 2010), at 9, available at www.icnl.org/research/trends/trends1-4.html.
7. The mechanics of providing tax benefits to donors also varies among countries. For example, in the UK a donor may elect to use *Gift Aid*, whereby a donor contributes after-tax funds rather than taking a tax deduction. The government then contributes to the charity an amount equal to the tax paid on those funds.
8. For summaries of tax incentives for philanthropy in a number of countries throughout the world, *see* "Global Institutional Philanthropy: A Preliminary Status Report," *supra* note 1.

9. The UK is one country that, as of the time of this book's publication, does not impose any cap on tax benefits for charitable giving. A 2012 government proposal to impose a cap was met with strong opposition from the charitable sector, and was ultimately withdrawn, in May 2012.

10. A 2006 Report commissioned by Charities Aid Foundation noted that, "there is yet no international research comparing the precise effects of different tax reliefs on levels of giving." CAF Briefing Paper, International Comparisons of Charitable Giving" (November 2006), 10, available at https://www.cafonline.org/publications/archive/international-giving.aspx.

    In the United States, proposals to cap the charitable deduction for wealthy taxpayers have generated extensive debate over the extent to which tax benefits motivate individual giving. In 2011, Indiana University published a study concluding that individual giving is affected by changes in tax benefits. *See* The Center on Philanthropy at Indiana University, "Impact of the Obama Administration's Proposed Tax Policy Changes on Itemized Charitable Giving" (October 2011), available at www.philanthropy.iupui .edu/research-by-category/tax-policy-and-giving-2011.

11. *See* CAF Briefing Paper, "International Comparisons of Charitable Giving," *supra* note 10, at 10.

12. Appendix B lists some resources for finding organizations, based in the United States and abroad, that support organizations and projects outside the United States.

13. More information about the Charities Aid Foundation is available at www .cafonline.org/about-us/international-network.aspx.

14. *See* David Moore and Douglas Rutzen, "Legal Framework for Global Philanthropy: Barriers and Opportunities," *The International Journal of Not-for-Profit Law* 13, no. 1–2 (April 2011), 9, available at www.icnl.org/ research/journal/vol13iss1/index.htm.

15. Ineke A. Koele, *International Taxation of Philanthropy* (IBFD: Amsterdam, 2007), 4.

16. David Moore and Douglas Rutzen, "Legal Framework for Global Philanthropy," *supra* note 14, at 9.

17. A 2011 report published by Charities Aid Foundation found that Canada, Australia, and the UK were seventh, third, and fifth in the world for charitable giving. Charities Aid Foundation (CAF), "World Giving Index," *supra* note 3, at 11.

18. *See* Canada Revenue Agency (*CRA*) Guidance: "Canadian Registered Charities Carrying Out Activities Outside Canada, Ref. No. CG-002, July 8, 2010, available at www.cra-arc.gc.ca/chrts-gvng/chrts/plcy/cgd/tsd-cnd-eng.html.

19. *Id.*

20. *See also* Patrick Boyle, Robert Hayhoe, Lisa Mellon, and LaVerne Woods, "Canada–U.S. Boundary Issues for Cross-Border Charitable Activities," *Taxation of Exempt Organizations* 18, no. 03 (WG&L) (November/ December 2006).

21. Detailed information about how an Australian organization can qualify to receive tax deductible contributions to support projects outside of Australia can be found on the Australian government website at www .ausaid.gov.au/publications/pages/oagds-guidelines.aspx.

22. The guidance is found at www.hmrc.gov.uk/charities/guidance-notes/ annex2/annex_ii.htm#9.

23. Convention Between The United States and Canada With Respect to Taxes on Income and Capital (1983) ("U.S.-Canada Income Tax Treaty"), Article XXI, available at www.irs.gov/Businesses/International-Businesses/ Canada—Tax-Treaty-Documents.

24. IRS Notice 99-47, I.R.B. 1999-36, 344 (September 1999).

25. For a discussion of the effect of Notice 99-47 on U.S. private foundations, *see* Patrick Boyle, Robert Hayhoe, Lisa Mellon, LaVerne Woods, "Canada–U.S. Boundary Issues for Cross-Border Charitable Activities," *supra* note 20.

26. Treasury Department, Technical Explanation of the Convention Between The Government of The United States of America and The Government of The United Mexican States for the Avoidance of Double Taxation (1992), Article 22, available at www.irs.gov/businesses/international/article/0,, id=169680,00.html.

27. Convention Between The Government of The United States of America and The Government of The United Mexican States for the Avoidance of Double Taxation ("U.S.-Mexico Income Tax Treaty") (1992), Article 22, available at www.irs.gov/Businesses/International-Businesses/Mexico— Tax-Treaty-Documents.

28. IRS Information Letter 2003–0158, March 17, 2003. For additional background and updates, *see* www.usig.org/countryinfo/mexico.asp.

29. As reported in "Enabling Reform: Lessons Learned from Progressive NGO Legal Initiatives," *Global Trends in NGO Law* 2, no. 3 (December 2010), 8, available at www.icnl.org/research/trends/trends2-3.html.

30. *See* "Beyond Borders: Observations for U.S. organizations considering nonprofit incorporation in Mexico," published by U.S.-Mexico Border Philanthropy Partnership (2010), found at www.borderpartnership.org/ membership/publications.html.

31. Convention Between The Government of The United States of America and The Government of the State of Israel with Respect to Taxes on Income (1975) ("U.S.-Israel Income Tax Treaty"), Article 15-A, added by Protocol I (1980), available at www.irs.gov/Businesses/International-Businesses/Israel—Tax-Treaty-Documents.

32. I.R.C. §§ 2055(a)(2), 2106(a), 2522(a)(2).

33. U.S.-Canada Tax Treaty, *supra* note 23, Article XXIX. A list of U.S. estate and gift tax treaties in force is available on the IRS website at www.irs.gov/ Businesses/Small-Businesses-&-Self-Employed/Estate-&-Gift-Tax-Treaties- %28International%29.

34. *Hein Persche v Finanzamt Lüdenscheid*, Case C-318/07, European Court of Justice (ECJ) Case C-318/07 (2009), available at http://bit.ly/fzDXb3. For additional information about the *Persche* case, and updates on its impact, *see* The European Foundation Center website, available at www.efc.be/programmes_services/advocacy-monitoring/Taxation-and-foundations/Pages/EU-level-tax-and-cross-border-issues.aspx.

35. *See* European Foundation Center, "Comparative Highlights of Foundation Laws: The Operating Environment for Foundations in Europe" (2011), available at www.efc.be/programmes_services/resources/Pages/Foundations-FAQ.aspx.

36. *See* European Foundation Center (EFC) Briefing, "European Commission refers Netherlands to court over discriminatory treatment of foreign public benefit organizations," April 15, 2011, available at www.efc.be/programmes_services/resources/Documents/befc1106.pdf.

37. *See* EFC Briefing, "UK Extends Tax Incentives to Cross-Border Giving," April 8, 2010, available at www.efc.be/programmes_services/resources/Documents/befc1025.pdf.

38. David Moore and Douglas Rutzen, "Legal Framework for Global Philanthropy," *supra* note 14, at 13.

39. For updates on the EFS, *see* www.efc.be/programmes_services/advocacy-monitoring/European-Foundation-Statute/Pages/default.aspx.

# CHAPTER 8

# Additional U.S. Laws and Reporting Requirements

It's important to know that, even if your U.S. organization is operating outside U.S. borders, the organization's activities are still subject to certain U.S. laws, such as those that prohibit supporting terrorism or bribing a foreign official. If you engage in cross-border grantmaking, you also need to be concerned with U.S. export controls.

This chapter provides an overview of various U.S. legal and practical considerations commonly faced by U.S. tax-exempt organizations with international activities. Some of these are specifically applicable to nonprofit organizations, and others have more general application. This is not a comprehensive list of all U.S. laws that may apply to any particular organization, and the descriptions below are mere summaries of complex legal subjects. It's important to consult a lawyer to understand how these considerations apply to your particular organization's activities, and to develop appropriate policies and procedures.

## 8.1 Anti-Terrorism Compliance

United States laws and regulations impose a variety of penalties on U.S. individuals and organizations that support terrorism, inadvertently as well as intentionally. U.S. nonprofit organizations are not exempt from these rules. In fact, following the attacks of September 11, 2001, the U.S. federal government became concerned that international terrorist organizations could exploit charitable organizations to raise and move funds.

For nonprofit organizations, the consequences of providing support for terrorist activities can include civil penalties, criminal penalties, loss of tax-exempt status, and freezing of an organization's assets. To protect themselves against any of these sanctions, all U.S. nonprofit organizations that make cross-border grants, or otherwise operate internationally, need to adopt appropriate policies and procedures to avoid supporting terrorist activities.

## Intentional Support of Terrorism

Since the September 11 terrorist attacks, U.S. federal criminal laws have been strengthened, imposing criminal fines and terms of imprisonment on individuals and organizations that support terrorist activity. Notably, the U.S.A. PATRIOT Act (the *PATRIOT Act*), enacted in 2001 and reauthorized in 2005, imposes criminal sanctions for intentionally or knowingly providing material support to terrorist organizations, or for use in committing terrorist acts. Support can be in the form of funds or goods.[1]

Nonprofit organizations, for the most part, do not intend to support terrorism. At the same time, if your organization disburses funds that wind up in the hands of terrorists, you could find yourself having to defend against an accusation of intentional support of terrorism. The nonprofit community has expressed concerns that an organization could be found to have acted intentionally, in support of terrorism, by making a grant to a highly suspicious organization. By implementing and following appropriate procedures, organizations should be able to avoid any risk of criminal penalties in the event that their grant funds or other materials fall into the wrong hands.

## Inadvertent Support of Terrorism

Of greater concern to U.S. nonprofit organizations are the sanctions, potentially severe, that can flow from inadvertent support of terrorist organizations and activities. An organization that, even inadvertently, provides financial support, other resources, or even technical assistance, may find itself unable to access bank accounts and other assets pending a federal investigation.

Consequences of inadvertently supporting terrorist organizations or activities include freezing of assets and civil penalties, and loss of tax-exempt status.

**FREEZING OF ASSETS AND CIVIL PENALTIES**   In 2001, President Bush issued an order, known as *Executive Order 13224* (the *Executive Order*),[2] aimed at cutting off resources to terrorist organizations by authorizing the federal government to block an organization's access to all of its assets. While asset blocking is an extraordinary measure, used only sparingly against nonprofit organizations, the threat is real and the consequences are harsh.

The federal office charged with enforcing the Executive Order is the U.S. Treasury Department's Office of Foreign Assets Control (*OFAC*). OFAC has broad authority to block an organization's access to assets, even before the organization has been notified of a possible violation. An organization can find itself unable to access its assets, including bank accounts, while the government investigates whether the organization provided any support to terrorism. Having a single board member whose name is on a government list of terrorist individuals can cause an organization to be designated as a terrorist organization, triggering blocking of assets.

A federal appellate court has concluded that some of OFAC's enforcement practices are unconstitutional, holding that the government must obtain a judicial warrant before blocking assets, and cannot deprive an organization of a meaningful opportunity to respond by withholding the reasons for blocking assets.[3] It remains to be seen whether OFAC will continue to block assets without any notice or prior judicial review, and conduct investigations without permitting access to funds to pay an attorney.

**LOSS OF TAX-EXEMPT STATUS**   A 501(c)(3) organization that inadvertently funds terrorist activity could lose its tax-exempt status, in addition to suffering any of the consequences previously described. This could occur even if the organization had no intention, or even knowledge, that it was funding prohibited activities. All 501(c)(3) organizations are prohibited from devoting more than an *insubstantial part* of their activities to those that are not in furtherance of their tax-exempt purposes.[4] There is no clear definition of the term *insubstantial part*. It is clear, however, that terrorist activity is not a tax-exempt purpose. An organization found to have inadvertently funded terrorist activity would need to establish that the diverted funds were not substantial in relation to the overall size and activities of the organization.

## Risk-Based Approach to Developing Policies and Procedures

It is critical to adopt and comply with policies and procedures, not only to avoid inadvertently supporting terrorist activity, but also to avoid or minimize sanctions should your funding find its way into the wrong hands.

OFAC's website states that, in the event of an inadvertent violation, OFAC will take into account whether the organization had adopted and followed policies and procedures that were appropriate for the size and nature of the organization. This may prompt you to ask: *What are appropriate policies and procedures for my organization?* Unfortunately, there are no clear rules.

The U.S. Treasury Department, and many organizations in the nonprofit sector, advise assessing the nature and level of risk that your organization might inadvertently support terrorist activities, and then creating policies and procedures appropriate for that risk.

Some critical factors to consider in assessing risk are:

- Is your grantee (or organization you support) working in countries where the risk of terrorist activity is high?
- How well do you know your grantee, or the organization you are supporting, and how long have you known the organization?

Additional factors are set forth in OFAC's *Risk Matrix for the Charitable Sector*.[5] Use of this matrix is voluntary, and OFAC's website states that the risk factors listed are not comprehensive.

## Know Your Grantee

For any organization involved in supporting foreign activities, whether through grantmaking or otherwise, it is critical to have sufficient familiarity with the organization you are supporting.

Steps in vetting an organization may include the following two:

1. *Adopting procedures to comply with, and possibly go beyond, IRS requirements for international grantmaking.*

   For grantmakers, a starting point is compliance with the IRS requirements regarding discretion and control, for public charities (*see* Chapter 2), or for private foundations, expenditure responsibility or equivalency determination (*see* Chapter 3). You may conclude that it's appropriate to go beyond these requirements, for example by gathering and documenting detailed information about a grantee's overall activities. This may include knowing where the organization operates, to whom it makes grants, and where and with whom it works. You may also consider gathering information about the organization's officers, board members, and management. Your assessment of risk factors will influence the extent to which you need to vet an organization before you provide funds or other support.[6]

2. *Checking the Specially Designated Names (SDN) list.*

   The SDN list, maintained by OFAC, is a comprehensive list of individuals and organizations it considers to be associated with terrorism (and certain other activities). The list is available to download from OFAC's website.[7]

   This list is extremely lengthy and constantly changing. It can be accessed by country, so that your organization can target certain areas where your grants or operations may involve higher risk. Financial institutions that engage in high volumes of transactions typically invest in software packages that automate review of the SDN list and compliance with OFAC rules. However, nonprofit organizations that make grants or operate internationally often find it is not economically feasible to purchase this software.

The U.S. Treasury Department (in its *Anti-Terrorism Financing Guidelines*, discussed later) suggests that an organization should check every potential grantee against the SDN list, and also confirm that none of a grantee's key employees, board members, or senior management have been subject to OFAC sanctions. In practice, some organizations conclude that these steps are not warranted in particular circumstances, for example when the grantmaker has a longstanding relationship with the grantee. Others forego this step, believing that the list contains errors that can prevent the delivery of aid to legitimate beneficiaries. Based on a risk analysis, you may conclude that you have sufficient familiarity with an organization that checking the SDN list is not necessary. This is a determination every organization should make with great care.

Be aware that if you do check the SDN list, that is not, in and of itself, sufficient to avoid sanctions in the event you are found to have provided material support to a terrorist organization. Note, also, that there are a number of additional lists, maintained by other U.S. government departments and the United Nations. Checking all of these lists would be impracticable for any organization.

## Guidance for Developing Policies and Procedures

Here are some important and useful resources for developing appropriate policies and procedures for your organization.

### U.S. DEPARTMENT OF THE TREASURY ANTI-TERRORIST FINANCING GUIDELINES: VOLUNTARY BEST PRACTICES FOR U.S.-BASED CHARITIES

These *Anti-Terrorism Financing Guidelines* (the *Treasury Guidelines*), found on the U.S. Treasury Department's website, were issued in 2002 and were subsequently revised in 2005 and again in 2006.[8] The introduction to the Treasury Guidelines states that they are intended to assist charitable organizations in complying with laws that prohibit supporting terrorist activities, and adherence to the Treasury Guidelines does not provide a defense against civil or criminal liability for violation of any law. While the Treasury Guidelines are voluntary (at least as of the time of publication of this book), they do represent the U.S. Treasury Department's position. If your organization engages in international activities, and is audited by the IRS, you may well have to respond to questions about your compliance with the Treasury Guidelines.

The Treasury Guidelines were criticized by representatives of the nonprofit sector, in part for imposing excessive requirements (despite being designated as voluntary), particularly with respect to information collection. There was a concern that these requirements would deter some U.S. organizations, and their U.S. funders, from engaging in or funding international charitable work.[9] Despite the criticisms, every U.S. organization engaged in international activity should review the Treasury Guidelines and take them into account in developing policies.

The Treasury Guidelines include the following recommendations (among others):

**Fundamental Principles of Good Charitable Practice** Charitable organizations should adopt practices in addition to those required by law to ensure that assets are used for legitimate purposes. Governance, fiscal and programmatic responsibility, and accountability are essential in all aspects of an organization's work.

**Governance, Accountability, and Transparency** An organization's board of directors is responsible to ensure compliance with applicable laws, and to oversee financial and accounting practices, including financial recordkeeping to safeguard financial assets. There is a recommendation that charities gather and maintain records of certain information pertaining to directors, key U.S. and non-U.S. employees, and directors of subsidiaries and affiliates.

**Financial Accountability and Transparency** The Treasury Guidelines provide detailed recommendations regarding financial controls and independent audits. They recommend making disbursements only by check or wire transfer and, where that is not possible (for example, in providing humanitarian assistance to remote areas of developing countries), cash disbursements should be made in the smallest increments sufficient to meet the need.

A charitable organization should issue an annual report, available to the public, describing programs, activities, and financial and other information. The Treasury Guidelines further recommend public disclosure of all branches, subsidiaries, and affiliates that receive resources from the charity.

**Programmatic Verification** The Treasury Guidelines set forth detailed recommendations to ensure fiscal responsibility when a charity is supplying resources or services, including gathering information about the recipient, monitoring (including through on-site visits), and maintaining written records.

**Anti-Terrorism Best Practices** A charity should vet its own key employees, its grantees, and the grantees' key employees, governing board, and other senior management. The recommended vetting process has an extensive list of steps, which include checking the Treasury Department's SDN list. It is noted that not all of the listed steps will necessarily be appropriate in all situations.

**PRINCIPLES OF INTERNATIONAL CHARITY, DEVELOPED BY THE TREASURY GUIDELINES WORKING GROUP OF CHARITABLE SECTOR ORGANIZATION AND ADVISORS** The *Principles of International Charity (Principles)*, released in March, 2005,[10] was prepared by a large, diverse group of representatives from the charitable sector (the *Working Group)* as an alternative to the Treasury Guidelines described above.

This document consists of eight Principles, with commentary, recognizing that, within those basic Principles, appropriate and effective policies and procedures will vary widely among organizations. The Principles stress fiscal responsibility in the international context, including the use of written grant agreements, monitoring the use of funds, and taking corrective action in the event of misuse of funds.

The eight fundamental Principles are:

1. Consistent with the privilege inherent in their tax-exempt status, charitable organizations must exclusively pursue the charitable purposes for which they were organized and chartered.
2. Charitable organizations must comply with both U.S. laws applicable to charities and the relevant laws of the foreign jurisdictions in which they engage in charitable work. Charitable organizations, however, are non-governmental entities that are not agents for enforcement of U.S. or foreign laws or the policies reflected in them.
3. Charitable organizations may choose to adopt practices in addition to those required by law that, in their judgment, provide additional confidence that all assets—whether resources or services—are used exclusively for charitable purposes.
4. The responsibility for observance of relevant laws and adoption and implementation of practices consistent with the principles contained herein ultimately lies with the governing board of each individual charitable organization. The board of directors of each charitable organization must oversee the governance practices to be followed by the organization.
5. Fiscal responsibility is fundamental to charitable work. Therefore, an organization's commitment to the charitable use of its assets must be reflected at every level of the organization.
6. When supplying charitable resources, fiscal responsibility on the part of the provider generally involves:
   a. In advance of payment, determining that the potential recipient of monetary or in-kind contributions has the ability to both accomplish

the charitable purpose of the grant and protect the resources from
diversion to non-charitable purposes;

b. Reducing the terms of the grant to a written agreement signed by both
the charitable resource provider and the recipient;

c. Engaging in ongoing monitoring of the recipient and of activities under
the grant; and

d. Seeking correction of any misuse of resources on the part of the
recipient.

7. When supplying charitable services, fiscal responsibility on the part of the
provider involves taking appropriate measures to reduce the risk that its
assets would be used for non-charitable purposes. Given the range of
services in which organizations engage, the specific measures necessarily
vary depending on the type of services and the exigencies of the
surrounding circumstances. The key to fiscal responsibility, however,
is having sufficient financial controls in place to trace funds between
receipt by the service provider and delivery of the service.

8. Each charitable organization must safeguard its relationship with the
communities it serves in order to deliver effective programs. This relationship is founded on local understanding and acceptance of the
independence of the charitable organization. If this foundation is shaken,
the organization's ability to be of assistance and the safety of those
delivering assistance is at serious risk.

The commentary to the Principles is highly recommended, as it describes
how the Principles might translate into concrete policies for organizations
engaged in a variety of activities.

Additional resources for complying with U.S. anti-terrorism requirements
for grantmakers are available on the website of the U.S. International Grantmaking project of the Council on Foundations.[11]

## Providing Humanitarian Aid in Sanctioned Countries

OFAC also maintains a country-based program that prohibits or restricts the
provision of funding and other resources to specified countries, or to certain
individuals and/or organizations in those countries. The list of countries, with
links to the specific prohibitions applicable to each country, can be found on
the U.S. Treasury Department's OFAC website.[12]

Organizations that make international grants, or otherwise conduct international activities, should be familiar with the OFAC list of sanctioned
countries. Violations can give rise to criminal penalties (if the violation was
committed knowingly or intentionally), or civil penalties, and OFAC has the
power to block assets of an organization pending an investigation (discussed
previously).

Under many of the sanctioned country programs, there are exceptions for the provision of humanitarian aid. Exceptions may also apply to certain informational materials, such as publications and photographs. Often, it is necessary to obtain a registration number or license. Whether, and under what conditions, a registration number or license is needed or available varies by country. OFAC's website provides extensive country-by-country information on the registration and licensing processes for the provision of humanitarian aid within sanctioned countries.

It is important to note that the exportation of certain items and technology is restricted by the U.S. Commerce Department. If you are exporting equipment, particularly technical equipment, it may be necessary to obtain a Commerce Department license, even if you have already obtained a license from OFAC. *See* section 8.2.

## USAID Funding Conditions

As a condition to receiving funding from the United States Agency for International Development (*USAID*), an organization is required to sign a *Certificate Regarding Terrorist Financing*.[13] The certificate requires a number of representations to establish that the organization has taken steps, including checking the SDN list, to ensure that funds will not be used to finance terrorist activities.

## 8.2   Export Controls

The United States imposes restrictions (*export controls*) on certain exports to other countries. Two major categories of export controls are:

1. Restrictions on commercial products and technology, which are regulated by the U.S. Department of Commerce.
2. Restrictions on equipment and technical data that can be used for military purposes, regulated by the U.S. State Department.

A number of other federal government departments have responsibility for additional export controls.[14] Steep civil fines, and even criminal penalties, can be imposed for violations.

It is important to note that, for purposes of export controls, exporting can take the form of an electronic, or even a verbal, transfer (for example, of restricted technical information), as well as a physical transfer of goods. An item that is donated can be subject to export controls, although the provision of humanitarian aid may fall under an exception. If an item is subject to export controls, a violation can occur where an individual merely carries that item into a particular country, without a license, for use while the visitor is there. In addition, both sets of export controls discussed in the following paragraphs regulate the *deemed export* of certain goods and technology, by prohibiting U.S. persons from sharing those items with non-U.S. persons who are physically in the United States.

### Restrictions on Exporting Certain Goods and Technologies

Certain commercial products and technologies may not be exported without obtaining a license from the U.S. Commerce Department's Bureau of Industry Security (*BIS*), which is charged with enforcing a set of regulations known as the *Export Administration Regulations* (*EAR*).[15] The EAR restrict certain exports according to classification of an item or technology, and according to the destination country, end user, and/or end use. The goods and technology subject to controls are those that are considered by the government to be *dual-use*. This means they are considered to have a military as well as ordinary commercial use, but have not been made to military specifications. It is critical that organizations sending goods overseas check the BIS regulations because the dual-use nature of an item may not be obvious. For example, while most medical supplies are not controlled, some vaccines are subject to restrictions when destined for certain countries.

The BIS website provides a primer for understanding the regulations, and a matrix of item classifications and countries for determining whether a particular item is restricted for export to a particular country.[16]

In cases of exports to certain countries that are under U.S. embargoes, it is sometimes possible to obtain a single license from OFAC.

### Restrictions on Military Equipment and Technical Data

The U.S. Department of Defense, Directorate of Defense Trade Controls (*DDTC*), administers the regulations known as *International Traffic in Arms Regulations* (*ITAR*), which impose export controls on certain items and technology that have military uses. Most nonprofit organizations will not be subject to these regulations, but if you violate them, penalties can be severe. Information about the items and technology covered under the ITAR is available on the DDTC website.[17]

## 8.3   Anti-Boycott Rules

It is illegal for U.S. citizens and residents, including 501(c)(3) organizations, to participate in, or cooperate with, international boycotts that are not sanctioned by the U.S. government. These restrictions were created to prohibit U.S.

companies from participating in the Arab League boycott of Israel. Today, the boycott of Israel remains a primary concern, although the prohibition applies to participation in any international boycott that is not sanctioned by the U.S. government.

The anti-boycott restrictions are found in two sets of laws, and they are enforced by two separate government agencies. The U.S. Department of Commerce Bureau of Industry Security (*BIS*) is responsible for enforcing the anti-boycott provisions of regulations under the *Export Administration Act*.[18] The Internal Revenue Service is responsible for enforcing Internal Revenue Code provisions that require reporting of operations in boycotting countries, and certain activities or actions treated as participation or cooperation in a boycott.[19]

Both the Department of Commerce rules and the IRS reporting rules are very complex, and the two sets of rules are not entirely consistent. If your organization has operations in any of the boycotting countries (*see* further on), it is important to seek legal advice. In addition, when operating in those countries, you should carefully review contracts to be sure you are not agreeing to refrain from supporting, or operating in, Israel or any other boycotted country, and that you are not agreeing to discriminate on the basis of race, religion, gender, or national origin.

## Commerce Department Rules

The Commerce Department *Export Administration Regulations* (*EAR*) prohibit participation in, or cooperation with, an international boycott that is not sanctioned by the U.S. government. The EAR anti-boycott provisions also prohibit discriminating, or agreeing to discriminate, on the basis of race, religion, sex, national origin, or nationality.[20] Penalties for violations of these rules may be criminal.

The receipt of one or more requests to participate in an international boycott is required to be reported to the U.S. Commerce Department, on Form BIS 621-P or BIS 6051P.

## U.S. Tax Rules

United States tax law requires that a U.S. organization file a report with the IRS if it participates in an international boycott that is not sanctioned by the U.S. government, or even receives a request to participate in a boycott.[21] As an example, a reportable event would occur if your organization, as a condition to registering an office in an Arab country, were required to agree not to conduct any activities in the State of Israel.

In addition, the U.S Treasury Department maintains a list of certain boycotting countries, and an organization that conducts operations in any of those countries is required to file a report with the IRS. As of this book's publication, these countries are:

Kuwait
Lebanon
Libya
Qatar
Saudi Arabia
Syria
United Arab Emirates
Republic of Yemen
Possibly Iraq[22]

Additional countries could become involved in boycotts at any time.

An organization may also be required to report any of these operations if conducted by a foreign organization in which the U.S. organization has a voting interest (such as a membership interest).

Reporting is made using IRS Form 5713. Failure to comply with the IRS reporting requirements can result in fines and even criminal penalties. An organization that participates in an international boycott also loses certain tax benefits, such as foreign tax credits. While a loss of tax benefits may not be of consequence to your 501(c)(3) organization, you will not want to incur penalties for failure to report.

## 8.4  Anti-Bribery Rules

Many nonprofit organizations find themselves operating in countries where corruption is the norm, and it is difficult to get things done without engaging in bribery. Yet it is not only possible, but essential, for U.S.-based organizations to avoid participating in corrupt activity, not only for ethical reasons but also because very steep U.S. sanctions can be imposed.

Before deciding to launch a program in any country, your organization should explore whether bribery is a common practice, and if so, assess the feasibility of conducting your activities without participating in corrupt practices. If it's too hard, you should not be operating in that country. Leave it to others and go elsewhere.

All U.S.-based tax-exempt organizations that engage in international activities need to be familiar with the law known as the *Foreign Corrupt Practices Act (FCPA)*, which prohibits the making of payments (bribes) to foreign officials for the purpose of obtaining or retaining a contract, concession, or other favorable treatment.[23] The FCPA's prohibitions extend to actions that occur entirely outside the United States.

In recent years, the U.S. Justice Department has become increasingly vigilant about detecting FCPA violations, and has imposed penalties, even where violations involved small dollar amounts. Steep penalties, criminal as well as cavil, can be imposed at the organizational and individual levels.

It is critical for any organization with international activities to adopt a compliance program that includes training for all officers and employees and monitoring of compliance. It is likely that your compliance program will need to take into account foreign anti-bribery laws as well. *See* section 9.6. In fact, in order to ensure compliance with all applicable laws, many organizations adopt a single policy that prohibits officers and employees from making even the kinds of payments that would be permitted under an exception to the FCPA.[24]

## Who Is Subject to the FCPA?

The FCPA reaches U.S. organizations and individuals, and in some circumstances even foreign organizations and individuals. For example:

- The FCPA applies to any tax-exempt organization or taxable business, established under a U.S. state law (or the District of Columbia, a U.S. possession, territory, or commonwealth) or having its principal place of business in the United States. It also applies to individuals who are U.S. citizens or residents.
- Penalties can apply to officers, directors, and employees of an organization that engages in bribery of a foreign official.

If a U.S. citizen or resident is employed by a foreign organization, that individual can be subject to FCPA sanctions if the individual engages in bribery of a foreign official on behalf of the foreign organization.

A U.S. organization (and in some circumstances, its employees or officers) can be subject to penalties for acts of a foreign organization, consultant, or other agent acting on behalf of the U.S. organization, if the U.S. organization authorizes an improper payment.

You cannot just look the other way while a bribe is being made on your behalf. A U.S. organization can be subject to penalties if it pays an agent, knowing that the agent will use the funds to make a bribe.

A foreign organization (taxable or tax-exempt) or individual can be subject to FCPA penalties if the foreign organization or individual engages in bribery of a foreign official within the United States.

## What Kinds of Payments Are Prohibited?

A violation of the FCPA can occur only if all of the following four elements exist:

1. *Offering, paying, or authorizing.* A violation can occur if an offer of payment is made, even if the payment is not actually made. A violation can also occur when a U.S. organization (or its officers or employees) authorizes an agent to make or offer a payment.
2. *Anything of value.* Payments need not be made with money. For example, providing meals or travel to government officials can be prohibited payments.
3. *To a foreign official.* A foreign official is a government employee of any level, a member or official of a foreign political party, or a candidate for foreign political office.
4. *For the purpose of securing any contract, concession, or other favorable treatment.* An FCPA violation can occur only if a payment was made, offered, or authorized with the intent to induce a foreign official to take action, neglect to take action, or otherwise use his or her influence to affect any act or decision. It is not necessary that the ultimate benefit pertain to a contract or other business with the government. For example, if a government official is bribed to use his or her official influence over a private party, that falls under the FCPA.

## Payments Made by Agents and Others: Do Not Turn a Blind Eye

United States organizations cannot afford to ignore what their foreign agents or consultants are doing. If an organization is paying another organization or individual to perform services in a foreign country, the U.S. organization can be sanctioned for the foreign agent or consultant's actions, if the U.S. organization knew or consciously disregarded what the foreign agent was doing. You cannot simply turn the other way. Rather, you need to have policies and procedures that extend to individuals and organizations you engage in foreign countries, and monitor what they are doing on your behalf.

## Exception: Payments to Facilitate Routine Governmental Actions

The FCPA contains an exception, allowing payments to facilitate or expedite *routine governmental action.* The law lists the following examples of routine governmental actions: obtaining permits and licenses; processing of governmental papers such as visas and work orders; provision of police protection; mail pick-up and delivery; provision of phone service, power, and water supply; loading and unloading cargo; protecting perishable products; scheduling inspections associated with contract performance or transit of goods across country.

Routine governmental action does not include any decision by a government official to award or continue business.

A decision to make use of this exception should be made with great caution. Officers, employees, and agents must be given very specific guidelines. Many organizations find it safer to prohibit all payments to government officials, rather than trying to enforce a narrowly drawn exception. Moreover, often local country laws, or international anti-bribery conventions, will prohibit payments that fall within the FCPA's exception.

## When Can You Pay for Government Officials' Travel Expenses?

Some organizations occasionally have legitimate needs to pay for government officials to travel. The FCPA permits the provision of entertainment (including meals) or travel to foreign government officials under certain circumstances. The expenses must be:

- Directly related to the promotion, demonstration, or explanation of products or services, or to the execution or performance of a contract with a foreign government or agency.
- Reasonable in amount.

This is called an *affirmative defense*, which means that, if challenged, your organization has the burden of establishing that the expenditure was made for a permissible purpose and was reasonable.

This should be an infrequent occurrence, and it must be planned in advance. In addition, it is critical to avoid any expectation, written or unwritten, that anything will be provided to your organization in return. In no event should any travel or entertainment be provided to an official who is in a position to award a contract, grant, or other business to your organization.

If you are going to provide any travel or entertainment to a foreign government official, address it in your anti-bribery policy, and include clear guidelines that prohibit payments of personal expenses (sightseeing or family travel). Payment for travel should be made directly to a governmental body where possible, and otherwise directly to the vendor. You should not make reimbursements directly to an individual government official. Also, you should reimburse actual expenses, rather than providing a *per diem* or other allowance.

In addition, note that payments of any expenses related to a government official's campaign are strictly forbidden to 501(c)(3) organizations. *See* section 8.5.

Finally, remember that even if something is permitted under the FCPA, it may be prohibited under the applicable foreign country's law. This means knowing what the local law actually says, not just whether it conforms to local custom.

### Payments Permitted under a Foreign Country's Law

The FCPA also provides an *affirmative defense* for payments that are permitted under the written laws of a foreign country. Local custom is not relevant. This will rarely be useful.

### Charitable Contributions Can Violate FCPA!

Your antennae should rise if your organization is told that you must contribute to a charity as a condition to registration in a foreign country, or to the receipt of some other government benefit. Of course, for many organizations, making charitable contributions is an integral part of, or at least consistent with, their tax-exempt purposes. However, you need to be sure that the foreign charity is not acting as an agent for a government official.

If you are told that you must make a contribution, determine whether this requirement is written into some law or regulation. Become very familiar with the prospective recipient charity, and whether it has ties to an individual government official. If you decide to contribute to a foreign charity, you will need to undertake careful due diligence and monitoring of the use of funds to comply with U.S. tax and anti-terrorism rules. *See* Chapters 2 and 3. Make the contribution directly to the charity, or to a governmental body. Do not make a direct payment to a government official.

### All International Organizations Should Have a Compliance Program

While any organization, operating anywhere in the world, can face challenges in avoiding corruption, the level of risk your organization faces will vary according to where you operate and the nature of your operations. Particularly when operating in countries where corruption is the norm, you will need to support a code of conduct with carefully crafted procedures aimed at eliminating opportunities for employees, officers, staff, directors, and volunteers to participate in corruption. *See* Case Study: Ashesi University, section 5.1.[25]

## 8.5  Lobbying and Political Activity

If your 501(c)(3) organization is directly conducting activities outside the United States, you need to be aware that the 501(c)(3) restrictions on lobbying (described in the following paragraphs) apply to the organization's foreign, as well as U.S., activities. If your organization is making grants to foreign organizations, you should take steps to be sure the organization does not contravene applicable restrictions on lobbying and political activity.

This section provides an overview of the restrictions on lobbying and political activities that apply generally to 501(c)(3) organizations. It then discusses challenges organizations face when attempting to comply with these rules while operating in a foreign country.

## Overview of Lobbying Restrictions for 501(c)(3) Organizations

The applicable restrictions on lobbying vary according to whether the 501(c)(3) organization is a public charity or private foundation (*see* Chapters 2 and 3).

- *Lobbying by public charities.* 501(c)(3) organizations that are treated as public charities (not private foundations) are permitted to lobby, as long as the lobbying is an *insubstantial* portion of the organization's overall activities, or satisfies a test that limits expenditures for lobbying.[26]
- *Lobbying by private foundations.* Private foundations are effectively prohibited from engaging in any lobbying activity.[27]

## Alternative Lobbying Tests for Public Charities

A 501(c)(3) public charity has the option of determining that its lobbying is insubstantial under either of two tests:

1. *Insubstantial part test.* If an organization does not elect the so-called *expenditure test* (below), it must meet the requirement that its lobbying activity is an insubstantial part of its overall activities. This is not clearly defined, and may be based on factors other than, or in addition to, expenditures. For example, expenditures may be quite small if your organization enlists a corps of volunteers to wage an online campaign in favor of a referendum, using a variety of social media. However, the time dedicated by the volunteers could be quite substantial.
2. *Expenditure test.* The so-called *expenditure test* is elective, and provides certainty because it allows an organization to expend specified amounts on lobbying activities.[28] Under the expenditure test, an organization's maximum annual lobbying expenditure is determined as a percentage of its annual budget (subject to certain adjustments). For organizations with a budget (after adjustments) of $500,000 or less, the maximum lobbying expenditure is 20 percent of that budget, and the allowable lobbying expenditure increases as the budget increases, based on a sliding scale, up to a maximum lobbying expenditure of $1 million.[29] A separate limitation applies to expenditures for so-called *grass roots lobbying,* which may not be more than 25 percent of the total maximum allowed.

If an organization exceeds the allowable limits under the expenditure test, an excise tax applies. In addition, the organization loses its tax-exempt status if, over a four-year period, its total or grass roots lobbying expenditures exceed 150 percent of the limit.

If two 501(c)(3) organizations are related in such a way that one has the ability to control the other's positions on legislation (as a result of provisions in governing documents or through overlapping board members), then the two organizations are combined for purposes of applying the expenditure test.

## What Is Lobbying?

It is important to understand that the definition of lobbying is rather narrow for purposes of the restrictions on lobbying by 501(c)(3) organizations.

ATTEMPTING TO INFLUENCE LEGISLATION    For purposes of both the insubstantial part test and the expenditure test, lobbying means attempting to influence *legislation*. Attempting to influence legislation includes a range of activities such as advocating for or against specific legislation, directly communicating with legislators, testifying at a legislative hearing, and urging the public to contact their legislators. General issue advocacy, and other activities that do not fall within the technical definition of lobbying, are not subject to the restrictions, although they must otherwise comply with 501(c)(3) requirements.

Legislation includes actions by Congress, a state legislature, a local council or similar governing body, and actions by the public in a referendum, initiative, constitutional amendment, or similar procedure.[30] Legislation also includes foreign legislation. Note, however, that administrative rules and regulations issued by government agencies are not treated as legislation. Actions by judicial and executive bodies are also excluded.

EXPENDITURE TEST DEFINITIONS OF DIRECT AND GRASSROOTS LOBBYING    For purposes of the expenditure test, the definition of influencing legislation is further defined as *direct lobbying* or *grass roots lobbying*.

- *Direct lobbying*. Direct lobbying means communication with a member of a legislative body, their staff, or other government official or employee, regarding specific legislation and reflecting a view on the legislation. Direct lobbying also includes communications with the general public regarding a specific ballot initiative or referendum, or similar item if the communication reflects a view on the item.
- *Grassroots lobbying*. Grassroots lobbying means communication with the general public regarding legislation if the communication takes a position on the legislation and urges the public to act, for example by contacting legislators.
- *Exceptions*. Exceptions include nonpartisan analysis or research, responding to a legislative request for technical advice, and communicating on

matters that affect the exempt organization's existence, powers, duties, or exempt status.

Regardless of whether you apply the insubstantial part test or the expenditure test, the rules for determining what is and is not considered lobbying are very technical and fact-specific. It is critical to obtain professional advice if you are venturing into the realm of legislative advocacy.

## Overview of Political Activity Prohibition

All 501(c)(3) organizations (public charities and private foundations) are prohibited from engaging in political campaign activities. Even a small amount of political campaign activity can jeopardize an organization's tax-exempt status.[31]

The political campaign prohibition applies to any participation or intervention in (including the publishing or distributing of statements) a political campaign on behalf of, or in opposition to, any candidate for public office.[32] The office may be federal, state, local, or even foreign.

The question of what constitutes participation or intervention in a campaign has not been clearly defined. The IRS takes a *facts-and-circumstances* approach, looking at whether the overall effect of a communication is to support or oppose a candidate, expressly or implicitly.[33]

## Lobbying in Foreign Countries

The lobbying restriction applies to activity aimed at influencing foreign legislation in the same way that it applies in the domestic realm.[34] You need to analogize to the U.S. legislative process in order to determine whether you are engaging in direct or grassroots lobbying in a foreign country. Do not simply rely on labels. In nondemocratic governments, the legislative process can look very different from that of the United States. For example, if your organization is communicating with a governmental body that has the power to issue laws or edicts, you need to look carefully at whether that is activity that is subject to the lobbying restrictions.

This is an area in which any organization is advised to proceed with extreme caution, and consult a knowledgeable attorney licensed to practice in the United States.

## Political Activity in Foreign Countries

The prohibition against participation or intervention in political campaigns also applies to foreign as well as domestic activity.[35] As with lobbying, you need to analyze the political process of the foreign country to which the activity or communication pertains. The prohibition applies only in the context of candidates for *public office*, and the IRS interprets that term to mean elective public office.

In the foreign context, it may not always be clear whether a candidate is running for elective office as defined by U.S. tax law. For example, in a single party system, would a candidate for a party position be considered a candidate for public office?

Given the high stakes (potential loss of tax-exempt status), it is critical to consult with an attorney licensed in the United States before engaging in any communications or other activities that could be seen as favoring or opposing a foreign public official.

Of course, even if the U.S. tax (and other) laws permit the activity, an organization must also understand any foreign law rules and restrictions related to engaging in the political process.

## Grants to Foreign Organizations

If a 501(c)(3) organization makes grants to a foreign organization, and if any of the grant funds are treated as used to support lobbying or political activities, those activities will be attributed to the grantor. To ensure that your organization does not inadvertently support prohibited political activity or exceed its lobbying limitations, you must build safeguards into your grant procedures.

All 501(c)(3) organizations (public charities and private foundations) should require foreign grantees to agree not to engage in any political activity that is prohibited under section 501(c)(3). While a U.S. public charity is permitted to engage in limited lobbying activity (as discussed previously), most public charities will want to prohibit foreign grantees from using any grant funds for lobbying activities. It is not always easy to determine, in the context of a foreign regime, whether particular activities fall within the 501(c)(3) definition of lobbying. Moreover, monitoring a foreign organization's lobbying expenditures may be difficult, if not impossible.

If the grantmaking organization is a private foundation and the grantmaker exercises expenditure responsibility (*see* Chapter 3), the terms of a cross-border grant must prohibit a grantee from engaging in prohibited lobbying activities.[36]

## Special Rule for Testamentary Gifts

A U.S. estate tax deduction, unlike the income tax deduction, is available for bequests made directly to foreign organizations that are organized and operated for 501(c)(3) purposes. The estate tax deduction is not available, however, if the foreign organization devotes a substantial portion of its

activities to lobbying, or engages in any political activities prohibited to 501(c)
(3) organizations.[37]

## 8.6 Foreign Funding of Lobbying and Propaganda

Any 501(c)(3) organization that receives funding from foreign sources to
engage in lobbying, or otherwise influencing of public policy, in the United
States should be aware of the *Foreign Agents Registration Act* (*FARA*).[38] This
broad-sweeping law is aimed at shedding light on foreign influences over U.S.
laws and public policy. When applicable, it requires registration with the U.S.
Department of Justice. It has been noted that, recently, websites and blogs
have been started to assert FARA violations by particular organizations that
take politically sensitive positions.[39] As a result, failure to register when
required may cause public embarrassment for an organization that is involved
with sensitive issues.

More importantly, failure to register under FARA can result in criminal
penalties. At the same time, an organization should not jump too quickly to the
conclusion that it needs to register.[40] Certain activities that are entirely
charitable in nature are exempt from the registration requirement. Once
registered, an organization will be required to disclose significant information
and to label information it disseminates.[41] Any organization that believes it
might be required to register under FARA should promptly seek legal advice.

## 8.7 U.S. Individuals Working in Foreign Countries

United States citizens and resident aliens (*see* section 6.4) are required to pay
U.S. income tax on their worldwide income, whether earned in the United
States or abroad. Income earned by a U.S. individual while working in a
foreign country may also be subject to tax in that country. There are, however,
some ways to avoid, or at least minimize, *double taxation*, or taxes imposed by
two separate countries on the same income.

### Claiming Exemption from Foreign Tax Under a Treaty

A U.S. resident working temporarily in a foreign country may be exempt from
that country's income tax under a treaty between the United States and the
country in which the individual is working. *See* section 6.3. In order to obtain a
treaty exemption from withholding on income earned in a foreign country, an
individual is often required to provide certification of U.S. residency. A U.S.
resident can obtain an official certification of U.S. residency in the form of a
letter (designated as Form 6166), printed on U.S. Department of Treasury

stationery. To obtain this certification, a U.S. resident files Form 8802 with the IRS.

Some countries may require that the individual furnish additional documentation for purposes of a treaty-based income tax exemption, or to establish eligibility for exemption from VAT.

## Claiming U.S. Tax Relief

If a U.S. citizen or resident alien is working in a foreign country, that individual may be able to reduce his or her U.S. tax liability by excluding some foreign income from U.S. taxable income. In addition, if a U.S. individual is required to pay income tax in a foreign country, that individual may be allowed to reduce a portion of U.S. tax liability by taking a credit for foreign taxes paid. *See* section 6.4.

- *Claiming the U.S. earned income or housing exclusion.* To claim the U.S. earned income exclusion or housing exclusion, or to claim a housing deduction (for independent contractors), an individual files Form 2555, or 2555 EZ, with the individual income tax return (Form 1040).
- *Claiming the individual foreign tax credit.* To claim a credit against U.S. federal income tax for income tax paid to a foreign government, an individual files Form 1116 with his or her U.S. federal tax return. The computation of the foreign tax credit is quite complex, and most individuals will hire a tax advisor to work through whether it is more advantageous to take a credit or a deduction for foreign taxes, and to compute and report the credit if claimed.[42]

## 8.8 Non-U.S. Individuals Working in the U.S.: Verifying Legal Status

If your U.S. organization wants to hire an individual to work in the United States, and that individual is not a U.S. citizen or permanent resident (*green card* holder), you need to be sure that individual has the required legal status. This is true even for short-term engagements.

United States organizations are required under federal law to verify the legal employment status of all employees, whether or not they are U.S. citizens, by completing and retaining Form I-9, issued by the U.S. Citizen and Immigration Services (*USCIS*). As part of completing the I-9, an employer is required to review certain specified documents to establish that the employee is legally employable in the United States. The form, and additional information are available on the USCIS website.[43]

## 8.9  Financial Reporting

Many U.S. 501(c)(3) organizations hire an independent auditor (*Certified Public Accountant*, or *CPA*) to audit their financial statements, either because they are required to do so under state law, or because foundations, governmental entities, and even individuals request audited statements as a condition of funding the organization. In the United States, audited financial statements are prepared using *U.S. Generally Accepted Accounting Standards* (*U.S. GAAP*).

If a 501(c)(3) organization operates in a foreign country through a branch office, the U.S. audited financial statements of the organization will include the branch operations. In most cases, the branch will also be required to maintain local country accounts, using local currency and local accounting standards. Some countries, such as Ethiopia, even require audited financial statements for a branch. In any event, it will be necessary to translate the foreign branch accounts into U.S. dollars for purposes of U.S. financial reporting.

By contrast, if you are operating in a foreign country through a separate legal entity, it is less likely that the U.S. and foreign entities will be consolidated for U.S. GAAP reporting purposes.[44]

## 8.10  U.S. Tax Reporting of Foreign Activities

All 501(c)(3) organizations, subject to limited exceptions, are required to file an annual information return with the IRS, using Form 990 or 990 EZ, or Form 990 PF (for private foundations).[45] The Form 990 EZ is available to certain smaller organizations.[46] A 501(c)(3) organization that conducts activities in a foreign country, makes cross-border grants, or engages in other transactions with foreign tax-exempt or taxable organizations, may be required to disclose information about those activities.

It is important to keep in mind that the Forms 990 and 990 EZ are public documents. Potential funders, and constituents of all types, will use this as a resource for learning about your organization. Be thoughtful about how you describe your activities.

In addition, before you decide how to structure the relationships between your U.S. organization and foreign legal entities, it is worthwhile understanding which U.S. reporting requirements will apply. For example, if your U.S. organization prefers not to publicly disclose the fact that you are operating in a particular country, you may want to avoid structuring a relationship in such a way that would require disclosure of a related foreign entity on Form 990 Schedule R (discussed later).

A foreign organization (whether or not exempt) that earns revenue from U.S. sources, but does not conduct a regular trade or business in the United States, may be subject to withholding taxes, and may need to obtain a U.S. tax identification number in order to avoid or reduce those taxes. *See* section 8.11.

## Reporting Foreign Grants, Offices, and Fundraising

Assuming your 501(c)(3) organization is required to file Form 990, and not 990 EZ, you will need to complete Schedule F to the Form 990 (if foreign activities meet certain dollar thresholds) to report and describe grants and other cash and noncash assistance to foreign organizations and foreign individuals, the operation of programs in foreign countries, and fundraising activities in foreign countries. All of this information is reported by region, not by individual country, with the regions defined by the IRS.

## Disclosure of Related Foreign Entities

Any 501(c)(3) organization that is required to file Form 990 must disclose, on Schedule R, the identity of foreign entities (taxable or tax-exempt) that are treated as related organizations. In addition to reporting the identity of a related organization, a U.S. Form 990 filer is required to report certain transactions with a related foreign entity. A U.S. organization that would otherwise qualify to file the shorter Form 990 EZ must file Form 990, along with Schedule R, if it is treated as having control over a foreign entity and engages in certain transactions with that entity. The rules for determining whether a foreign organization is related to, or controlled by, the 501(c)(3) filing organization, are technical and complex.

Some examples of a controlling interest are a U.S. organization that serves as the sole member of a foreign membership organization, or where a majority of a foreign organization's directors are officers, directors, or employees of the U.S. organization. It is critical to parse carefully through the definitions of related organizations.

## Additional IRS Forms That May Be Required

You may also be required to file any of the following IRS forms to report particular types of foreign investments or transactions with foreign legal entities:

- *Form 5471: Information Return of U.S. Persons with Respect to Certain Foreign Corporations*. A U.S. 501(c)(3) organization may have to file this form if it owns, acquires, or transfers 10 percent or more of the voting interests of a foreign legal entity. U.S. citizens and residents who are officers or directors of the foreign entity may also have to file this form.[47]
- *Form 926: Return by a U.S. Transferor of Property to a Foreign Corporation*. This form must be filed under certain circumstances when a U.S. citizen or resident (including a 501(c)(3) organization) transfers funds or other assets to a foreign corporation.
- *Form 3520 or 3520-A: Transactions with Foreign Trusts*. Form 3520 is required to report certain transactions with foreign trusts, and 3520-A

is a required annual information return for a foreign trust with a U.S. owner.

- *Form 8865: Interest in a foreign partnership.*
- *Form 8621: Interest in a Passive Foreign Investment Company.*[48]

If your U.S. organization has a voting (such as a membership) interest, or owns stock, in a foreign entity, you are well advised to work with an experienced lawyer or accountant to determine which U.S. tax reporting requirements apply. It is not always easy to determine which, if any, of these forms are required given a particular set of facts.

### IRS Reporting Requirements for Foreign Legal Entities

Some foreign legal entities are required to file U.S. federal tax forms. Notably, a foreign entity that qualifies as a 501(c)(3) organization may be required to make annual filings with the IRS, even if it has minimal activity or investments in the U.S.[49] A foreign organization that does not qualify as a 501(c)(3) organization for U.S. purposes, and earns revenue by conducting a regular trade or business in the United States (for example, through an office that it maintains), is required to file a U.S. tax return.

## 8.11   U.S. Tax Withholding on Payments to Non-U.S. Citizens or Residents

If your U.S. organization makes payments to a foreign organization or individual, for example as royalties for the use of copyrighted material, you may be required to withhold U.S. tax and remit that tax to the IRS. Even grant funds can be subject to withholding under certain circumstances.

Payments made to nonresident aliens (*see* section 6.4) and foreign entities are generally subject to U.S. *withholding tax* if the payments are treated as made from U.S. sources, and are not treated as effectively connected with a trade or business in the United States (that is, not otherwise subject to U.S. federal income tax reporting by the payee).[50]

The responsibility for collecting and paying the tax generally belongs to the individual or entity making the payment to the foreign recipient. This is called a withholding tax because the payor is required to withhold the applicable tax from the payment and remit the tax to the IRS.

When withholding is required, the amount is a flat percentage of the payment made, except that a nonresident alien who is working in the United States as an employee, rather than an independent contractor, is generally subject to withholding at graduated rates.[51]

A flat withholding tax is generally a final tax payment, not an advance payment of tax, as in the case of wage withholding. However, a nonresident alien who is working in the United States as an employee, and is subject to graduated withholding tax, is treated as conducting a business in the United States and may claim certain deductions on a tax return.

## Types of Payments Subject to Withholding Tax

Here are some types of payments, commonly made by U.S. nonprofit organizations, that are subject to withholding, unless there is an applicable exemption:[52]

**COMPENSATION FOR PERSONAL SERVICES**  Compensation for personal services performed in the United States is treated as income from U.S. sources, and is therefore subject to withholding. This category includes payments a U.S. organization makes directly to individual service providers, as well as payments to a foreign organization for services performed in the United States by staff of the foreign organization. For example, if your U.S. organization pays a foreign organization to send one of its employees to do some work for your organization in the United States, the payment you make to the foreign organization will be subject to U.S. withholding.

Under some circumstances, grants made by a U.S. organization to a foreign grantee may be subject to U.S. withholding, if the grantee organization sends staff to the United States. *See* section 3.4.

A narrow exception to the withholding requirement applies when a nonresident alien, working in the United States, is physically present in the United States for no more than a total of 90 days during the year, is paid directly by a foreign entity, or by a foreign office or branch of a U.S. organization, and receives less than $3,000.[53]

**Compensation Paid to Nonresident Alien Employees**  Compensation paid to a nonresident alien, whom your U.S. organization hires as an employee, is subject to the same graduated wage withholding as wages paid to U.S. residents. You are also required to withhold Medicare and Social Security taxes.

Of course, before you hire a nonresident alien employee, it is critical to ensure you can legally employee the individual, by collecting the required documentation (*see* section 6.7).

**Compensation Paid to Nonresident Alien Independent Contractors**  If your U.S. organization pays compensation to nonresident alien independent contractors (whether individuals or entities) for services performed in the United States, you are required to withhold U.S. tax at a flat rate, unless an exception applies. Most individual contractors are eligible to claim only one personal exemption, by providing the payor with an IRS Form 8233.[54]

**Reimbursement of Travel Expenses**  Your organization can reimburse expenses incurred by a nonresident alien for travel to the United States, without withholding, as long as the travel is for the benefit of your organization, and you require the individual to provide detailed documentation of the expenses. For example, you may have a foreign branch or foreign affiliate with staff who can lend valuable expertise to your U.S. operation. Travel to the United States would have a business purpose, and travel expenses could be reimbursed without withholding, as long as appropriate documentation is gathered and maintained by the U.S. organization.

**Special Rules for Scholarship and Fellowship Grants**   Scholarship and fellowship grants for study, training, or research that meet certain conditions may be entirely exempt from withholding, subject to a reduced rate of withholding, or subject to withholding at the regular rate of 30 percent.

**ROYALTIES**   Royalties are payments for the use of intangible property such as trademarks, copyrights, and patents. *See* section 9.7. Gains from the sale of this category of property are also treated as royalties, for purposes of withholding, if the payments are based on the use of the property, for example, based on sales of a copyrighted publication.

Royalty payments made to nonresident alien individuals and foreign entities are treated as income from U.S. sources, and therefore are subject to U.S. withholding, if the intangible property is used in the United States. For example, if your U.S. organization licenses the right to copyrighted materials owned by a foreign organization, and those materials are used in your U.S. operations, the royalties you pay will be subject to withholding unless an exemption applies.

**RENTS**   Rental payments made to a nonresident alien individual or a foreign entity are treated as income from U.S. sources if the leased property is situated within the United States. For example, if your U.S. organization leases a building, situated in the United States and owned by a foreign entity, the rents you pay to the foreign lessor will be treated as U.S. source income and subject to withholding unless an exemption applies.

**INTEREST**   Interest paid to a nonresident alien individual, or an entity established outside the United States, is treated as income from U.S. sources if paid by a U.S. resident. For example, if your U.S. organization borrows from a foreign organization, the interest is treated as U.S. source income, and is subject to withholding unless an exemption applies.

## Withholding Exception: Income Connected with a Trade or Business in the United States

An individual nonresident alien or foreign entity that is engaged in a trade or business in the United States is required to file a U.S. income tax return and compute U.S. income tax liability on a net income basis. This means that a person who is conducting business in the United States, generally through an office or other regular location, is entitled to claim deductions properly allocable to the business. Withholding does not apply to payments of income that is effectively connected with a trade or business carried out in the United States, as long as the nonresident alien or foreign entity provides the appropriate documentation to the payor.

To be exempt from withholding on income that is connected with a U.S. trade or business, the nonresident alien or foreign entity must obtain and provide:

- An IRS Employer Identification Number (*EIN*).
- IRS Form W-8 ECI.

## Eliminating or Reducing Withholding Under a Treaty

Any individual or entity claiming to be eligible for a withholding exemption or reduction under an applicable treaty must obtain and provide to the payor the following three types of documentation:

1. An IRS Taxpayer Identification Number (*TIN*). A TIN may be a social security number (*SSN*) for U.S. citizens and eligible residents; an Individual Taxpayer Identification Number (*ITIN*) for individuals not eligible for SSNs; or an Employer Identification Number (*EIN*) for anyone who is not an individual (such as a legal entity), anyone who is an employer, or anyone who is engaged in a regular trade or business in the United States.
2. IRS Form 8233 for an individual claiming a treaty exemption for personal services as an employee or an independent contractor, or Form W-8BEN.
3. Additional documentation for students, teachers, and researchers. A number of U.S. treaties provide special exemptions for students, teachers, and researchers working in the United States, subject to specific conditions that vary by treaty. The IRS has issued a publication that sets forth the statement to be provided with Form 8233 in order to qualify for the withholding exemption under each applicable treaty.[55]

## Withholding Exemption: Foreign Tax-Exempt Organizations

A foreign organization that is tax-exempt in its own country is not automatically exempt from U.S. withholding. Rather, a foreign organization may be eligible for exemption from U.S. withholding on payments it receives from U.S. sources if it satisfies the requirements for tax-exempt status under U.S. law.

To qualify for exemption as a tax-exempt organization, a foreign organization must:

- Obtain a TIN from the IRS and provide it to the payor.
- Provide the payor with a completed Form W-8 EXP.
- Provide documentation to establish that the foreign organization qualifies for U.S. tax-exempt status, in the form of either an IRS determination letter (confirming recognition of tax-exempt status), or an opinion of counsel.
- Provide an affidavit setting forth financial information to determine that the organization is not a private foundation, if the foreign organization qualifies as a 501(c)(3) organization and claims to be a public charity.[56]

A foreign organization that qualifies as a tax-exempt organization under U.S. law does not use this procedure for payments that are treated as UBTI (*see* section 4.9), or payments that are treated as income effectively connected with a trade or business that the foreign organization operates in the United States.

## Exemption under a Treaty's Reciprocity Provision for Tax-Exempt Organizations

The U.S. treaties with Germany, the Netherlands, Canada, and Mexico afford U.S. tax-exempt status for tax-exempt organizations established under the laws of those countries. If a foreign organization is relying on one of these treaties to claim exemption from withholding, it must follow the procedures described previously for exemption under a treaty, rather than providing the payor with a Form W-8EXP. In addition, each of these treaties contains specific conditions, and the procedures for claiming exemption vary by country. A U.S. payor should consult with an attorney if a payee is claiming exemption as an exempt organization under one of these treaties. *See* section 4.8.

## Exemption as an International Organization

Organizations designated as *international organizations* are exempt from U.S. withholding. International organizations for this purpose are certain public international organizations that have been designated, through an Executive Order, as organizations entitled to enjoy privileges, exemptions, and immunities under the *International Organizations Immunities Act*.[57] A payor is not required to obtain a Form W-8 EXP from these organizations, as long as the payor can determine that the international organization is the beneficial owner of the payment (receiving the payment on its own behalf).

## Reporting Payments Subject to Withholding

If your U.S. organization makes any payments of U.S. source income (*see* Types of Payments Subject to Withholding Tax, earlier in this section) to nonresident alien individuals or entities established outside the United States, you need to report those payments to the IRS on Form 1042-S, and file Form 1042. The timing of required deposits of withholding taxes varies according to the amounts withheld.[58]

## 8.12  Reporting of Foreign Financial Assets

U.S. individual citizens, residents, and organizations (taxable and tax-exempt) may be subject to either or both of two separate U.S. federal reporting requirements for financial assets held in foreign countries. The *Report of Foreign Bank and Financial Accounts*, known as *FBAR*,[59] serves as yet another weapon in the U.S. arsenal against financial support of terrorism, as well as money laundering and other illegal activities. The *Foreign Account Tax Compliance Act* (*FATCA*),[60] enacted in 2010, is aimed at reducing tax evasion by U.S. taxpayers who hide financial assets in offshore accounts.

While these reporting requirements have somewhat different purposes, in some cases their reporting requirements overlap. The IRS has published a comparison chart summarizing the key features of each.[61]

### Foreign Bank Account Reporting (FBAR)

FBAR is administered by the U.S. Treasury Department's *Financial Crimes Enforcement Network* (*FinCEN*). U.S. citizens, individual residents, and entities established in the United States are required to file an annual report to disclose interests they hold in foreign bank accounts and certain other foreign financial accounts. Failure to file this report, even if inadvertent, can result in steep civil penalties and intentional failures can result in criminal fines and imprisonment.[62]

**WHO IS REQUIRED TO FILE?**   The filing requirement applies to:

- Any *U.S. person* who has a *financial interest* or *signature authority* over a *foreign financial account,* if the aggregate value of all accounts over which the U.S. person has a financial interest or signature authority exceeds $10,000 at any time during a calendar year.
- A *U.S. person* is defined as an individual citizen or resident alien (*see* section 6.4) or entity created, organized, or formed under the laws of the United States, any State, or District of Columbia. Individuals and entities are also subject to FBAR if they are residents of the Territories and Possessions of the United States, or the Indian Tribes established in the United States.
- *Foreign financial accounts* are bank accounts, securities accounts, and certain other financial accounts located outside the United States. An

account with a foreign branch of a U.S. financial institution is considered a foreign account, while an account with a U.S. branch of a foreign institution is not considered foreign. The mere fact that an account contains foreign assets (such as securities of foreign corporations or foreign currency) does not make it a foreign account.

- A *financial interest* exists when the U.S. person owns the account or is the legal titleholder.
- *Signature authority* exists when an individual has authority to communicate, in writing or orally, with the financial institution regarding the disposition of funds. Only individuals (not legal entities) can be treated as having signature authority. If the institution is authorized to act on the instructions of an individual (or an individual in conjunction with other individuals), then that individual has signature authority.

Foreign legal entities and individuals are not subject to these reporting requirements. However, a foreign legal entity may have officers or employees who are U.S. residents, and if they have signature authority they are required to report, assuming the $10,000 threshold is met.

In addition, a U.S. entity that controls a foreign entity (by holding more than 50 percent of the voting or equity interests) is treated as having a financial interest in the foreign entity's accounts.

For example, if a U.S. tax-exempt organization is the sole (or more than 50 percent) member of a foreign entity that has a foreign bank account, the U.S. organization is treated as having a financial interest in the foreign entity's bank account. The U.S. organization must report that interest, assuming it reaches the $10,000 threshold.

There are limited exceptions to the FBAR requirement, but there is no general exception applicable to tax-exempt entities.

HOW AND WHEN TO FILE    FBAR reporting must be made on Form 90-22.1. It is important to note that this is not a tax filing. While some IRS forms (including the Form 990 filed by tax-exempt organizations) ask about foreign bank accounts, it is necessary to file the separate Form 90-22.1 in order to be in compliance with FBAR. The form and instructions can be found on the FinCEN website. FBAR is due (must be received) by June 30 of each year, to report for the previous calendar year. Unlike most tax returns, no extensions are available.

## Foreign Account Tax Compliance Act (FATCA)

FATCA imposes a foreign asset reporting requirement, applicable only to individuals, and a withholding requirement applicable to organizations that make certain types of payments.

**INDIVIDUAL REPORTING OF FOREIGN FINANCIAL ASSETS**  FATCA requires U.S. citizens and resident aliens (and some nonresident aliens) to file Form 8938 with the IRS to report certain financial assets held in foreign countries. Unlike FBAR, FATCA's reporting requirement does not apply to tax-exempt organizations or business entities.[63]

**WITHHOLDING REQUIREMENTS**  FATCA imposes additional withholding requirements on U.S. organizations (taxable and tax-exempt), and in some cases individuals, that make certain types of payments to foreign entities.[64] When applicable, FATCA requires withholding even if a treaty exemption would otherwise apply. Most types of payments made by U.S. 501(c)(3) organizations to foreign entities and individuals will not be subject to withholding under FATCA, as it applies to payments of a financial nature, such as interest paid to a bank, if treated as paid from U.S. sources. It does not apply to payments an organization makes in conducting regular, nonfinancial activities.

For example, a U.S. 501(c)(3) organization would not have to withhold under FATCA (although withholding might still be required as described above) on grants, fees for services performed by a foreign organization or individual, or royalties it pays to license intellectual property. On the other hand, if a U.S. tax-exempt organization makes a payment of interest on a loan from a foreign entity, it may have to withhold and remit U.S. tax, even if a treaty exemption applies. Keep in mind that, if your organization operates in a foreign country through a branch, the branch is treated as part of a U.S. entity for U.S. federal tax purposes. If the branch borrows money from a local bank, you may have a FATCA withholding obligation.

There are a number of exceptions to the withholding requirements, based on the payee's status as a financial or nonfinancial institution, and a number of other factors. These rules are highly complex.[65]

While it is likely that most U.S. tax-exempt organizations will have few withholding obligations under FATCA, some organizations may be surprised to learn that they do have withholding requirements. As penalties for noncompliance can be steep, all U.S. organizations that make cross-border payments are well advised to consult with their accountants or lawyers to be sure they do not fail to comply.

## 8.13  Review and Further Considerations

This chapter has provided an overview of additional U.S. legal and practical considerations that international nonprofit organizations often encounter. This is intended as a starting point for organizations and their lawyers in developing policies and procedures to comply with applicable laws.

The following chapter provides an overview of foreign legal and practical considerations your organization may face when operating in foreign countries. References to foreign laws are intended to illustrate the range of issues and challenges an organization may face. The specific application of any of those laws will vary according to an individual organization's particular circumstances. If your organization is contemplating conducting activities in a foreign country, you should always consult a competent lawyer in the particular country. To underscore the importance of this point, Chapter 9 begins by addressing how to find the right lawyer for your organization in a foreign country.

# Notes

1. Uniting And Strengthening America By Providing Appropriate Tools Required To Interrupt And Obstruct Terrorism, Pub. Law 107-56, 107th Cong. (2001), as amended ("The USA PATRIOT Act of 2001").
2. EO 13,224, 66 Fed. Reg. 49,079 (September 23, 2001), as amended, available at www.treasury.gov/resource-center/sanctions/Pages/eolinks.aspx.
3. *Al Haramain Islamic Foundation Inc. v. United States Dep't of the Treasury*, No. 10-35032 (FED9), February 27, 2012. The Ninth Circuit denied a request for re-hearing, and the U.S. Solicitor General decided not to request U.S. Supreme Court review of the Ninth Circuit's decision. As a result, the Ninth Circuit's holding, that OFAC's procedures were unconstitutional, stands.
4. Treas. Reg. § 1.501(c)(3)-1(c).
5. United States Treasury Department Office of Foreign Assets Control, Risk Matrix for the Charitable Sector (2007), available at www.treasury.gov/resource-center/sanctions/Pages/regulations.aspx.
6. For a chilling description of one organization's ordeal with OFAC, and recommended policies and procedures to facilitate a defense in the event of an OFAC investigation, *see* Lon E. Musslewhite, "How OFAC Shut Down a Charitable Organization," *Taxation of Exempts/* (WG&L) 21, no. 02 (September/October 2009).
7. www.treasury.gov/resource-center/sanctions/SDN-List/Pages/default.aspx.
8. www.treasury.gov/resource-center/terrorist-illicit-finance/Pages/protecting-charities-intro.aspx.
9. *See* Treasury Guidelines Working Group Letter to the U.S. Treasury Department, December 18, 2006, available at www.usig.org/legal/TreasuryGuidelinesLetter.asp.
10. *Principles of International Charity,* Developed by the Treasury Guidelines Working Group of Charitable Sector Organizations and Advisors (March 2005), available at www.usig.org/legal/anti-terrorism-resources.asp#pub7.

11. www.usig.org/legal/anti-terrorism.asp.

12. www.treasury.gov/resource-center/sanctions/Pages/default.aspx.

13. Information can be found on the USAID website, available at www.usaid .gov/policy/ads/300.

14. A list of U.S. federal government departments responsible for various export controls is available on the U.S. Department of Commerce website at www.bis.doc.gov/about/reslinks.htm.

15. 15 C.F.R. chapter VII, subchapter C.

16. *See* www.bis.doc.gov/licensing/exportingbasics.htm.

17. www.pmddtc.state.gov/index.html.

18. 15 C.F.R. § 760.

19. I.R.C. § 999.

20. For more information about the Commerce Department's anti-boycott rules, *see* www.bis.doc.gov/complianceandenforcement/antiboycott compliance.htm.

21. I.R.C. § 999.

22. *See* IRS Publication 514, *Foreign Tax Credit For Individuals* (April 2012), 9, available at www.irs.gov/publications/p514/index.html.

23. 5 U.S.C. §§ 78dd-1, *et seq.*

24. More information about the FCPA, including the U.S. Department of Justice's "A Resource Guide to the Foreign Corrupt Practices Act" (November 2012), is available on the Department of Justice website at www.justice.gov/criminal/fraud/fcpa/guidance.

25. A starting point for finding resources on risk assessment and anti-corruption policies is the website of the organization, Transparency International, available at www.transparency.org.

26. The U.S. Supreme Court held that the 501(c)(3) lobbying restriction does not violate the guarantee of freedom of speech under the First Amendment to the U.S. Constitution because extensive lobbying can be conducted through an organization that is tax-exempt (although ineligible to receive tax-deductible contributions) under section 501(c)(4) of the Internal Revenue Code. *Regan v. Taxation with Representation of Washington*, 461 U.S. 540 (1983).

27. Private foundations are subject to onerous penalties for engaging in lobbying activities. *See* I.R.C. § 4945.

28. I.R.C. §§ 501(h), 4911; Treas. Reg. § 56.4911.

29. For more information about electing the expenditure test, and computing allowable lobbying expenditures, *see* IRS Publication 557, *Tax-Exempt Status For Your Organization* (December 2011), 44–45, available at www.irs.gov/publications/p557/index.html.

30. Treas. Reg. §§ 1.501(c)(3)-1(c)(3)(ii) and 56.4911-2(d)(1).

31. Other types of U.S. tax-exempt organizations, notably 501(c)(4) social welfare organizations and 501(c)(6) business leagues, are permitted to

engage in political activity, subject to certain limitations. A so-called *section 527 fund* is a form of tax-exempt fund dedicated to political campaign activity. Of course, there are additional federal and state (non-tax) laws that regulate campaign activities.

32. I.R.C. § 501(c)(3).

33. In Rev. Rul. 2007-41, 2007-1 C.B. 1421, the IRS provides 21 examples to illustrate activities that will and will not be treated as political campaign participation or intervention. The IRS also provides an online mini-course on political campaign activities for tax-exempt organizations, available at www.stayexempt.irs.gov/Mini-Courses/Political_Campaigns_and_Charities/political-campaigns-and-charities.aspx.

34. *See* Rev. Rul. 73-440, 1973-2 C.B. 177. Lobbying of tribal governments is also considered lobbying for purposes of the 501(c)(3) lobbying restrictions. IRC §7871.

35. This was confirmed in a recent IRS Priv. Ltr. Rul. 20124035 (April 6, 2012).

36. Treas. Reg. § 53.4945-5(b)(5). Under a limited exception, a private foundation, or public charity electing the expenditure test, that makes a grant to a foreign organization that qualifies as a 501(c)(3) public charity (as a result of having received an IRS determination letter or because an equivalency determination has been made), may be able to make a general purpose or specific project grant, with no part of the grant attributed to lobbying activity, subject to certain conditions. *See* Treas. Reg. § 53.4945-2 (a)(6), Private Letter Ruling 200943042 (July 29, 2009).

37. *See* I.R.C. § 2055(a); Treasury Regulation § 20.2055-1(a).

38. 22 U.S.C. § 611 *et seq.*

39. *See* D.E. Wilson, Jr. and Andrew E. Bigart, "What Nonprofits Need to Know about the Foreign Agents Registration Act," *Taxation of Exempts* (WG&L) (March/April 2011), 9.

40. Even if not required to register under FARA, an organization that lobbies may be required to register at the federal and/or state level under any number of laws, notably including the federal Lobbying Disclosure Act of 1995, 2 U.S.C. § 1601 *et seq.*

41. Further information is available on the Department of Justice FARA website page, available at www.fara.gov.

42. For detailed information about computing and claiming the foreign tax credit, *see* IRS Publication 514, *Foreign Tax Credit For Individuals, supra,* note 22.

43. www.uscis.gov.

44. Under U.S. GAAP, the financial statements of two legal entities are required to be consolidated when one of the entities is treated as having a certain degree of control over, and economic interest in, the other entity. In the case of a U.S. 501(c)(3) organization and a foreign entity, the

required economic interest required by GAAP for purposes of consolidation may be inconsistent with 501(c)(3) requirements. This is an issue to be discussed with your auditors.

45. Exceptions apply to organizations that qualify as churches and certain types of church-affiliated organizations. Organizations with minimal revenues are required to make a minimal electronic filing using a Form 990 N. *See* IRS Form 990 Instructions, available at www.irs.gov/instructions/i990/index.html.

46. 501(c)(3) public charities (with some exceptions) that have $200,000 or less in gross receipts and $500,000 or less in total assets, file the shorter Form 990 EZ (or the very brief 990 N, if revenues are $50,000 or less). These thresholds apply as of the time of this book's publication, and may change in subsequent years. Some organizations are required to file the longer Form 990, even though they satisfy the thresholds for 990 EZ. For example, an organization that qualifies to file 990 EZ under these thresholds is nevertheless required to file the larger Form 990 if it is treated as having control of a foreign entity and has engaged in certain transactions with affiliates.

47. *See* IRS Form 5471 Instructions, available at www.irs.gov/instructions/i5471/index.html. Membership interests in a foreign membership organization may be considered *stock* for purposes of the Form 5471 filing requirements. *See* I.R.C. § 7701(a)(8).

48. The so-called *Passive Foreign Investment Company (PFIC)* reporting rules apply to U.S. individuals and organizations that hold interests in certain foreign entities that earn most of their revenue through investment income (such as dividends and interest), or hold most of their assets in the form of investment assets. These highly technical rules are found in I.R.C. §§ 1291–1298.

49. As of 2011, the IRS determined that any foreign organization that qualifies for U.S. 501(c)(3) status (and is not a private foundation or supporting organization) is not required to file a Form 990 or 990 EZ if the organization has no significant activity (including lobbying activity) in the United States, and its annual gross revenues from U.S. sources (determined by averaging a specified number of years) do not exceed $50,000. However, even an organization that meets this test may have to make an annual online filing, using Form 990N, to identify itself. Rev. Proc. 2011-15, I.R.B. 2011-3, 322 (January 13, 2011).

50. For more information about U.S. withholding, *see* IRS Publication 515, *Withholding of Tax on Nonresident Aliens and Foreign Entities* (April 2012), available at www.irs.gov/publications/p515/index.html.

51. It is beyond the scope of this book to delve into the factors that determine whether an individual is properly treated as an employee or independent contractor for U.S. federal income tax purposes. The IRS website provides

information, available at www.irs.gov/businesses/small/article/0,, id=99921,00.html.

52. This list is representative. It does not include every type of payment that may be subject to withholding. In addition, the discussion does not address payments to certain types of payees, such as partnerships, trusts, and estates. For complete sourcing and withholding rules, *see* I.R.C. §§ 861 and 1441, and Treas. Reg. §§ 1.861 and 1.1441. Also see IRS Publication 515, *Withholding of Tax on Nonresident Aliens and Foreign Entities*, *supra* note 50.

53. I.R.C. § 861(a)(3).

54. Residents of Canada, Mexico, and South Korea are allowed to claim additional exemptions. I.R.C. § 873; Convention between The United States of America and The Republic of Korea for the Avoidance of Double Taxation (1976) ("U.S.-South Korea Income Tax Treaty"), Article 4, available at www.irs.gov/Businesses/International-Businesses/Korea—Tax-Treaty-Documents.

55. *See* IRS Publication 519, *U.S. Tax guide for Aliens* (Feb. 2012), Appendices A and B, available at www.irs.gov/publications/p519/index.html.

56. Treas. Reg. § 1.1441-9. A foreign corporation that, since its creation has received at least 85% of its support (including contributions, grants, dues, and earned revenue but excluding investment income) from U.S. sources can qualify as a 501(c)(3) organization without applying for tax-exempt status, as long as it has not engaged in certain so-called *prohibited transactions*. I.R.C. § 4948(b). However, if a foreign organization does not establish that it is a public charity (and therefore is treated as a private foundation (*see* Chapter 3), it will be subject to U.S. withholding on its investment income from U.S. sources at the rate of 4 percent rather than the 1 or 2 percent rate that applies to investment income of domestic private foundations. IRC § 4948(b); Treas. Reg. § 53.4948-1.

57. 22 U.S.C. 288; Treas. Reg. § 1.1441-8(d).

58. *See* IRS Publication 515, *Withholding of Tax on Nonresident Aliens and Foreign Entities*, *supra* note 50.

59. FBAR originated under the Financial Recordkeeping and Reporting of Currency and Foreign Transactions Act of 1970, known as the *Bank Secrecy Act* or *BSA*, 31 U.S.C. § 5311 *et seq.*

60. I.R.C. §§ 1471-1474, enacted by The Foreign Account Tax Compliance Act of 2010, Pub. L. 111-147, § 501.

61. IRS, Comparison of Form 8938 and FBAR Requirements, available at www.irs.gov/Businesses/Comparison-of-Form-8938-and-FBAR-Requirements.

62. Information about the FBAR filing requirements is available on the FinCEN website at www.fincen.gov/statutes_regs/guidance.

63. I.R.C. § 6038D.

64. I.R.C. §§ 1471, 1472, and 1473.

65. In February 2012, the U.S. Treasury Department issued proposed regulations. For more information about FATCA, *see* Paul D. Carman, "International Exempt Organizations and FATCA, *Taxation of Exempts* (WG&L) 22, no. 2 (September/October 2010).

# CHAPTER 9

# Additional Foreign Legal and Practical Considerations

This chapter explores some of the most common legal and practical considerations faced by nonprofit organizations operating in foreign countries. As discussed throughout this book, laws are constantly changing, particularly in developing countries, and governmental bodies may have wide discretion in interpreting and enforcing laws. In some countries, an organization's operations are affected by local laws as much as, or more than, by national level laws.

For all of these reasons, this chapter does not attempt to provide specific foreign country information. The foreign laws that are referenced and described in this chapter, and throughout this book, are intended as examples, to help you frame the right questions while you're deciding how best to further your mission.

One of the first steps an organization should take when planning foreign operations is to find good local counsel. *See* section 9.1. Some organizations may find it helpful to use this chapter as a checklist when consulting with local counsel.

## 9.1  Finding the Right Local Counsel

Finding the right lawyer to help you weave your way through unfamiliar territory can be more difficult than you might imagine. The nature of relationships between attorneys and clients, and between attorneys and government officials, varies widely among countries. There is an abundance of stories among international nonprofits that discovered they wasted valuable time, money, or both, and did not necessarily get the result they wanted. Even worse, some have discovered after the fact that they were advised to do things that were not legal.

Here are a few guiding principles for finding and working with an attorney in a foreign country:

- *Get recommendations.* The best way to find the right advisor is to network with other nonprofits that are working in the area. When speaking with references, ask whether the lawyer is practical. Many countries, particularly in the developing world, do not have clear written laws and regulations setting forth all of the requirements and restrictions that may apply. You want a lawyer who understands how organizations like yours operate, and knows how to achieve the result you want.
- *Locality matters.* In many countries, you will need to register in a local jurisdiction, or at least comply with local as well as national laws. Make sure to find an attorney who has experience working in the geographical area in which you are working. That means knowing the local laws and regulations, and also having relationships with the relevant governmental bodies.
- *Request a step-by-step outline, from A to Z.* Your attorney should be able to lay out the steps required to achieve your goal. If the goal is to register a legal entity and obtain certain tax exemptions, the attorney should be able to give you a list of the documents you will need and an estimated timeframe. You should have a list of the required approvals before you start the registration process. This seems obvious, but too many organizations have had the experience, particularly in developing countries, of having to resubmit applications and documents due to simple omissions that could have been prevented.
- *Make sure your lawyer is honest.* This too may seem obvious, but cultural norms vary from country to country. You want a lawyer who has working relationships with the relevant government officials, but you don't want one who gets things done through bribery. Not only is that unethical, but bribery is illegal in virtually all countries. Turning a blind eye toward corrupt actions taken on your behalf could result in steep sanctions against your organization or its leaders, under local and/or U.S. laws. Moreover, reputation is critical to nonprofit organizations, and you don't want to risk being associated with a scandal.
- *Use common sense!* You need to ask lots of questions to be sure that the advice you are getting is sound and legal. Don't just accept that something is legal because you are told that everyone does it that way.

## 9.2 Anti-Terrorism Restrictions

During the decade following the attacks of September 11, 2001, governments across the globe became concerned that nonprofit organizations could be used, with or without their knowledge, to finance terrorist operations. Nonprofit organizations that engage in cross-border activities now need to be aware of a dizzying array of laws, regulations, and voluntary guidelines issued by governments and international bodies. Indeed, it has been said that the fight against international terrorism and money laundering is becoming the single greatest force behind regulation of the nonprofit sector worldwide.[1]

In 2001, the United Nations Security Council passed a resolution calling for states to take actions to combat international terrorism, including updating anti-terrorism laws to prevent the use of nonprofit organizations to fund terrorism, and freezing assets of terrorist organizations.[2]

Similarly, the *Financial Action Task Force (FATF)*, an intergovernmental body devoted to promoting national and international policies to combat terrorist financing and money laundering, has identified several ways in which nonprofit organizations can be misused for terrorist purposes:

- By terrorist organizations posing as legitimate entities.
- By exploiting legitimate entities as channels for financing terrorist activities.
- By concealing the diversion of funds, intended for legitimate purposes, to terrorist organizations.

The FATF published recommendations, revised in 2012, encouraging countries to adopt policies that prevent such misuse, for example by promoting a high degree of transparency in the management and operation of nonprofit organizations.[3]

Many countries in the developed and developing world did indeed enact anti-terrorism legislation between 2001 and 2011, with varying impact on the activities of nonprofit organizations. New or heightened suspicion of nonprofit organizations translates, in many countries, into enhanced financial regulations, requirements that nonprofits check official terrorist lists, and other restrictions and reporting requirements. Some countries have followed the lead of the United States and FATF by issuing regulations or voluntary guidelines.

In some countries, regulations or guidelines are aimed at preventing terrorist financing and money-laundering by promoting best practices in areas such as governance, transparency, and fundraising, to name a few.[4] On the other hand, in some countries, counter-terrorism measures have empowered government officials to obstruct the work of legitimate organizations considered by government officials to be politically threatening.[5]

## Specific Country Examples

A few examples will help to illustrate the range of impact anti-terrorist legislation has had on the activities of nonprofit organizations.

**ENGLAND AND WALES**  The Charity Commission of England and Wales has published guidance for nonprofit organizations, in the form of an online *toolkit*, setting forth the steps charities, and their trustees, are required to take to avoid furthering terrorist activities.[6] The toolkit makes clear that UK legislation prohibiting financing of terrorist activities is very broad.[7] For example, a charitable organization's trustees, employees, and even volunteers, can be criminally liable for failing to report possible terrorist financing activities that they become aware of in the course of their work for the charity. Charities that operate in England and Wales need to be very familiar with their grantees and other partners, including knowing about the directors and officers of those organizations, and other organizations with which they associate.

The toolkit recommends that charities adopt a risk-based approach, and it lists voluntary measures, including governance practices, that the Charity Commission deems best practices to avoid inadvertently supporting terrorist activities.

**AUSTRALIA**  Australia's anti-terrorism legislation also criminalizes a broad range of activities deemed to be in support of terrorism.[8] Criminal offenses include:

- Directing the activities of a terrorist organization.
- Being a member of a terrorist organization.
- Providing training to or receiving training from a terrorist organization.
- Receiving funds from or making funds available to a terrorist organization.
- Providing support or resources that would help a terrorist organization directly or indirectly engage in preparing, planning, assisting in, or fostering a terrorist act.

**CENTRAL ASIA: UZBEKISTAN AND KYRGYZSTAN**  Uzbekistan and Kyrgyzstan are examples of countries that have responded to the post-September 11 U.S. war on terror by becoming suspicious of nonprofit organizations, and particularly of foreign funding.[9] Uzbekistan enacted a series of measures restricting the activities of international NGOs and making it difficult, if not impossible, to receive foreign funding. Kyrgyzstan implemented restrictions targeted at certain sectors, such as religious organizations.

**UGANDA**  Uganda is one of at least 27 developing countries that enacted anti-terrorist legislation within the first few years following the September 11 attacks. The Ugandan legislation imposes criminal penalties for, among other things, directly or indirectly financing terrorist acts or activities. Even legitimate contributions to local organizations can fall within the definition of criminal activity if the recipient is subsequently found to have terrorist ties.[10]

**INDIA** India's restrictions on foreign funding predate the September 11 attacks, going back to the 1976 enactment of India's *Foreign Contribution Regulation Act (FCRA)*. The FCRA was amended, effective May 1, 2011, to give governmental authorities greater discretion to reject applications for permission to receive foreign funding where an organization has been prosecuted (even if on frivolous grounds) for creating communal tension. The new law also makes organizations of a political nature ineligible for permission to receive foreign funding, but does not define the term, *political nature*.[11]

### Developing Policies and Procedures

As a fundamental matter, every nonprofit organization that operates across borders must have policies and procedures to ensure that the organization does not inadvertently support terrorist activities, and that it complies with applicable anti-terrorism laws. Many organizations will need to comply with the laws of multiple countries.

In developing appropriate policies and procedures, a good starting point is to make an assessment of the risk that your organization could find itself inadvertently supporting terrorism. The degree and nature of risk will vary based on a number of factors, including geography, the nature of your organization's activities, and its familiarity with foreign and domestic grantees and collaborators. Of course, compliance will often require more than a commonsense approach to managing risk.

In addition to complying with the letter of the law, many organizations have expressed concerns that so-called *voluntary guidelines* issued by government bodies will be treated as *de facto* legal requirements. It's important to be aware of any voluntary guidelines issued by the government of a country in which your organization is operating.

## 9.3  Restrictions on Cross-Border Funding

Cross-border flows of funds can be subject to a variety of restrictions from the recipient's, as well as the transferor's, country.

### Foreign Country Restrictions on the Inflow of Funds

While very few countries impose general prohibitions against the receipt of foreign funds by nonprofit organizations, the receipt of funds can be restricted in a variety of ways. These restrictions can take several forms:

- Advance approval requirements.
- Restrictions on the purposes for which foreign funds can be received.
- Mandatory use of designated banks.
- Burdensome reporting requirements.
- Imposition of taxes on the receipt of funds.[12]

This is an area in which rapid change is occurring. During the years 2011 and 2012, a large number of countries enacted, or considered enacting, constraints on the receipt of foreign funding by nonprofit organizations.[13] The foreign country restrictions listed in the following sections are intended to provide examples of the kinds of constraints your organization may face. It is critical to do your homework. In addition to knowing the applicable laws, you should inquire about proposed legislation in the country you are targeting.

**ADVANCE APPROVAL REQUIREMENTS**    As an example of advance approval requirements, India's *Foreign Contribution Regulation Act (FCRA)* requires that all nonprofit organizations in India register with the central government in order to receive foreign contributions. The FCRA further requires that a recipient organization route foreign funds through designated banks, and make reports setting forth the amount and source of each contribution received, the manner in which it was received, the purpose for which it was intended, and the manner in which it was used. If an Indian organization receives foreign funds, and wishes to contribute those funds to another Indian organization, the second organization must also comply with the FCRA. Under a 2011 amendment to the FCRA, organizations of a political nature are prohibited from receiving foreign funds.

Other countries that require advance approval for the receipt of foreign funds include China, Indonesia, Egypt, Algeria, Jordan, Eritrea, Belarus, and Uzbekistan.[14]

**RESTRICTIONS ON THE USE OF FOREIGN FUNDS**    Some countries prohibit the receipt of foreign funds for political or other purposes that are considered threatening to the government. *See* section 9.6. In Russia, a law enacted in 2012, which was aimed at preventing foreign influence over internal policy, designates many foreign-funded NGOs as foreign agents. As a consequence, those organizations may no longer receive foreign funding and, in many cases, will have to leave Russia. Violations can result in fines and even imprisonment.[15]

**MANDATORY USE OF DESIGNATED BANKS**    Some countries seek to monitor and control the receipt of foreign funds by requiring that foreign funds be routed through designated (usually government-controlled) banks or governmental bodies. Two examples are Uzbekistan and Eritrea. India's FCRA also includes such a requirement.[16]

**REGISTRATION AND REPORTING REQUIREMENTS**    Like India, a number of countries, including China, Azerbaijan, and Indonesia, impose burdensome registration and reporting requirements related to the receipt of foreign funds. Registration may include the filing of a written grant agreement with government officials, often with notarization.[17]

**IMPOSITION OF TAXES**    While taxes are rarely imposed on the receipt of grants and contributions made for philanthropic purposes, there are exceptions. Some countries of the former Soviet Union impose a tax on the receipt of funds from foreign organizations that are not included on a government list of approved grantmakers.[18]

## Foreign Country Restrictions on the Outflow of Funds

If your U.S. organization is funding, or collaborating with, one or more legal entities in one or more foreign countries, it may be necessary or desirable to charge royalties or service fees to other entities. Or, you may decide to make a loan to, or investment in, a foreign organization as a program-related investment. *See* section 3.3. All of these arrangements involve cross-border payments by a foreign organization.

Before you enter into such arrangements, be sure that the foreign entity will be allowed to transfer funds for the agreed upon purpose. Understand whether any government approvals are required and, if so, whether there are legal or practical hurdles. Be sure to know whether any taxes (such as withholding taxes or VAT) will be imposed on the outbound transfer of funds.

Note that we are not talking here about cross-border grantmaking. If you want to solicit charitable contributions in a particular country for use outside that country, another set of rules may apply. *See* Chapter 7.

## 9.4  Restrictions on Sending Goods across Borders

Before you decide to send goods to a foreign country, make sure you know whether any restrictions are imposed, by either the sender's or the recipient's country.

## Foreign Country Restrictions on Importing Goods

You should not assume that you can legally import goods into a foreign country, even when the goods are intended for charitable use. For example, Mexico has strict prohibitions on the importation of used clothing, textiles, medicines, and medical equipment (among other items), even when destined for charitable use within Mexico or another country.[19] Violations of these rules can result in confiscation of goods and/or large fines.

Importation of technical and communications equipment can be particularly challenging in many countries, and can result in unanticipated expenses and delays for a charitable organization. If you are working with other organizations in one or more foreign countries, it will be critical to have the capability to communicate across borders, and that may entail importing technical and communications equipment, particularly in developing countries. Technical and telecommunications equipment may be subject to restrictions such as those aimed at preventing terrorist activities, resulting in the need to obtain special permission, with consequent long delays.

Understanding the importation process in advance may avoid delays that can be costly as well as inconvenient. If your shipment is delayed at the border, you could end up paying storage fees that exceed the value of the goods!

### Foreign Country Restrictions on the Outflow of Goods

If you are considering shipping goods from one foreign country to another, for example for purposes of humanitarian aid, you should be aware that organizations established outside the United States can be subject to export restrictions imposed by their own countries or by international bodies. For example, the Canadian government maintains a list of countries to which the export of goods or technology is restricted. As of 2011, the list consists of Burma (Myanmar), Belarus, and North Korea.[20] A Canadian organization wishing to export humanitarian supplies to countries on the list may be able to do so but must apply for a permit.

As another example, organizations established within the European Union (*EU*) are, like their U.S. counterparts, subject to restrictions on the provision of funds to Iran. In 2010, the EU imposed sanctions on Iran, which in certain cases, require advance permission and/or reporting of funds sent into Iran.[21]

## 9.5  Anti-Bribery Laws and Avoiding Corruption

Bribery and other corrupt activities are a way of life in some countries, and it can be difficult to operate ethically in an environment where corruption is the norm. Indeed, U.S. organizations operating in foreign countries have often complained that the strict U.S. anti-bribery laws place them at a disadvantage relative to foreign organizations. *See* section 8.4.

First and foremost, avoiding corruption is simply good policy. You don't want your organization to suffer the embarrassment of being publicly identified with a corruption scandal. In addition to the threat of U.S. sanctions for bribery of foreign officials, local country laws may apply to your organization's foreign activities. As your organization expands its activities into multiple countries, whether directly or through separate legal entities, you may have to comply with the anti-bribery laws of multiple countries. It's critical to know the laws that apply to your organization's activities, and to develop policies and procedures to avoid running afoul of these laws.

## Foreign Country Anti-Bribery Laws

While the United States has recently stepped up enforcement of its anti-bribery laws, foreign countries increasingly have adopted their own legislation against bribery and corruption, often with criminal penalties. Individual country anti-bribery laws vary in their reach. Some countries impose sanctions for acts committed beyond their borders, and some do not. These laws also vary in scope. For example, there may or may not be exceptions for small facilitating payments, as is the case under U.S. law.

In addition, a number of international conventions, or treaties, have been created by international organizations, including the *Organisation for Economic* Cooperation and Development (*OECD*), the United Nations, and the Organization of American States (OAS).[22] These international organizations have been working toward international cooperation in countering bribery, by encouraging individual countries to sign on to the various treaties and adopt implementing legislation.

To date, approximately 37 countries have signed onto the OECD treaty, and 160 countries have signed on to the United Nations treaty. At the same time, *Transparency International*, an organization whose mission is to fight international corruption, has found that corruption continues to exist across the globe, and enforcement of anti-corruption laws is uneven, even among countries that have signed onto international treaties.[23]

A number of countries have recently enacted legislation criminalizing bribery committed beyond their borders. A few examples are Spain, Russia, and the UK.[24] These laws may apply to the activities of a legal entity you form in a foreign country, such as the UK, even when it is conducting activities outside the UK.

The UK's anti-bribery law is particularly broad in scope.

**THE UK BRIBERY ACT OF 2010**   The UK's anti-bribery law (known as the *UK Bribery Act*), which came into effect in July 2011, like that of the United States and a number of other countries, reaches acts committed anywhere in the world. However, the UK law is even broader in scope, in that it prohibits bribery of private parties, while the U.S. law applies only to bribery of foreign officials. *See* section 8.4. In addition, while the U.S. FCPA, contains an exception for facilitating routine government functions, the UK Bribery Act has no such exception. Violations can result in criminal fines, and even imprisonment.

The UK Bribery Act applies to charitable organizations, as well as business entities, formed, headquartered, or operating in the UK. It proscribes four general activities:

1. Bribing another person.
2. Bribing a foreign official.
3. Accepting a bribe.
4. Failing to prevent bribery.

The UK Ministry of Justice has issued guidance for compliance with the UK Bribery Act of 2010.[25] In addition, the organization, *Transparency International UK*, published a set of principles and guidance to help nonprofit organizations assess the risks that their organizations will encounter corruption, and to help them develop appropriate policies and procedures to comply with the UK Bribery Act.[26]

## Avoiding Other Forms of Corruption

Of course, corruption is not limited to bribery, kickbacks, and financial fraud. Nonprofit organizations, particularly those working in the areas of development and humanitarian aid, have too often been surprised to learn that their employees, volunteers, or foreign partners have engaged in a variety of corrupt practices. The organization called Transparency International defines corruption as "the abuse of entrusted power for private gain," including not only bribery and kickbacks, but also:

> *Non-financial forms of corruption, such as the manipulation or diversion of humanitarian assistance to benefit non-target groups; the allocation of relief resources in exchange for sexual favors; preferential treatment in assistance or hiring processes for family members or friends (nepotism and cronyism); and the coercion and intimidation of staff or beneficiaries to turn a blind eye to or participate in corruption.*[27]

According to Transparency International, private gain occurs when resources are diverted to individuals, families, government officials, or any other groups that are not the intended beneficiaries of an organization's resources. Gain need not be financial; it may involve, for example, social or political gain.

## Adopt Policies and Procedures

The critical point here is that every organization with international activities must adopt policies and procedures to avoid participation in any corrupt practices. Start by identifying the particular risks you face, based on the nature and location of your operations.

Establish an organizational culture that has zero tolerance for corruption. Develop and implement a code of conduct. Train employees, officers, board members, staff, and volunteers. Then be prepared to devote adequate resources to ongoing monitoring of foreign activities, even when they are in remote locations. Take the time and effort to find trusted partners, and continually monitor relationships.[28]

# 9.6   Restrictions on Political Activity and Lobbying

Many countries restrict nonprofit organizations from engaging in political activity and/or lobbying, often defining these terms more broadly than they are defined under U.S. law for 501(c)(3) purposes. *See* section 8.5. For example, prohibitions may extend to a broad range of advocacy on public policy matters, or engagement in issues relating to human rights. Some countries ban these activities altogether, regardless of nonprofit or tax-exempt status, and some prohibit foreign individuals, and/or foreign-controlled organizations, from engaging in certain activities. You need to understand specifically which activities are, and are not, permitted for your organization.

The rules may not always be clear, and you need to understand whether and how your organization's intended activities may create risks for local country staff and volunteers, as well as for organizations and individuals with whom you're collaborating. In the United States, we may consider loss of 501(c)(3) status as a draconian consequence for engaging in political activity, but in many countries sanctions are far worse and may include jail time for individuals.

## Types of Restrictions on Political Activity and/or Lobbying

Restrictions on lobbying and/or political activity can take any of a number of forms, including the following.

BAN ON ACTIVITIES PERCEIVED AS THREATENING TO THE GOVERNMENT   Many countries prohibit nonprofit organizations from engaging in activities the government considers threatening, such as the promotion of democracy or advancement of human rights. Often, the prohibited activities are only vaguely defined, leaving government officials with broad discretion to deny or revoke an organization's registration, or to impose other sanctions.

For example, Russian law prohibits advocacy of extreme political positions, and affords government officials broad discretion to identify extremist activity.[29] Malaysia prohibits the registration of any organization that is deemed likely to be used for "any purpose prejudicial to or incompatible with peace, welfare, good order, or morality in the federation."[30] Equatorial New Guinea prohibits NGOs from engaging in human rights activities.[31] In 2012, Algeria adopted a law allowing the government to suspend an organization's registration if the organization's activities are deemed to interfere with the "internal business" of the country.[32]

## BAN ON THE USE OF FOREIGN FUNDS TO SUPPORT POLITICALLY SENSITIVE ACTIVITIES   Some countries aim to prevent foreign influence over sensitive issue areas, such as promotion of democracy or human rights, by restricting foreign funding of particular activities. For example, in Ethiopia, an organization that receives more than 10 percent of its income from foreign sources is prohibited from advancing human rights, the rights of children and the disabled, gender equality, nations and nationality, good governance and conflict resolution, and the efficiency of the justice system.[33]

.Bolivia prohibits foreign funding that entails any "implied political or ideological conditions."[34] Tanzania prohibits international NGOs "from doing any act which is likely to cause misunderstanding among indigenous or domestic NGOs."[35] Kenya prohibits a nonprofit organization from becoming a branch of, or affiliated or connected with, any foreign organization of a political nature, unless the organization is able to obtain prior written consent from government authorities.[36]

## BAN ON CERTAIN TYPES OF ASSOCIATION OR COMMUNICATION   Some countries seek to prevent nonprofit organizations from influencing public policy, or communicating about politically sensitive issues, by restricting association and/or communication, including use of the Internet.

Uzbekistan, Cuba, and Zambia are among countries that prohibit activities of associations or groups of people, absent formal registration as an organization. In some cases, sanctions can include imprisonment.[37] In Singapore, it is illegal for five or more people to gather for other than social purposes. Zimbabwe authorizes the government "to intercept mail, phone calls, and emails without having to get court approval."[38]

Of course, freedom of speech, as it exists in the United States, is nonexistent in many countries. In recent years, legal barriers aimed at use of the Internet have arisen. During the year 2011, a number of countries enacted a variety of Internet restrictions that impede the work of nonprofit organizations. These countries include Egypt, Libya, Tunisia, Sudan, Iran, Syria, China, Cuba, Ethiopia, and Vietnam.[39] Vietnam prohibits "taking advantage of the web to disrupt social order and safety," in addition to generally prohibiting any distribution of harmful information.[40]

DENIAL OF TAX BENEFITS TO ORGANIZATIONS THAT ENGAGE IN LOBBYING OR POLITICAL ACTIVITY   Some countries, like the United States, deny tax benefits (such as tax-exempt status and/or the ability to attract tax-favored contributions) to organizations that conduct, or exceed an allowed threshold for, certain legislative or political activities. These countries include Canada, the UK, and Australia. It's important to be aware that each country has its own rules and definitions. Do not make the mistake of assuming that, for example, the term *political activity* has the same meaning from one country to another.

### Operating or Funding Organizations in Countries That Allow Political Activity or Lobbying

In some countries, a U.S. organization, or a local country entity, may be free to engage in lobbying or political activities. For example, in Sweden, where social services are provided by the government, nonprofit organizations are commonly formed to influence public policy through a variety of activities that include lobbying.[41]

Where foreign law permits lobbying or political activity, you need to be careful that your U.S. organization complies with U.S. 501(c)(3) requirements, as well as the foreign country's laws. If you are funding a separate entity in such a country, you should take steps to be sure that the grantee's activities do not cause your organization to run afoul of 501(c)(3) restrictions. *See* section 8.5.

## 9.7   Protecting Trademarks, Copyrights, and Other Intellectual Property

Every organization owns and/or uses intellectual property. Names, logos, slogans, written material (whether in tangible or electronic form), films, photographs, and the content of your website are examples of intellectual property. An organization that owns rights to those items should protect those rights in the United States and abroad.[42]

### Types of Intellectual Property

Most intellectual property falls into the following four categories and can be protected in the United States in various ways.

TRADEMARKS   A trademark (or service mark) protects a distinctive mark that identifies and associates certain goods or services with a particular organization, or brand. The purpose of trademark protection is to avoid confusion. Nonprofit organizations, like for-profit businesses, have valuable brand identity that requires protection. For example, a logo typically can be protected as a

**FIGURE 9.1 Service Mark Example.**
*Source:* Half the Sky Foundation (HTS).

trademark. The name or initials of your organization, written in a distinctive way, can also be protected. The name itself may or may not be eligible for protection, depending on how distinct it is. Generic terms that are commonly associated with a general category of goods or services generally are not eligible for protection.

Figure 9.1 shows an example of a service mark, used by Half the Sky Foundation (HTS), which is the subject of Chapter 10. HTS has created separate legal entities in several countries, each of which has the right to use this service mark.

In the United States, trademarks and service marks can be registered under state or federal law, with federal registration affording greater projection.

To preserve your rights in a trademark or service mark, it is critical to continuously use it and actively look for misuse of your trademark by others. This includes checking to see whether your trade name is being used in a domain name without your permission.

**COPYRIGHTS**  In general, original works such as writing, art, music, film, photography, software code, and even a school's unique curriculum, are eligible for U.S. copyright protection. You can think about owning a copyright as owning a bundle of sticks. This bundle includes the right to exploit the material for the owner's own use and profit, to license the use of it to others, and even to sell all of the rights (at least in the United States and some other countries).

While not required, it is generally advisable to use the symbol ©, or the word *Copyright*, together with the date of creation and name of the owner, in order to put others on notice that you claim rights. In addition, it is often advisable to register with the U.S. Copyright Office.[43]

Under U.S. law, the creator of an original work generally owns all of the rights in that work. For example, an individual author normally owns all of the rights to the material he or she creates. However, you will probably want your organization, rather than an individual, to own works that are created for use by your organization. Under U.S. law, if a U.S. employee creates a work for your organization while doing his or her job, that work belongs to the organization. If you hire an independent contractor, or engage a volunteer to create something for your organization, you should generally enter into a so-called *work for hire* agreement, to be sure that your organization, rather than the individual, is the owner of those rights.

In addition, if you create multiple legal entities in various countries, with separate entities creating or contributing to works that are used by the group, you may want an agreement that assigns the rights from one entity to another, so that all rights are owned by a single entity. That way, you know which entity has the rights, should you choose to license or otherwise dispose of them.

If employees, independent contractors, or volunteers who are creating works for your organization are situated outside the United States, you'll need to be sure to have an agreement that achieves the desired result under the applicable foreign and U.S. laws. Always seek legal advice in the particular foreign country, as well as in the United States.

**PATENTS**  Patent protection is available for non-obvious discoveries such as inventions, processes, formulas, and in some instances for algorithms used in software programs. Of the four types of intellectual property protection, patents are the most difficult to acquire, requiring registration with the U.S. Patent and Trademark Office.

**TRADE SECRETS**  Trade secrets include a range of proprietary information that is not protectable under any of the above. For example, a membership or mailing list may be a trade secret. In the United States, protection for trade secrets is exclusively under state, and not federal, law, and this protection is weaker than that afforded to the other three types of intellectual property described previously. There is no registration process in the United States for trade secrets. What is critical to protecting a trade secret is to keep it confidential. Make sure that only those who need the information have access to it, even internally. You can license a trade secret, but a license agreement should always require that the licensee maintain confidentiality.[44]

## Five Basic Steps

A U.S. organization that operates internationally, either directly or through separate legal entities, should take the following steps.

**IDENTIFY YOUR INTELLECTUAL PROPERTY**  This may seem obvious, but it isn't always. You may be using logos or slogans without realizing they have become important identifiers of your organization or the services you provide. Your website may contain content that was posted by users, or you may be using content that was created by volunteers and contractors. As you enter the international arena, it will be increasingly important to identify your intellectual property so that you can take steps to protect it.

**MAKE SURE YOUR ORGANIZATION HAS THE NECESSARY RIGHTS**  Whenever you're using intellectual property, you need to be sure you have the right to do what you want to do with it.

Before you choose a name for your organization, as well as a logo and other identifying images, be sure that you're not infringing on something that's already in use. You don't want to have to change your name, domain name, and/or logo once the organization has developed some public awareness.

If your organization wants to use content it didn't create through its own U.S. employees, you may need to acquire rights through a license or assignment. If you engage someone to create something for you, be sure that you end up with the rights you expect to have.

When making grants, if the grantee is creating intellectual property with your grant funds, be clear about the rights to that intellectual property, and document it in a grant agreement.

In addition, you should post *Terms of Use* on your website, to ensure that you provide users with appropriate rights to the use of content while protecting your rights in content you make available to users. If users are also posting content on your site, such as reviews or comments, you need to be sure you have rights to that content.

**Example**  A U.S. organization (*U.S. Org*) seeks to improve the lives of orphans in a number of foreign countries by providing expertise in the area of early childhood education. U.S. Org hires a foreign entity (*Developer*) to create a unique early learning curriculum, which is aimed at the needs of institutionalized children. U.S. Org may need to enter into an agreement with Developer, whereby Developer assigns the copyright in the curriculum to U.S. Org. Absent such an assignment, U.S. Org may not have the rights to make the curriculum available as it deems appropriate, for example by licensing the curriculum to foreign orphanages, posting parts of the curriculum on its website for download by educational institutions (with or without a fee), and producing and selling educational materials based on the curriculum.

The U.S. organization (*U.S. Org*) makes a grant to a foreign organization (*Foreign Org*) to help Foreign Org develop a unique curriculum for institutionalized children. Foreign Org wants to own the copyrights worldwide, including the right to license the curriculum, and to sell educational materials based on the curriculum. U.S. Org wants the right, in perpetuity, to use and distribute the curriculum within the United States. It also wants to develop additional materials, based on the curriculum, for particular foreign populations, and it wants to own the copyrights on those materials. A written grant agreement should explicitly set forth the respective rights of each party in the curriculum, and in the works developed by each party based on the curriculum. Absent a clear written agreement, one or both of the organizations may be surprised to learn later that they do not have the rights they thought they had.

**PROTECT INTELLECTUAL PROPERTY RIGHTS IN THE UNITED STATES**   If someone else uses your name or logo, that can cause confusion among your supporters, potential supporters, and other constituents, resulting in loss of funding, or harm to the organization's reputation. Some organizations claim to have lost donors to other organizations that adopt similar names and logos.[45]

Of course, intellectual property may also be a direct source of revenue, such as where an organization licenses rights to use written materials (in tangible or electronic form), or where it sells publications containing written content. Some nonprofit organizations also hold rights in valuable patentable discoveries or processes. An organization's membership list may also be a valuable asset, even one that can generate revenue through licensing rights to its use.

**ENTER INTO WRITTEN AGREEMENTS**   An important piece of protecting your intellectual property is making sure that others use it only when you grant permission. If your organization is making any intellectual property (trademarks, copyrights, patents) available for use by a separate legal entity outside (as well as within) the United States, a written license agreement is critical to protecting your organization's rights. For example, if you establish a network of legal entities in multiple countries, you may want all of them to use a common trademark. You must, however, have written agreements setting forth the terms of use. Without that, you run the risk of losing the ability to protect your rights against misuse by others.

When licensing intellectual property to a foreign entity, you need to decide whether to charge a royalty and, if so, whether the royalty will be subject to any U.S. or foreign taxes. *See* section 5.5. When making grants, your written grant agreement should address the rights in any intellectual property developed with the grant funds, as well as any grant of rights from one party to the other. *See* section 2.3.

**TAKE APPROPRIATE STEPS TO PROTECT YOUR RIGHTS IN FOREIGN COUNTRIES** It's important to seek legal advice about protecting your rights in every country in which your intellectual property is used, whether you are using the rights directly or licensing them to a foreign entity. Be aware, however, that even if you take appropriate steps to protect your rights in foreign countries, the enforceability and scope of those rights can vary from country to country. In some countries, it can be virtually impossible to enforce your rights. Once you know what's at stake, and the likelihood of success in protecting your rights, you can decide how far you're willing to go to assert your rights.

## Protecting Trademarks Outside the United States

In contrast to the United States, most foreign countries require registration in order to protect a trademark, and often there is more than one option for protecting a trademark in a particular foreign country. Filing registrations in each country in which trademarks are used can be costly and time consuming.

An international trademark registration system, referred to as the *Madrid Protocol*, provides a streamlined, less expensive process for protecting trademarks in multiple countries. It allows a U.S.-based organization (or one based in any other country that is a party to the Protocol) to register in the United States, and have that registration extended into any additional countries that have joined the Protocol. As of the time of this book's publication, 84 countries have joined. In order to take advantage of this system, a U.S. organization must first file a trademark application with the U.S. Patent and Trademark Office, then file an international application designating the countries to which it intends to extend, or register, the trademarks. Any country has the right to refuse to recognize a trademark registration through this process (as it could in the case of a country-specific registration). Once accepted, however, the registration has the same effect in a foreign country as if a separate, country-specific registration had been made.[46]

**THE IMPORTANCE OF WRITTEN LICENSE AGREEMENTS**  If you allow separate legal entities to use your trademarks, make sure you enter into written license agreements. This is critical, even if your U.S. organization controls the other entity. In the absence of a written license agreement that contains appropriate standards of use to ensure quality control and consistency, you could lose your U.S. trademark protection. An informal arrangement with a trusted party may serve your purposes, but in the absence of a properly drafted written trademark license, a U.S. court may find that you have a *naked license*, and declare your trademark invalid. It is worth your while to find a U.S. lawyer who can provide you with a properly drafted trademark agreement.[47]

## Protecting Copyrights Outside the United States

In general, it is not necessary to register in a foreign country in order to protect a copyright. However, the extent to which your rights are protected, if at all, varies greatly from country to country. Some countries afford virtually no protection for works originating in other countries. Even where rights are protected, enforcement against infringement may or may not be feasible.

In addition, the nature and scope of copyright protection differs among countries. Notably, most European countries, Japan, and a number of other countries, recognize so-called *moral rights*, which are rights that belong to the author or creator of literary and artistic works. These rights remain with the author, even if he or she transfers economic rights (rights to exploit the work for revenue). Although the scope of moral rights varies among countries, in general they include the right to claim authorship of the work (the right of *attribution*), and the right to object to any modification or distortion of the work, which might undermine the author's reputation (the right of *integrity*), among others. The important thing to note is, if your organization is engaging, or acquiring rights from, an author in one of these countries, you should be aware that the author may necessarily retain certain rights in the work.

If your organization believes it will be important to protect copyright rights in a foreign country, you should consult a qualified lawyer in that country. If possible, you should look into foreign protection and enforcement before publishing a work in your home country (or anywhere).[48] At the least, copyright notices should be placed on all works that may be distributed or viewed outside the United States.

## Protecting Patents Outside the United States

A U.S. patent affords exclusive rights to the owner within the United States. An organization that wishes to protect rights in a patentable discovery or creation in a foreign country will generally need to register in that country. Timing can be very important. Unlike the United States, which awards patents on the basis of *first to invent*, most countries award patents on the basis of *first to file*. Patent applications, in the United States and elsewhere, tend to be quite complex and generally should be done with the assistance of a qualified lawyer.[49]

## Protecting Trade Secrets Outside the United States

While many countries afford protection for certain proprietary information (often referred to as *undisclosed information* in the international setting), the scope of protectable rights, and feasibility of enforcement, varies greatly among countries.[50] As with other forms of intellectual property, an organization that intends to use or license valuable rights in a foreign country should consult with local counsel in advance.

## 9.8  Data Privacy Laws

Many, if not most, nonprofit organizations will gather personal data related to the beneficiaries of their services, donors, members, employees, and/or customers (if providing services for fees). Your organization may well be collecting personal data through its website, for example through online giving.

## Data Privacy in the United States

In the United States, the collection and use of individuals' personal information is governed by a patchwork of state and federal laws and regulations, and in many cases it is left to self-regulation. Regardless of whether there is any applicable law or regulation, if your organization collects any personal data online, it's critical to take appropriate steps to protect the integrity of the data you collect. In addition, you should post a privacy policy on your website to alert users as to what data you are collecting and how you are protecting it. Do not simply copy one you find online, as you may not be able to adhere to all of its premises. Having a policy you can't comply with can be worse than having no policy at all, so consult a lawyer and get it right. Of course, it's essential to have adequate procedures to ensure the protection of any personal data you collect offline, as well as online.

While it's important for all organizations to have sound privacy policies, U.S. organizations that operate internationally need to be aware that many countries have far more stringent privacy laws than what we are accustomed to in the United States.

## Data Collection across Borders

Organizations that operate across borders can find it challenging to identify and comply with all applicable laws. Given that data is generally stored and transmitted electronically, it is not always clear which country's laws apply. Moreover, legislation tends not to keep up with the pace of technological change, so the application of existing rules to newer technologies can be unclear.

Despite the uncertainties, organizations that operate across borders need to devote resources to ensuring that they comply with applicable data protection laws. Failure to do so can result in civil and, in some cases even criminal, penalties. Of course, a data breach that results in a loss of confidence can be equally, if not more, devastating than government sanctions.

**EXAMPLE: THE EUROPEAN UNION**   U.S. organizations can be surprised to learn that they are subject to foreign privacy laws, even when a U.S. organization has no physical presence in the foreign country. For example, each of the EU countries imposes particularly onerous restrictions on the use of personal data.

The *EU Data Protection Directive* requires that each of the 27 Member States (countries) enacts and enforces laws that protect individuals against unauthorized use or misuse of personal information.[51] The Directive is very broad, restricting the so-called *processing* (collection, use, and transfer) of personal information including name, address, telephone number, and employment-related information. Certain sensitive information, such as religion and sexual orientation, is subject to additional restrictions.

Nonprofit organizations may become subject to the EU Directive when, for example, they manage employee information, membership lists, or donor data.

If an EU-based organization processes personal information, it is required to take security measures to protect the privacy of the individual whose data is used, must provide individuals with the opportunity to correct inaccuracies, and must obtain consent (often through a so-called *opt-out* clause) for any transfer of personal data to third parties.

Transfers of data from within the EU to the United States are subject to additional restrictions, and the mere use of an EU-based server to store and transfer data can trigger these rules. As a result, a U.S. organization, with no EU physical presence at all, can be subject to the Directive's restrictions if it collects and stores personal information pertaining to EU residents. A data transfer can also occur when a U.S. organization operates through an EU branch, or when affiliated organizations in the EU and the United States share data by maintaining a common database.[52]

Because the European Commission believes that U.S. laws inadequately protect the privacy of individuals, U.S. organizations and their EU affiliates have to comply with cumbersome requirements when transferring (or treated as transferring) personal data out of the EU.[53] These requirements, which vary by country, may include the use of specific language to obtain individuals' consent.

If your organization operates directly in Europe, or shares any personal information with an EU entity, it is critical to consult with a lawyer in the country in which you operate to be sure you are complying with the EU requirements.

## 9.9  Privacy

What international organization doesn't want to post photographs from the field to demonstrate the great work it's doing? Photographs of people are compelling, and those of children often succeed in tugging at the heartstrings of donors.

It's important to be aware that, in many countries, it's illegal to publish (including by Internet) photographs taken of people without their permission. A few countries prohibit the mere taking of a photograph without permission. Make sure you know what permissions are needed, and obtain the necessary consents before taking photos and posting them on a website.

## 9.10  Managing Multiple Currencies and Currency Controls

Managing investments and cash flows in multiple currencies is challenging and often expensive. The more countries in which an organization works, the more complex the legal and practical currency issues become. Many organizations find they need to create a paid treasury position by the time they are operating in more than two or three different currencies. To do the job well requires a high degree of sophistication, and it is not inexpensive to hire experienced treasury personnel.

Challenges related to managing multiple currencies include the following:

### Working with Non-Marketable or Thinly-Traded Currencies

While foreign exchange risk is always present, currencies fluctuate widely in some countries. A plan for funding a foreign project from the United States, or elsewhere, can suddenly become more expensive.

### Steep Transaction Costs and Bank Fees

Wire transfers are expensive, but transferring funds can be even more expensive where wire transfer is not available. If you are funding small organizations in remote rural areas, it may not be possible to use wire transfers. You may have to arrange for checks to be hand delivered, and that in turn may require taking some security measures. You may even have to assist fund recipients with establishing local bank accounts.

### Artificially Low Exchange Rates

Some countries impose below-market exchange rates on the exchange of funds received as grants from foreign sources. For example, Venezuela requires recipients of foreign funding to exchange currency through the Central Bank of Venezuela, at an exchange rate that significantly devalues the Venezuelan Bolivar relative to the market exchange rate. Recipients of funds who bypass the Central Bank are subject to serious penalties, including imprisonment.[54]

### Prohibitions Against, or Prohibitive Costs on, Investment Income

Some countries impose tax on investment income, while others restrict the accumulation of funds in other ways. If you can't maintain the appropriate reserves in the country in which you're operating, you may end up accumulating the necessary reserves outside that country, in another currency. This poses an additional layer of cost for your organization, as you will incur incremental costs each time you transfer funds across borders.

## 9.11　International Travel and Security

If your organization plans to operate in a foreign country, whether directly or through collaboration with a local entity, it's important to consider the costs of international travel. Technology may help you to communicate regularly with staff and volunteers, but monitoring foreign operations will require travel. Transporting people from headquarters to remote locations can be expensive and complex.

Security is another critical concern for organizations that send people to developing countries. In some cases it may be necessary to take security measures for travelers, adding expense to the budget.

It's important to have travel policies and procedures in place to ensure that logistics and security concerns are addressed. In addition, staff, board members, and volunteers who travel to developing countries should receive appropriate training, including information about cultural norms, and health and safety matters.

## 9.12　Insurance Matters

It is critical to maintain adequate insurance coverage for foreign as well as U.S. operations, whether the operations are conducted through branches or separate legal entities. You should carefully consider whether, and the extent to which, you need to obtain coverage for:

- Directors and officers
- Vehicles
- General liability
- Employees (workers' compensation or the equivalent)

If your organization is operating directly in a foreign country, you should find out whether your policy covers those activities. It's also important to understand whether the policy covers a lawsuit brought in a foreign court.

In some cases, it may be possible, and more efficient, to obtain insurance in a local country. Workers may be covered through national social programs.

If your organization decides to form separate legal entities to operate programs in foreign countries, you may be able to obtain a global insurance policy that covers related entities. This may be possible, for example, if your organization is the sole, or majority, member of a foreign membership organization. *See* Chapter 5. If you choose to go this route, you should have an attorney review the policy to be sure you are purchasing the desired coverage. In particular, the policy presented to you will likely require some revisions to ensure that foreign legal entities are covered. For example, the definition of an affiliate will typically contemplate stock ownership, and without revisions, may not cover legal entities that are related through membership or overlapping directors.

## 9.13  Acquiring Real Estate

If your organization is buying real estate (land or buildings) outside the United States, you must exercise due diligence to be sure that you are acquiring the rights you expect to hold. Purchasing land in a foreign country can be fraught with traps for the unwary. For example, in some African countries there are multiple layers of jurisdiction over land. You might enter into a contract to acquire land, only to discover that some other individual or entity holds rights to the property. The bottom line here is, find a local lawyer, and proceed with extreme caution.

In addition, it's likely that you will want, or need, to form a separate legal entity to own real estate in a foreign country. Some countries prohibit foreign entities from owning real property, particularly land. Even if your U.S. organization is permitted to own property in a particular country, that may cause your organization to become subject to liabilities, including taxes, in the country in which the property is situated. You may be better off forming an entity in that country to hold the property rights and carry out activities in that country. *See* Chapter 5.

## 9.14  Value Added Tax (VAT)

Approximately 135 countries throughout the world (excluding the United States) have some form of Value Added Tax (*VAT*) or its cousin, Goods and Services Tax (*GST*). Japan uses the term *consumption tax*. Put simply, a VAT or GST is a form of tax commonly referred to as a consumption tax. This is a tax imposed on transactions such as sales of goods and often sales of services. The tax is typically computed as a percentage of the purchase price. Rates can be as high as 25 percent, and are typically highest among Scandinavian countries, while Japan's rate of 5 percent is one of the lowest. Many countries apply different rates to different categories of goods and services.

For simplicity, the term *VAT* will be used here to refer to VAT, GST, and Japanese consumption tax.

### How Does VAT Work?

In the United States, most states and many localities impose a retail sales tax on sales and goods and sometimes on services. Like a retail sales tax, VAT is imposed on transactions, not on individuals or organizations. However, a retail sales tax is typically triggered only at the time of final sale to the consumer. By contrast, a VAT is imposed at multiple stages, but the economic cost is ultimately borne by the final consumer. In most countries, VAT is imposed at the national level. India is an exception, with each Indian state maintaining its own VAT regime. Canada has a national GST, but the so-called *Provincial Sales Tax* is also imposed at the provincial level. Typically, export sales are exempt from VAT, while VAT is collected when a product (or service) is imported into a country that has a VAT.

**EXAMPLE** While there are many variations on VAT, the following simple example illustrates the general principle.

Consider a hypothetical foreign NGO (*Foreign NGO*) that makes bicycles available to individuals, charging a price considerably less than the commercial market price. Foreign NGO assembles the bicycles from components that it purchases from *Components Supplier*. Components Supplier makes the components from scrap metal, which it purchases from *Scrap Dealer*. Assume Scrap Dealer scavenges for the scrap metal and does not pay anything.

If VAT is imposed upon each transaction, at the rate of 10 percent, the result is as follows in Table 9.1.

In this simple example, each of the sellers along the chain, including Foreign NGO, pays VAT when it makes a purchase. Each then charges VAT when it sells a product. Each seller is entitled to reimbursement of the VAT it paid when it made a purchase. This is called an *input tax credit*. The seller remits to the government the amount of VAT it collects upon sale (*output VAT*), minus the amount of the input tax credit. As you can see, in the simple example above, the entire burden of the VAT is borne by the final consumer.

TABLE 9.1

| | Purchase Price (before VAT) | VAT Paid on Purchase (input tax credit) | Sales Price | VAT Collected on Sale (output tax) | VAT Remitted to Government (after input credit) |
|---|---|---|---|---|---|
| Scrap dealer | 0 | 0 | 100 | 10 | 10 |
| Components supplier | 100 | 10 | 120 | 12 | 2 |
| Foreign NGO | 120 | 12 | 140 | 14 | 2 |
| Individual | 140 | 14 (no input credit) | | | |

## How Does VAT Affect Nonprofit Organizations?

A nonprofit organization that operates in a country that has VAT may incur additional costs as follows:

- VAT itself is an additional cost that is often borne by nonprofit organizations.
- The administrative cost of complying with a complex VAT regime can be significant.

Many countries, notably throughout most of Europe, provide exemptions from VAT on some or all goods and services provided by charitable, or public benefit, nonprofit organizations. This serves the purpose of relieving the ultimate consumer, such as the beneficiary of the nonprofit's charitable work, from bearing the burden of VAT. However, it can also have the effect of imposing the economic burden on the nonprofit organization. In the above example, if Foreign NGO does not charge VAT to the consumer, it may have no way to recover the VAT it paid when it purchased the components.

Note, also, that VAT can apply to goods that an organization imports into its country, even if the goods are donated. As a result, unless an exemption applies, an organization that imports supplies for the purpose of providing charitable services could have to pay and bear the burden of VAT.

Some countries, including Canada and Australia, have mechanisms that allow a nonprofit organization to recover all or some of the VAT it pays, even when it does not charge VAT to consumers. While this relieves the nonprofit organization from the economic burden of the tax, it does not eliminate the administrative burden of maintaining systems to comply with a complex VAT regime.[55]

Indeed, for many nonprofit organizations, the administrative burden of complying with a VAT regime is significant, even if an organization does not bear the ultimate burden of the tax itself.

## 9.15  Other (Non-Income) Taxes

A nonprofit organization can be subject to a variety of taxes in foreign countries other than, or in addition to, income taxes and VAT. These taxes may be imposed at the national or local level, or both. You should not assume that exemption from income tax automatically brings exemption from other taxes. In some countries, an organization that qualifies for income tax exemption is exempt from some other taxes. In others, it may be necessary to qualify separately for exemptions from other taxes, and in still others there may be no exemption from other taxes.

Nonprofit organizations often find that, regardless of whether they are exempt from income taxes, the impact of other taxes is more significant. If your organization is contemplating activities in a foreign country, it is important to be aware of the various foreign taxes that may be imposed.

## Import Duties/Tariffs

Before you ship goods into any country, you should determine whether import duties (also known as *tariffs*) will be imposed by the destination country. Make sure that you understand the importation process, timing, and total costs, and the risk of delays.

Duties can be quite steep. It is often more efficient to send money and arrange for the goods to be procured locally. Of course, that is not always possible.

Some countries afford limited exemptions from import duties for certain nonprofit organizations. Often, the exemption is based on the purpose for which the goods are imported. For example, some countries, including India, provide exemptions from duties on goods imported for disaster relief purposes.

You may be able to have goods imported into a particular country, free of duties, by working with a local NGO to arrange importation. If your organization does not have a relationship with a trusted party in the country to which you are shipping goods, you will probably need to hire a customs broker to handle the importation process. It's critical to arrange this before you ship the goods.

Even if an organization is importing exempt goods, in many counties the process of clearing customs can be hopelessly delayed if the necessary clearances have not been obtained in advance. In addition, the importer may be charged for steep storage costs while the legal process is proceeding.

## Withholding Taxes on Cross-Border Payments

Cross-border payments are often subject to so-called *withholding taxes* imposed by the country of the payor. A withholding tax is a tax that is required to be deducted, or withheld, from a payment and remitted to the government. For example if a royalty payment of $100 is subject to a 10 percent withholding tax, the payor must withhold $10 and remit that amount to the payor's government. The payee (which may be a legal entity or an individual) receives $90, instead of the $100 it expected.

Withholding taxes can be imposed on a wide variety of types of payments, depending on the country. Often, this type of tax is imposed on investment income (interest and dividends), royalties, and compensation for services performed. *See* section 8.11 for a description of withholding taxes imposed by the United States.

Withholding taxes may be eliminated or reduced where a tax treaty exists between the country imposing the tax and the payee's country of residence.

## Taxes Related to Employment

If you hire employees to work in a foreign country, it is likely that your organization will have to comply with income tax and social tax withholding and reporting. Employment-related taxes may be imposed on the organization as well. These kinds of taxes and reporting requirements can apply regardless of whether the employer is a foreign entity or a foreign branch of a U.S. entity. They may apply to U.S. citizens working in the foreign country, as well as to nationals of that country.

If you intend to employ staff in a foreign country, you should understand, and budget for, the costs associated with any employment-related taxes, including the administrative costs of compliance with reporting obligations.

## Other Foreign Taxes

A variety of additional taxes may apply to a nonprofit organization operating in foreign countries. These may include real or personal property taxes, as well as a variety of excise taxes. Increasingly, taxes are imposed on the consumption of gasoline, electricity, and other forms of energy consumption.

# 9.16  Governmental Reporting Requirements: Financial, Tax, and Others

Before deciding to establish a regular presence in any foreign country, you should understand what will be required in the way of financial, tax, and other government reporting. If your organization registers a legal presence in a foreign country, whether as an office, branch, or a separate legal entity, you will undoubtedly be subject to some reporting requirements in that country. These may be relatively easy or they may be quite burdensome.

Many countries require locally prepared and audited financial statements for separate legal entities, and this entails hiring a local country auditor. Some countries, such as Ethiopia, require audited financial statements for branches as well. A foreign entity or branch may be required to use accounting standards that are different from those used by a U.S. entity for purposes of U.S. financial reporting.[56]

You should not only consider the burdens of financial reporting requirements, but also understand how much information you will have to disclose to government officials and the public, as a result of operating through a branch or legal entity in a foreign country. In some countries, operating through a branch may trigger a requirement to provide financial statements for the entire legal entity, including the U.S. operations.

A variety of additional reports may be required by a foreign government, including tax filings, employment-related filings, reports regarding the use of foreign funds, and a variety of reports specific to the nature of activities. For example, a school may be required to apply periodically for re-accreditation.

## 9.17 Market and Political Impact of Foreign Direct Services

As a practical matter, it's important to consider, and anticipate, the direct and indirect impact your activities may have in a foreign country. For example, you may find that, while your intention is to deliver a narrowly defined health benefit to a small segment of the local population, your services are viewed as a threat to an established system. You may suddenly find your services constrained by protective laws.

Building relationships and alliances in the country in which you intend to operate will help your organization to find the optimal way of working within and serving a foreign culture.

## 9.18 Review and Further Considerations

Chapters 8 and 9 have provided an overview of additional U.S. and foreign legal and practical considerations that international nonprofit organizations often encounter. The purpose of these chapters is to provide a starting point for organizations and their lawyers in developing policies and procedures to comply with applicable laws. Some organizations may use these chapters to make checklists for discussions with their legal advisors.

In the final chapter of this book, we return to the big picture. Chapter 10 consists of a case study of one organization, *Half the Sky Foundation (HTS)*, that became a multinational organization within just 13 years.

## Notes

1. *See* David Moore and Douglas Rutzen, "Legal Framework for Global Philanthropy: Barriers and Opportunities," *International Journal of Not-For-Profit Law* 13, No. 1–2 (April 2011), 15, available at www.icnl.org/research/journal/vol13iss1/index.htm, *citing* Ineke A. Koele, *International Taxation of Philanthropy* (Amsterdam, The Netherlands: IBFD, 2007), 373.

2. United Nations Security Council Resolution 1373, "Threats to International Peace and Security Caused by Terrorist Acts" (2001), available at www.un .org/Docs/scres/2001/sc2001.htm.

3. The FATF Recommendations, "International Standards on Combating Money Laundering and the Financing of Terrorism and Proliferation," (February 2012), Special Recommendation VIII, available at www.fatf-gafi.org/topics/ fatfrecommendations/documents/fatfrecommendations2012.html.

4. For additional information about the impact of various countries' anti-terrorism policies on nonprofit organizations, *see* Howell, Jude and Jeremy Lind, editors, *Civil Society Under Strain: Counter-Terrorism Policy, Civil Society and Aid Post-911* (Sterling, VA: Kumarian Press, 2010).

5. *See* Jude Howell, "Civil Society, Aid and Security Post-9/11," *International Journal of Not-For-Profit Law* 12, no. 4 (November 2010), 21–22, available at www.icnl.org/research/journal/vol12iss4/special_2.htm.

6. Charity Commission of England and Wales, "Compliance Toolkit: Protecting Charities from Harm" (2009), available at www.charity-commission .gov.uk/Our_regulatory_activity/Counter_terrorism_work/protecting_ charities_landing.aspx.

7. The Charity Commission of England and Wales has regulatory authority over charitable organizations established in those two countries. However, organizations under the jurisdiction of the Charity Commission are subject to UK anti-terrorism legislation.

8. Australia's anti-terrorism laws are available on the Australian government's website at www.nationalsecurity.gov.au/agd/www/nationalsecurity.nsf/ AllDocs/826190776D49EA90CA256FAB001BA5EA?OpenDocument. For further discussion of the impact of Australia's anti-terrorism legislation on nonprofit organizations (as of 2008), *see* Howell, Jude and Jeremy Lind, eds., *Civil Society Under Strain, supra* note 4, at 75.

9. *Id.* at 93.

10. *Id.* at 209.

11. For a summary of the 2011 changes to the FCRA *see* Government of India Press Information Bureau, "Salient Features of FCRA, 2010 Comes into Effect from May 1, 2011" (May 6, 2011), available at http://pib.nic.in/ newsite/erelease.aspx?relid=71995. *See also*, Noshir Dadrawala, "Foreign Contributions Regulations Bill 2010 Becomes Law in India," April 7, 2011, available at www.icnl.org/news/2011/7-Apr.html.

12. *See* David Moore and Douglas Rutzen, "Legal Framework for Global Philanthropy: Barriers and Opportunities," *supra* note 1, at 17.

13. *See* Douglas Rutzen, "Practice Note: Egypt and the Catalyst Constraint," *International Journal of Not-for-Profit Law* 14, no. 1–2 (April 2012), 49–51, available at www.icnl.org/research/journal/vol14iss1/index.html.

14. David Moore and Douglas Rutzen, "Legal Framework for Global Philanthropy: Barriers and Opportunities," *supra* note 1, at 18–20.

15. *See* Patrick Henningsen, "Russia Lowers the Boom on NGOs and Other Foreign Agents" (August 1, 2012), available at www.globalresearch.ca/index.php?context=va&aid=31901.

16. "Defending Civil Society," co-authored by International Center for Not-for-Profit Law and World Movement for Democracy Secretariat at the National Endowment for Democracy, *International Journal of Not-for-Profit Law*, 14, no. 3 (September 2012) ("Defending Civil Society Report"), 29, available at www.icnl.org/research/journal/vol14iss3/art1.html; David Moore and Douglas Rutzen, "Legal Framework for Global Philanthropy: Barriers and Opportunities," *supra* note 1, at 17–23.

17. Defending Civil Society Report, *supra* note 16, at 28.

18. *See* David Moore and Douglas Rutzen, "Legal Framework for Global Philanthropy: Barriers and Opportunities," *supra* note 1, at 24.

19. Information about bringing charitable supplies into Mexico can be found on the website of the U.S. Consulate General of Matamoros Mexico, available at http://matamoros.usconsulate.gov/service/travel-information/mexican-customs.html.

20. *See* www.international.gc.ca/controls-controles/about-a_propos/expor/destination.aspx?view=d.

21. *See* David Moore and Douglas Rutzen, "Legal Framework for Global Philanthropy: Barriers and Opportunities," *supra* note 1, at 17.

22. These treaties include the Organization for Economic Cooperation and Development Convention on Combating Bribery of Foreign Officials in International Business Transactions (1997), the United Nations Convention Against Corruption (2005), and the Organization of American States Inter-American Convention Against Corruption (1996). Information about these and other anti-bribery treaties is available at www.transparency.org.

23. *See* Transparency International, *Annual Report 2011* (June 2012), at 12, available at www.transparency.org/whatwedo/publications.

24. *See* Velasco Lawyers, "A Business Law View of the New Criminal Law 2010 in Spain, available at www.velascolawyers.com/en/company-law/112-a-business-law-view-on-the-new-criminal-law-2010-in-spain.html. For information about Russia's legislation, *see* OECD Newsroom, "OECD Welcomes Russia Introducing Law to Make Foreign Bribery a Crime," May 5, 2011, available at www.oecd.org/document/36/0,3746,en_21571361_44315115_47769508_1_1_1_1,00.html.

25. UK Ministry of Justice, Bribery Act 2010 Guidance, available at www.justice.gov.uk/legislation/bribery.

26. Bond Anti-Bribery NGO Working Group, *Anti-Bribery Principles and Guidance for NGOs*, available at www.transparency.org.uk/our-work/publications/128-anti-bribery-principles-and-guidance-for-ngos.

27. Transparency International, *Pocket Guide of Good Practices: Preventing Corruption in Humanitarian Operations*, 6, available at www .transparency.org/whatwedo/pub/pocket_guide_of_good_practices_ preventing_corruption_in_humanitarian_operat.

28. Transparency International's Pocket Guide of Good Practices, *supra* note 27, contains extensive examples of types of corruption and guidance for identifying risks and developing policies and procedures.

29. *See* Defending Civil Society Report, *supra* note 16, at 18.

30. *Id.* at 17.

31. *Id.* at18.

32. *See* Douglas Rutzen, " Practice Note: Egypt and the Catalyst Constraint," *supra* note 13 at 50.

33. *See* David Moore and Douglas Rutzen, "Legal Framework for Global Philanthropy: Barriers and Opportunities," *supra* note 1 at 21.

34. Id.

35. *See* "Defending Civil Society Report," *supra* note 16, at 18.

36. *See* David Moore and Douglas Rutzen, "Legal Framework for Global Philanthropy: Barriers and Opportunities," *supra* note 1, at 27.

37. *See* "Defending Civil Society Report," *supra* note16, at 15.

38. *Id.* at 26, 24.

39. *See* Douglas Rutzen, "Practice Note: Egypt and the Catalyst Constraint," *supra* note 13, at 50.

40. "Defending Civil Society Report," *supra* note 16, at 24.

41. *See* Alyssa Dirusso, *American Nonprofit Law in Comparative Perspective*, *Wash. U. Global Stud. L. Rev.* 10, no. 1 (2011), 50, available at http://law .wustl.edu/WUGSLR/pages.aspx?id=8832.

42. For an overview of U.S. legal aspects of intellectual property, *see* Lesley Rosenthal, *Good Counsel: Meeting the Legal Needs of Nonprofits* (John Wiley & Sons 2012), Chapters 4 and 8.

43. Further information about ownership and protection of copyrights in the United States is available on the website of the U.S. Copyright Office at www.copyright.gov.

44. There are many resources available for understanding the basics of intellectual property law. *See*, e.g., *Intellectual Property Deskbook for the Business Lawyer: A Transactions-Based Guide to Intellectual Property Law*, 2nd ed. (American Bar Association Business Law Section Committee on Intellectual Property 2009), available for purchase at http://apps.americanbar.org/ abastore/index.cfm?section=main&fm=Product.AddToCart&pid=5070623.

45. *See* Clifford M. Marks, "Nonprofits Aren't So Generous When a Name's At Stake," *Wall Street Journal*, August 5, 2010, available at http://online.wsj.com/ article/NA_WSJ_PUB:SB10001424052748703700904575390950178142586 .html.

46. Madrid System for the International Registration of Marks, WIPO IP Services, available at www.wipo.int/madrid/en. Additional information about the process and effect of registration under the Madrid Protocol can be found on the U.S. Patent and Trademark Office website at www.uspto .gov/trademarks/law/madrid/madridfaqs.jsp.

47. *See*, e.g., *Eva's Bridal Ltd. v. Halanick Enterprises, Inc.*, 639 F. 3d 788 (7th Cir. 2011), rehearing denied 2011 U.S. App. LEXIS 11560 (2011). In this case, the trademark owner licensed to relatives and did not enter into written agreements that imposed standards and supervision because the owner trusted the licensees. The trademark was found invalid because the licenses lacked standards to ensure consistent, predictable quality.

48. Further information about protecting copyrights outside the United States can be found on the U.S. Copyright Office website, available at www .copyright.gov/fls/fl100.html.

49. A basic overview of the U.S. patent process can be found on the website of the U.S. Patent and Trademark Office, available at www.uspto.gov/ patents/process/index.jsp.

50. For more information, *see Intellectual Property Deskbook for the Business Lawyer: A Transactions-Based Guide to Intellectual Property Law*, *supra* note 44 at 144–145.

51. Directive 95/46/EC of the European Parliament and the Council of 24 October 1995 on the protection of individuals with regard to the processing of personal data and on the free movement of such data [1995] OJ L 281/31. In January 2012 the EU Commission proposed sweeping data protection reform. If and when that reform goes into effect, it is expected to make compliance easier for organizations and businesses by adopting a single set of rules throughout the EU. Further information about the current EU data protection regime, and the proposed reforms, is available at http://ec.europa.eu/justice/data-protection/index_en.htm.

52. For a detailed explanation of the application of the EU Data Protection Directive to non-EU organizations, *see* Lokke Moerel, "Back to Basics: When Does EU Data Protection Law Apply?" *Oxford International Data Privacy Law Journal* 1, no. 2 (January 2011), available at http://idpl .oxfordjournals.org/.

53. It should be noted that the so-called *U.S.-European Union Safe Harbor Program*, which provides a streamlined framework for certain U.S. companies to comply with the European Commission Directive on Data Protection, is not available to nonprofit organizations because they do not fall under the jurisdiction of the U.S. Federal Trade Commission. *See* the Department of Commerce website at http://export .gov/safeharbor/. Note, however, that for-profit affiliates and subsidiaries of nonprofit organizations may qualify for the Safe Harbor. A similar safe

harbor framework applies to U.S. companies seeking to comply with Swiss requirements.

54. *See* David Moore and Douglas Rutzen, "Legal Framework for Global Philanthropy: Barriers and Opportunities," *supra* note 1, at 24–25.

55. For a detailed explanation of the impact of various VAT regimes on nonprofit organizations, *see* Harley Duncan and Walter Hellerstein, "VAT and the Tax-Exempt Sector: Unique U.S. Issues," *Tax Notes*, December 20, 2010.

56. Currently, many nonprofit organizations formed in the U.S. are either required or choose to report their financial results using U.S. Generally Accepted Accounting Principles (*U.S. GAAP*), while many other countries use either their own standards or International Financial Reporting Standards (*IFRS*). The United States is considering transitioning to IFRS for publicly traded business corporations, but IFRS does not specifically address nonprofit organizations. It is unclear whether IFRS will be specifically adapted for the use of nonprofit organizations in the United States. In addition, in many foreign countries, there are no accounting standards specifically applicable to nonprofit organizations, and those organizations often use accounting standards developed for business entities. For more information on this topic, *see* www.ifrs.com.

# CHAPTER 10

# Evolution of a Global Organization: Half the Sky Foundation

I n this final chapter we look at how one organization evolved into a global nonprofit within just 13 years. I chose *Half the Sky Foundation (HTS)* for this final chapter, not only because it is an inspiring success sorry, but also because its evolution into a global nonprofit highlights a number of the major themes of this book.

In China, where HTS provides direct services, it has had to navigate an uncertain and ever-changing legal environment. As HTS developed a multinational fundraising network, it had to balance the benefits of expansion with the inevitable legal and operational complexity. HTS's founder/CEO and its board of directors did their homework. They looked at large organizational models. Ultimately, they charted their own path by creating a multinational structure that meets the organization's needs. That structure, and the relationships among the legal entities in multiple countries, will continue to evolve as the organization grows and individual country laws change.

## 10.1 Seeing a Need and Addressing It with Passion

HTS founder Jenny Bowen first visited a Chinese orphanage in 1997, when she and her husband adopted their first daughter. Watching her own Chinese daughter blossom within a loving family, Jenny became convinced that the infants and young children in Chinese orphanages would thrive if only they had more caregivers who were trained extensively in a more nurturing approach to care. She was determined to make that a reality.

In 1998, Jenny created HTS (www.halfthesky.org) as a California non-profit corporation that describes its mission as follows:

> *Half the Sky was created to enrich the lives and enhance the prospects for orphaned children in China. We establish and operate infant nurture and preschool programs, provide personalized learning for older children and offer loving permanent family care, medical care and guidance for children with disabilities. It is our goal to ensure that every orphaned child has a caring adult in her life and a chance at a bright future.*

The organization quickly applied for and received 501(c)(3) status. Meanwhile, Jenny immersed herself in learning about early childhood development and education. She consulted with experts, and worked to develop programs that would blend the best of Western early childhood learning with Chinese educational methods. Once the infant nurture and preschool programs were established, HTS developed additional programs for older children and children with significant special needs.

Within 13 years after its founding in 1998, HTS was operating five programs for orphans in more than 50 cities across China: infant nurturing, preschool, individualized learning for older children, family living environments for children with significant physical and mental challenges, and life-saving surgeries for medically fragile orphans. By 2011, these programs were annually reaching 6,000 children in 21 of the 31 provinces of China, and had transformed 60,000 young lives.

Also by 2011, HTS had developed close working relationships with Chinese government officials at the national, provincial, and local levels, and it had entered into a partnership with the Chinese government to train every child welfare worker in the country. In addition, HTS had become one of approximately 16 non-Chinese nonprofit organizations to obtain official national registration in China. It had established legal entities or funds for attracting tax-deductible contributions in five countries, including the United States, and had applications pending in two more. This is a highly complex structure for an organization with an annual budget of approximately $10 million.

How did HTS achieve all of this in 13 years? The short answer is that it took a highly passionate and visionary founder, the determination and patience to cultivate trusted relationships with a multitude of government officials, and a cause that lent itself to building a global community of supporters. The remainder of this chapter is devoted to a longer explanation of how HTS became a global organization in such a brief period of time.

## 10.2  Half the Sky's Experience in China

Forming a California nonprofit corporation and obtaining 501(c)(3) status were the easy parts of creating HTS. The next step was to obtain permission to work in government-operated Chinese orphanages. In addition, as a non-Chinese organization, HTS would have to figure out how to obtain legal status in China.

### Early Days: Developing Relationships

In 1998, there were very few legally recognized foreign (non-Chinese) NGOs in China. Those few, including the Ford Foundation, had long-term government relationships in China and were effectively grandfathered. At the same time, many foreign NGOs were working in China without legal recognition. While there was no way for those organizations to become legally sanctioned, government officials generally tolerated them when they were providing useful human services, so long as they were not perceived as making trouble.

HTS could not fly under the radar, as did so many foreign NGOs, because it needed permission to work in government-run welfare institutions. Meanwhile, by 1998, the Chinese central government had severely restricted foreigners' visits to orphanages. Thus, the likelihood of obtaining permission to conduct programs in orphanages, and to obtain legal status, appeared remote.

Knowing that orphanage directors (who are government employees) and other government officials would not welcome HTS with open arms, founder Jenny Bowen needed to find an existing NGO to partner with, and it had to be one that was government-sanctioned, a so-called *GONGO* (government operated nongovernment organization). Partnering with a GONGO that had a similar mission to HTS's would provide HTS with the necessary introductions to government officials, and would facilitate the development of trusting relationships. Through some contacts in the United States, Jenny was introduced to China Population Welfare Foundation (*CPWF*), a GONGO that was providing assistance to rural women through a project called the *Happiness Project*.

CPWF embraced HTS's mission, and it introduced Jenny to officials in China's Ministry of Civil Affairs, the central government authority which, at that time, was responsible for overseeing all orphanages.

Having found a Chinese partner and made some key government contacts, in late 1999 HTS received permission to make its first official orphanage visit. In early 2000, HTS received permission to introduce pilot programs in two orphanages.

Jenny Bowen quickly raised $29,000, and HTS officially launched its pilot programs with two groups of volunteers. The volunteers flew from the United States to China and spent a month hiring and training nannies, renovating rooms, and creating nurturing environments for young children in two orphanages. Within a short time, there were noticeable changes in the children's alertness and activity levels. The pilot programs demonstrated that institutionalized children, like all children, are resilient, and those who receive intensive, hands-on attention from well-trained, loving caregivers will thrive in ways not usually seen among institutionalized children.

From the very beginning, Jenny devoted large portions of her time and effort to developing relationships with government officials at all levels, from orphanage directors to the officials at the local, provincial, and national levels. Maintaining those relationships at multiple levels was, and continues to be, enormously complex, due in part to constant flux in the government, and in part to the political dynamics among governmental bodies.

In the early days, working with the Ministry of Civil Affairs was challenging, in part because the Ministry was responsible for domestic matters and was not accustomed to working with foreigners. After HTS had been operating for about a year, the Ministry of Civil Affairs created a new GONGO, China Social Workers Association, in part to work with HTS, which then had to juggle two partnerships. A few years later, national-level responsibility for orphanage oversight shifted to another GONGO, China Center for Adoption Affairs (*CCAA*). HTS was again challenged to develop a new set of relationships.

Those efforts to develop and maintain relationships were rewarded when, in 2005, HTS was invited to collaborate with the CCAA on the development of national guidelines for the education and nurture of orphans. In 2007, HTS was invited to become a direct partner with the central government's Ministry of Civil Affairs in order to make HTS's programs available to children in 300 orphanages throughout the country. Interestingly, as of that time, HTS still had no formal legal status in China.

In 2008, HTS signed a formal cooperative agreement with the Ministry of Civil Affairs' new *Blue Sky Program*, in which HTS would establish model children's centers with training facilities in each of China's 31 provinces and municipalities. The training centers would train and mentor at least 300 state-run institutions throughout the country to establish their own HTS programs.

By late 2010, HTS had been so successful in establishing new standards of care and education for institutionalized children that, together with the Ministry of Civil Affairs, it announced a plan to turn over the operation of its programs to the orphanages themselves. The plan would also allow HTS to realize its goal of transitioning from a direct service provider into a training and mentoring organization.

In 2011, China's Ministry of Civil Affairs, HTS, and CCWA (formerly CCA, now China Center for Child Welfare and Adoption) entered into a new national agreement, an integrated national training plan called the *Rainbow Program*, through which they would co-train every child welfare worker in the nation.

This unprecedented cooperative program was launched at China's Great Hall of the People on China's Children Day, June 1, 2011.

## How Can Foreign NGOs Operate in China?

As of the time of this book's publication, the legal landscape for foreign (non-Chinese) nonprofit organizations in China remains highly complex. Although legislation enacted in 2004 opened the door to greater foreign participation in the Chinese nonprofit sector, the landscape is still in flux. For non-Chinese individuals and nonprofit organizations, it is still difficult and often impossible to obtain permission to operate legally. Even those NGOs that have legal status are subject to significant scrutiny and restrictions. Without legal status, however, it is impossible for a nonprofit to hold a bank account, hire employees, or obtain visas for non-Chinese employees.[a]

### Notable Features of Chinese Nonprofit Law

Three significant features of Chinese nonprofit law continue to make it difficult, and often impossible, for non-Chinese individuals and organizations to form nonprofit organizations in China.

1. *There is no right to form a legal entity.* Unlike in the United States and many other countries, where registration of an entity is automatic once the legal requirements are satisfied, this is not the case in China. Government authorities can, and frequently do, deny an application for registration even if all of the legal requirements are met.
2. *Need to find a sponsoring agency.* China has a so-called *dual management system*, whereby an organization must find a governmental body willing to sponsor and oversee the organization. The term *dual* refers to the fact that a nonprofit organization must also obtain approval, and submit to continuing oversight, by the government body responsible for registration. Finding a sponsoring agency is often an obstacle to forming an entity, particularly for foreign organizations.
3. *Fundraising laws are not well developed.* With regard to fundraising, on the one hand very few organizations, and almost no foreign organizations, are granted the right to raise funds from within China. At the same time, there is an absence of regulations governing fundraising practices and, as a result, reports of fraudulent fundraising practices are common. There have been calls for reform of fundraising laws, both to protect donors and, at the same time, to allow more organizations to engage in fundraising.

### Legal Forms Available to Foreign Organizations

As of the time of this book's publication, non-Chinese NGOs can operate legally in China in the following ways.

## Representative Office

A representative office is not a separate legal entity. It does not have its own governance structure. Representative office status allows an organization to hold a bank account and hire employees, but it does not afford the right to solicit funds, or even to accept contributions from within China.

A 2004 change in Chinese law has allowed foreign foundations (but no other form of nonprofit legal entity) to establish representative offices in China. While there is no legal entity in the U.S. that corresponds to the Chinese foundation, as of this book's publication a number of U.S.-based nonprofit organizations have received permission to register representative offices. In addition, many international nonprofit organizations have chosen to use representative offices as business entities, rather than as nonprofit organizations, finding that route to be easier.

A nonprofit representative office is subject to the dual management system described above. As a result, a foreign NGO must find a government ministry that is willing to sponsor, or take responsibility for, the foreign NGO's activities in China. This sponsorship requirement can be an insurmountable obstacle for a foreign organization. Once a sponsor is found, the Beijing-based Ministry of Civil Affairs must approve the application. Despite lacking legal entity status, a representative office is subject to onerous requirements including filing annual reports. Representative offices can also be subject to a high degree of government scrutiny.

## Foundation

Unlike a representative office, a foundation can receive contributions from within China, and for this reason many international organizations operating in China would like to form foundations.

- The foundation form, under Chinese law, bears certain similarities to the foundation form in many other countries in Europe and elsewhere (*see* section 5.3), in that it must be formed for public benefit purposes and it does not have members.
- However, unlike the foundation form in other countries, the Chinese foundation is the only form of Chinese nonprofit entity permitted to engage in public fundraising, and it is often used as a vehicle for directing state funds toward public benefit purposes.

Moreover, there are two types of foundation under Chinese law, so-called *endowment* (or *private*) foundations, and *fundraising-oriented* (or *public*) foundations. While the former are permitted to receive contributions from individuals, foundations, and business enterprises within China, only the latter are permitted to engage in public solicitation, for example by holding public fundraising events.

## Affiliating with a Chinese Organization

This is an arrangement somewhat analogous to fiscal sponsorship. A non-Chinese NGO finds a domestic Chinese foundation (or other form of nonprofit organization) that is willing to function as a host, receiving funds for the foreign NGO's project in China. The host foundation must obtain approval from its sponsoring government ministry as well as the Ministry of Civil Affairs. Once the necessary approvals are obtained, funds can be raised for the project from within China to the extent that the host organization is authorized to raise funds.

## The Rapidly Changing Legal Landscape

It's important to be aware that the legal landscape for nonprofit organizations in China is changing rapidly. As of this book's publication, there has been significant attention among government officials to the need to develop philanthropy by implementing legal reforms. Reforms under discussion include eliminating the sponsoring agency (dual management) requirement, creating clear rules for fundraising, and imposing transparency requirements (such as obligations to disclose financial results) on organizations to improve accountability in the sector.[b] In some cases, provincial governments are being allowed to experiment with implementing their own legal reforms, for example by doing away with the separate sponsorship requirement.

In July 2012, the Ministry of Civil Affairs implemented regulations requiring that Chinese foundations publish details of donations and expenditures, and limiting the extent to which public donations may be used to pay administrative expenses. The Ministry of Civil Affairs has also submitted a new draft Charity Law for review and approval by the State Council and National People's Congress. The draft law addresses the tax deductibility of donations and how donations can be used, requires certain disclosures by charities that receive donations, and creates a system for government supervision of charity work. These developments are significant steps toward imposing accountability in the Chinese charitable sector.

If your organization seeks to work in China, it is critical to understand the state of the law and impending changes at the national, provincial, and local levels where you intend to operate. You should talk to organizations already operating there to understand the practical as well as formal legal obstacles you are likely to face.

---

[a] For a summary of the ways foreign NGOs can operate in China, see David Livdahl, Jenny Sheng, Henry Li, and Jack Tse, "What's Next for Foundations in China," *The Online China Business Review*, October 2010, available at www.chinabusinessreview .com/public/1009/livdahl.html. For detailed information about the various forms of nonprofit entities that exist in China, most of which are currently unavailable to foreign founders, *see*, von Hippel, Thomas and Knut B. Pissler, eds., *Nonprofit Organizations in the People's Republic of China: Comparative Corporate Governance of Non-Profit Organizations* (Cambridge, UK: Cambridge University Press 2010), 428–477.
[b] In April 2012, China released draft regulations for foundations, aimed at improving transparency and accountability for the use of donor funds. *See* International Center for Not-for-Profit Law, "China Releases Draft Rules on Foundations," April 25, 2012, available at www.icnl.org/news/2012/25-April-china.html.

---

## 10.3  Legal Status of HTS in China

For the first 10 years of its existence, from 1998 until 2008, HTS operated in China with the approval of government agencies, but without any formal legal status. Without legal status, HTS was unable to hire employees, but it could engage local consultants to help run the programs. The first consultant (still with HTS as of 2011) was a former government employee who had also worked for and retired from CPWF.

HTS also funded the compensation of caregivers and preschool teachers in many orphanages, but the orphanages were always the legal employers. These arrangements were informal. Because it lacked legal status in China, the only way HTS could bring funds into China was through bank accounts owned by individual consultants. Due to exchange controls, only small amounts could be wired at a time, and the process of wiring funds was quite cumbersome.

### Representative Office

In 2004, a new law went into effect, allowing foreign NGOs to create representative offices in China. A few of the largest U.S. foundations, including the Bill and Melinda Gates Foundation, the William J. Clinton Foundation, and World Wildlife Fund, immediately took advantage of the new law.

In 2008, HTS applied for and received permission to form a registered office. This meant that HTS could hold a bank account in its own name and could directly employ managers. Caregivers and preschool teachers working in the orphanages continued to be employed directly by the orphanages, with compensation funded by HTS.

Upon registration of the representative office, HTS's presence in China became legally sanctioned. However, there were no clear rules regarding the tax status of a foreign NGO's representative office. So, when HTS opened its own bank account, even as exchange controls loosened, it was careful to avoid accumulating funds. As result, the U.S. office had to wire funds to China on a regular basis, a cumbersome and costly process.

In addition, the representative office is permitted to receive funds only from the U.S. head office (its owner), and only from a U.S. bank account. This prevents the various HTS fundraising entities in other countries (described further on) from remitting funds directly to China. Rather, they have to send funds to HTS U.S., which in turn remits them to China, adding further cost and complexity.

By 2011, exchange controls had loosened, allowing foreign organizations to accumulate more Chinese renminbi (*RMB*) than was previously the case. At the same time, there was talk in the banking sector of the likelihood of significant appreciation in the Chinese currency. HTS responded with a decision to accumulate RMB in a Hong Kong bank account, owned by its Hong Kong affiliate (discussed later). However, before those funds are remitted to China, they must be transferred back into a U.S. dollar bank account, again adding complexity and cost.

An additional restriction on the representative office is that it is prohibited from receiving any contributions from within China.

## Fundraising in China

During 2011 and 2012, as HTS prepared for the transition from operating programs to conducting a nationwide training program, the organization saw opportunities to raise funds within China. Many Chinese nationals had become aware of HTS's efforts in China, and in particular its collaboration with the Chinese government to train every caregiver in the Chinese child welfare system using HTS's approach to caring for vulnerable children. Increasingly, Chinese individuals and companies wanted to help, but HTS, while legally registered in China, did not have the legal status needed to attract their contributions. This would require forming a Chinese foundation.

## Forming a Foundation

Legislation enacted in 2004 opened the door for non-Chinese nationals to form foundations in China, although as of 2011 no such foundations had been reported. Undaunted by yet another seemingly impossible feat, in 2012 HTS submitted an application to form the Chun Hui Bo Ai Child Welfare

Foundation (*Chun Hui*) in Beijing to allow Chinese individuals and corporations to support child welfare initiatives as inspired by the mission of HTS.

The Chun Hui foundation was approved in October 2012, and is reportedly the first Chinese foundation to be formed by non-Chinese nationals. The foundation is required to be governed entirely by Chinese nationals, and it may not operate HTS's programs. Jenny Bowen, HTS's founder, is permitted to sit on the board, but only as a nonvoting member.

HTS attributes its success in forming the foundation to the fact that HTS has demonstrated to the government that its programs make a valuable contribution to the public welfare. In addition, at a time when donor trust has been undermined by repeated scandals in China, and government regulators strive to introduce accountability into the nonprofit sector, Chun Hui aims to gain the confidence of donors by introducing levels of transparency and accountability that have traditionally been lacking in the Chinese nonprofit sector.

## 10.4   What Has HTS Learned about Working in China?

HTS has undergone a remarkable evolution in China. It began by bringing volunteer groups into two orphanages to provide intensive care for orphans. In 13 short years, HTS succeeded in persuading China's central government about the benefits of applying international best practices for the care of orphans and other marginalized children.

Here is what HTS learned about operating a program in China:

- *Cultivate government relationships.* Relationships with governmental officials are critical to success in China. This means identifying the layers of government you will need to work with, and working hard to develop and maintain those relationships. There will likely be dynamics among government officials that you will not understand. You need to navigate the maze and strive to stay on good terms with everyone. You will likely find yourself attending many banquets, toasting continuously, and eating unfamiliar food.
- *Remain as flexible as possible.* China is continually changing, and the rules will change as soon as you put something in place. This is true in many developing countries and particularly in China. Try to avoid creating a structure that is hard to change.
- *Choose board members who can live with uncertainty.* All nonprofit organizations need board members who pay attention and ask the hard questions. When you are operating in China, you will often lack certainty. There is an absence of clear laws governing the nonprofit sector. HTS is doing things that have never been done before in China. Caution and good judgment are always needed. Boards must be able to evaluate a situation, and ultimately live with a degree of uncertainty in order to move forward.

## 10.5   Developing a Global Fundraising Network

If you have already read Chapter 7, you may be wondering whether the fundraising potential justifies the expense and effort required to establish and maintain fundraising entities in multiple countries. For HTS, the answer was yes, because HTS views the development of a global support community as serving multiple purposes.

### Why Go Global?

For HTS, one purpose of creating fundraising entities in multiple countries is, of course, raising funds to support programs. However, the funds raised would not alone justify the maintenance of separate fundraising entities, at least not in some countries. The second purpose is to ensure that the world does not forget about the children languishing in orphanages, even as the Chinese government assumes responsibility for HTS's programs. The third is to provide a platform for the many (approximately 90,000) individuals around the world who were adopted from China, mostly after 1992. As these children become teenagers and young adults, HTS believes it can play a unique role by helping them to connect with each other and with the children living in Chinese orphanages.

HTS's global structure also allows it to employ the best people, even if they do not reside in the United States or China. For example, HTS's finance director, an invaluable part of the team, had to relocate from the United States to Hong Kong for personal reasons. She was able to continue working as finance director for the organization from Hong Kong because HTS had established a legal presence there.

### Balancing Central Control versus Local Autonomy

Since its inception, HTS has attracted supporters from many countries, largely from within the community of adoptive families. During HTS's early years, groups of supporters in various countries initiated fundraising projects to help support HTS programs. Though well intentioned, these projects were often informally organized. HTS's board of directors became concerned that informal groups of supporters were using HTS's name and logo to raise funds, implying that HTS was responsible for the efforts. At the same time, HTS had no control over compliance with local laws, nor did it have control over the consistency or accuracy of communications.

The board recognized the potential for developing communities of supporters in a number of countries, but it also saw the need for central oversight to ensure legal compliance and consistency of communications. The board decided that HTS should indeed work to develop a global network of supporters, but that it needed to have some control over fundraising efforts in each country. Focusing on those countries where HTS had the strongest base of support, the board decided to create fundraising entities in Hong Kong, the UK, Canada, and Australia. As a result, supporters in those countries would be able to obtain tax benefits for their contributions. In the Netherlands, HTS was able to register in a way that affords Dutch contributors with tax benefits for making contributions directly to the U.S. entity.

Founder Jenny Bowen and the board recognized that a degree of central control over the fundraising entities helps ensure that they devote their funding in a way that's consistent with HTS's strategy, even as that strategy evolves. Without such control, groups of supporters might become attached to, and continue funding, a particular project they previously sponsored, even as the organization's needs have migrated elsewhere. In addition, central control helps protect the brand by maintaining consistent messaging.

HTS has chosen to forgo some of the safeguards typically used in larger organizations in favor of maintaining a more nimble, informal culture. In contrast to World Vision International (*see* section 5.7), there is no formal partnership or federation agreement, and no formal agreement that sets forth values, ethics, or strategy. Rather, at this stage in the organization's evolution, some overlapping directors, along with strong communication among the leaders and boards of the separate entities provide an acceptable level of assurance to HTS U.S.

## Specific Country Experiences

**HONG KONG AND THE UK**   In Hong Kong (where the legal system is still largely based on the British system) and the UK, HTS formed a company limited by guarantee, with HTS U.S. as the sole member of each entity. *See* section 5.3. As the sole member, HTS U.S. has the right to elect the board of directors. This gives HTS U.S. effective control over the operations of the Hong Kong and UK entities. While the directors are responsible for governance of the organization, HTS U.S. has the power to replace directors if they deviate from the mission and policies of HTS U.S.

HTS's Hong Kong entity, Half the Sky Foundation (Asia) Limited, was HTS's first fundraising affiliate. Formed in 2006, it is exempt from Hong Kong tax (income, or profit, and certain other taxes), and is able to attract tax-deductible contributions from Hong Kong taxpayers

Similarly, Half the Sky (UK) Limited is registered with the UK Charity Commission, which regulates charities in England and Wales. It has qualified for charity status in the UK, which affords exemption from tax (income and other certain other taxes), and allows it to attract tax-favored contributions.

Hong Kong and the UK have fairly liberal regimes with regard to charities funding foreign programs. After paying their own expenses, HTS's Hong Kong and UK entities remit the balance of funds raised to Half the Sky U.S. for use in HTS's China programs.

CANADA    Half the Sky (Canada), Inc. became a registered charity in Canada in late 2009. A nonprofit membership corporation, it is not controlled by Half the Sky U.S. Jenny Bowen, founder and CEO of HTS U.S., serves as board chair of HTS Canada while the remainder of the board is comprised of Canadian nationals. There is, however, nothing in the bylaws or other organizing documents of HTS Canada that requires any representation from HTS U.S.

Cross-border giving is far more difficult in Canada than in the United States, Hong Kong, or the UK. *See* Chapter 7. A Canadian charity is permitted to fund only its own programs outside Canada. One way to satisfy this requirement is for a Canadian charity to enter into a joint venture or partnership agreement with the entity that directly operates foreign programs. Taking this approach, HTS Canada has entered into an operating agreement with HTS U.S. The agreement sets forth the rights of each party, and provides HTS Canada with, among other rights, the right to participate in governing the particular projects it chooses to fund.

Whenever a new project is to be funded by HTS Canada, a new schedule must be created, setting forth in detail the scope of the project, the budget, the objectives, evaluation methods, and requirements for reporting to HTS Canada. HTS Canada always retains the right to provide instructions regarding the use of its funds.

This is a very cumbersome process for any organization. For HTS, however, the value is not only in the financial support it receives but also in building a global community.

AUSTRALIA    Half the Sky Foundation Australia Limited was registered in 2009 as a public company limited by guarantee. As of the time of this book's publication, it had obtained tax-exempt status, and was awaiting registration as an *Overseas Aid Gift Deduction Scheme* (*OAGS*). Once approved as an OAGS, the Australian entity will need to apply to the Australian Tax Office for endorsement as a Deductible Gift Recipient (*DGR*), allowing it to attract tax-deductible contributions from Australian taxpayers. As a condition to this registration, an Australian entity must have a strong presence in Australia, with the membership and board of directors reflecting the community. As a practical matter, this means that the membership and board of HTS Australia are entirely comprised of Australian nationals. HTS U.S. retains the right to appoint up to one-third of the board. The CEO of HTS U.S. does not sit on the board of HTS Australia.

Of the countries in which HTS conducts fundraising, Australia presents the greatest complexity for an organization that wants to raise funds for foreign projects. Under Australian law, as in Canada, an organization that seeks tax-deductible contributions may not merely make cross-border grants. Rather, it must actively participate in foreign projects. Like HTS Canada, HTS Australia has to cooperate with HTS U.S. to identify projects, and must participate in the governance of those projects. Detailed agreements are required, setting forth the responsibilities of the parties, budget, and timelines. In addition, HTS Australia must be given detailed reports and project evaluations, and the project must be branded and promoted in China in such a way that identifies HTS Australia. For example, the first project funded by HTS Australia involved the refurbishment of facilities and staff hiring and training at an orphanage in the city of Changsha, China. Upon completion of the refurbishment, hiring, and training, a plaque was placed conspicuously at the facility identifying HTS Australia as the project sponsor.

While HTS Australia would appear to be quite autonomous, given the local composition of its membership and board, in reality it is constrained by the need to enter into detailed project agreements with HTS U.S. In fact, Australian law prevents HTS Australia from making unilateral decisions about funding of projects in China.

**THE NETHERLANDS**   Unlike the other countries in which HTS raises funds, the Netherlands does not require a separate legal entity with an independent governance structure in order to attract tax-deductible contributions. Rather, HTS U.S. was able to register as a foreign charity, obtaining so-called *ANBI* (*Legmen Nut Betokened Instelling*, or Institution for General Benefit) status. The funds raised in the Netherlands are owned by HTS U.S. and can be used in HTS's China programs. Dutch tax law affords the greatest tax benefits to Dutch taxpayers who make commitments to donate to the organization over a period of at least five years.

## Balancing Complexity with Informality

As of 2011, HTS had approximately 30,000 supporters globally, and was engaged in fundraising in five countries, with an application pending in a sixth. HTS also plans to develop a community of supporters within China, using the new foundation, "Chun Hui." Beyond that, HTS will continue to work on developing a global community that cares and spreads the word about HTS programs. It does not, however, have plans to expand into new countries.

Maintaining a network of separate legal entities in multiple countries is highly complex. As we have seen in this chapter and in other case studies throughout this book, maintaining the optimal balance between central control and local autonomy requires constant attention, as organizational needs shift and local country laws change. The relationship between HTS U.S. and each of its fundraising entities is somewhat different, largely due to differences in local country requirements. At the same time, HTS has opted for relatively informal methods of control in order to avoid having to manage complex intercompany agreements.

The success of this approach may be due, at least in part, to the fact that there is a strong, charismatic founder to keep everyone marching in the same direction. Time will tell whether a more formal structure will eventually be needed. For now, the organization will continue to straddle complexity and informality. Jenny Bowen, HTS's founder and CEO, summed it up saying, *HTS is remarkably complex for an organization its size in which the CEO still gets to hug babies.*

## 10.6   Closing Thoughts

The inspiring story of HTS demonstrates that it is possible to create an international nonprofit organization. HTS's experience also shows that, in order to succeed, it's necessary to have more than a great idea and a lot of determination. It's critical to do your homework before launching into a foreign country. Develop local relationships with NGOs and others. Find a good lawyer in the foreign country. Work with legal advisors, within and outside the United States, to determine the optimal legal structure for your activities. Put the right policies and procedures in place. If you are prepared to devote the necessary time and resources to do things right, you will greatly enhance the likelihood of success.

At the same time, we have seen throughout this book that there are multiple ways to further a charitable purpose outside the United States. In many cases, working with an existing organization, rather than creating a new one, is the most efficient way to make use of scarce resources.

Above all, if you are informed and thoughtful about how to pursue your mission, you will be more likely to succeed in turning your passion into reality.

*Unless someone like you cares a whole awful lot, nothing is going to get better. It's not.*

*From* The Lorax *by Dr. Seuss*

# Glossary of Terms

**501(c)(3) organization.** An organization that qualifies as tax-exempt, for U.S. federal income tax purposes, under section 501(c)(3) of the Internal Revenue Code. To qualify for 501(c)(3) status, an organization must be formed for one of the following purposes: religious, charitable, scientific, testing for public safety, literary, educational, or fostering amateur national or international sports competition, or the prevention of cruelty to children or animals. Additional requirements apply.

**American Friends of organization.** A 501(c)(3) organization established in the United States for the primary purpose of supporting a foreign nonprofit organization by attracting tax-deductible contributions from donors who are U.S. taxpayers.

**branch (or branch office).** A legal presence that an organization may have in a country other than the one in which the organization is established. For example, an organization formed in the United States may conduct operations in a foreign country through a branch. A branch is not a separate *legal entity*, and therefore does not have a separate governing body such as a board of directors.

**Central and Eastern European countries (CEE).** The CEE countries referred to in this book are: Albania, Bosnia and Herzegovina, Bulgaria, Croatia, Czech Republic, Estonia, Hungary, Kosovo, Latvia, Lithuania, Macedonia, Montenegro, Poland, Slovakia, Slovenia, and Serbia.

**charity.** In some countries (including the UK, Canada, and Australia), the term *charity* is used to refer to a nonprofit organization that qualifies for the most tax-favored status, which often includes the ability to attract tax-deductible or other tax-favored contributions. While the criteria for qualifying as a charity vary from country to country, typically a charity must benefit a broad category of people. The term charity is also sometimes used to refer to a U.S. organization that qualifies for 501(c)(3) status.

**civil society organization (CSO).** While the precise definition of a CSO can vary, the term is generally used to refer to an organization (or even collective action) that is independent from any governmental body, and is operated primarily for a purpose other than profit making. The purposes of a CSO may vary from country to country and may include a wide range of activities.

**copyright.** A form of legal protection, provided under the laws of the United States and other countries, for the creator of an original work such as a writing, artistic expression, film, photograph, and software code, among others. A copyright gives the creator a number of rights, including rights to control the distribution, sale, and reproduction of a work, and rights in so-called *derivative works* based on the original work. Individual countries vary with respect to the scope of copyright protection, and the procedures for establishing and enforcing a copyright.

**donor-advised fund.** A *donor-advised fund* is defined in section 4966 of the U.S. Internal Revenue Code as a fund or account, separately identified with respect to contributions of a particular donor, owned by a 501(c)(3) public charity, whereby the donor has advisory privileges with respect to the distribution of funds for 501(c)(3) purposes. This means that a U.S. taxpayer may make a contribution to a public charity and receive an immediate tax deduction (subject to limitations). At a later date, the donor may request, but may not require, that the funds be used to support a particular organization.

**dual employment arrangement.** An individual employee may be working for two separate legal entities, each of which enters into an employment agreement with and separately compensates the individual. This type of arrangement is often useful when an individual is working for separate legal entities that are established in separate countries.

**earned revenue.** For purposes of this book, *earned revenue* refers to revenue earned by a nonprofit organization from sources other than contributions and grants from individuals, other nonprofit organizations, corporations, and governmental bodies. Common types of earned revenue are proceeds from the sale of goods and fees for services. Investment income (such as interest, dividends, and gains on sale of stocks, bonds, and other financial instruments) are generally considered passive and not as earned revenue.

Earned revenue may be attributable to an organization's tax-exempt functions, as in the case of entrance fees charged by a museum. Alternatively, earned revenue may be attributable to an organization's operation of business activity. Earned revenue (and in some cases even investment income) may be taxed differently from contributions and grants, and may even cause an organization to become ineligible for tax-exempt status.

**European Commission (EC).** The EC is comprised of 27 commissioners, representing each of the countries (*Member States*) of the European Union (EU). It is responsible for upholding and implementing EU policy by drafting proposed laws, managing the EU's budget and allocating funding, enforcing EU law (together with the *European Court of Justice*), and representing the EU internationally, for example by negotiating treaties.

**European Court of Justice (ECJ).** The ECJ interprets European laws to ensure that they are applied consistently throughout the EU, and settles disputes between EU countries and institutions.

**European Economic Area (EEA).** As of this book's publication, the EEA consists of Iceland, Lichtenstein, and Norway, along with the 27 EU Member States. The non-EU EEA countries are bound by the EU principles of free movement of goods, persons, services, and capital, but they are not represented in the *European Commission*.

**European Foundation Statute (EFS).** The EFS would allow a new or existing public benefit organization to operate and raise funds throughout the EU without having to comply with separate EU country requirements. As of the date of this book's publication, the EFS has been proposed by the *European Commission*. It requires unanimous approval by the 27 EU *Member States*.

**European Union (EU).** The EU is a political and economic partnership consisting of 27 European countries (*Member States*) as of this book's publication:

| | |
|---|---|
| Austria | Latvia |
| Belgium | Lithuania |
| Bulgaria | Luxembourg |
| Cyprus | Malta |
| Czech Republic | Netherlands |
| Denmark | Poland |
| Estonia | Portugal |
| Finland | Romania |
| France | Slovakia |
| Germany | Slovenia |
| Greece | Spain |
| Hungary | Sweden |
| Ireland | United Kingdom |
| Italy | |

One of the major tenets of the EU is to facilitate the free flow of people, services, goods, and capital among the *Member States* as if they were a single country. As of 2012, efforts to achieve these objectives have lagged in the philanthropic sector relative to the market sector, but recent rulings have required some legislative changes in a number of countries.

**FARA.** The U.S. *Foreign Agents Registration Act*, 22 U.S.C. § 611 *et seq.*

**FATCA.** The U.S. *Foreign Account Tax Compliance Act*, I.R.C. § 6038D.

**FBAR.** Foreign bank account reporting requirements, imposed on U.S. citizens, individual residents, and entities established in the United States. The program is administered by the U.S. Treasury Department's *Financial Crimes Enforcement Network (FinCEN)*.

**FCPA.** The U.S. *Foreign Corrupt Practices Act*, 15 U.S.C. §§ 78dd-1, *et seq.*

**foundation.** Under the laws of many countries, a *foundation* is a form of nonprofit legal entity, typically having no members. The characteristics of a foundation vary among countries. The term *private foundation*, as used in the United States, is not a form of legal entity under state law, but rather, this is a federal income tax designation.

**IFRS.** *International Financial Reporting Standards*. IFRS is the standard used for the preparation of financial statements in many countries outside the United States. A U.S. nonprofit organization that is not required to use *U.S. GAAP* may choose to prepare its financial statements using IFRS.

**international NGO (INGO).** *International nongovernmental organization*, or *International NGO*, is often used to distinguish an NGO that operates across borders from one that operates in a single country.

**intellectual property (IP).** *Intellectual property*, or IP, refers generally to something created through intellectual effort. The major categories of intellectual property are trademarks and service marks, copyrights, patents, and trade secrets. In the United States, and in most foreign countries, the creator of intellectual property has certain legal rights that are protected against unauthorized use and misuse by others. It is often necessary to take certain steps, such as registering with a governmental body, to establish those rights.

**internal controls.** Procedures an organization implements to safeguard an organization's assets, as well as to ensure accurate financial reporting and compliance with applicable laws and regulations. An important part of internal controls is making sure there are checks and balances. For example, an organization might adopt a policy that prohibits the same individual from writing checks and entering payments in the financial accounts.

**Internal Revenue Service (IRS).** The U.S. federal governmental bureau, within the U.S. Department of the Treasury, charged with the collection of federal taxes and administration of U.S. federal tax laws. While the acronym IRS is used to designate the tax collection or administration body in some other countries (for example, Ghana), in this book it is used solely to refer to the U.S. federal bureau.

**legal entity.** A separate organization, formed under the laws of a particular U.S. or foreign jurisdiction, with its own organizational documents (such as articles of incorporation and bylaws) and governing body (such as a board of directors). For example, in the United States. legal entities include nonprofit and for-profit corporations. For purposes of this book, the term legal entity also includes a trust, although a trust may technically be considered not a legal entity because the trustee, rather than the trust, holds title to property. The laws of other countries provide for a variety of types of nonprofit and for-profit legal entities.

**Member State.** As used in this book, the term *Member State* refers to one of the 27 countries that are members of the *European Union*.

**Middle Eastern and Northern Africa Region (MENA).** This term is used by the World Bank as well as by academic institutions and businesses. While the list of countries included in the MENA region varies, as of the date of this book the MENA region commonly includes:

| | |
|---|---|
| Algeria | Jordan |
| Djibouti | Lebanon |
| Egypt | Libya |
| Gulf States | Morocco |
| Israel | Syria |
| Iran | Tunisia |
| Iraq | Yemen |

**national (of a particular country).** For purposes of this book, an individual is considered a *national* of a particular country if the individual is a citizen of that country.

**nongovernmental organization (NGO).** While the precise definition of an NGO can vary, the term is generally used to refer to an organization (or even collective action) that is independent from any governmental body and is operated primarily for a purpose other than profit making. The purposes of a NGO may vary from country to country and may include a wide range of activities. The term NGO is often, but not always, used interchangeably with the term CSO.

**nonprofit organization (NPO).** The term *nonprofit organization* generally refers to an organization that has a purpose other than earning profits for its owners or members. This can include a wide variety of purposes. A nonprofit organization can take a variety of forms. It may be a legal entity, or it may be an informal group of individuals. This book is focused primarily on a subset of nonprofit organizations that have 501(c)(3) purposes, or similar purposes if established in a foreign country.

**nonresident alien.** In the context of U.S. federal income tax, a *nonresident alien* is an individual who is not a U.S. citizen and does not meet the tests for *resident alien* status (*see* section 6.4). Unlike a U.S. citizen or resident alien, a nonresident alien is not subject to U.S. federal income tax unless that individual performs services while physically in the United States as an employee or independent contractor, conducts a regular trade or business in the United States, or earns other income that is considered to be from U.S. sources.

**not-for-profit organization.** The term *not-for-profit organization* is often used interchangeably with the term *nonprofit organization*, although it is often said that the former is more accurate. A not-for-profit (or nonprofit) organization is not prohibited from earning a profit, but rather, does not have profit making as its purpose.

**Organization of American States (OAS).** The OAS has, as of the date of this book's publication, 35 members comprised of countries situated in North, South, and Central America. Among its purposes is the promotion of economic, social, and cultural development of the member countries.

**Organisation for Economic Cooperation and Development (OECD).** As of the date of this book's publication, the OECD is comprised of 34 member countries, spanning the globe, from North and South America to Europe and the Asia-Pacific region. They include many of the world's most developed countries, but also emerging countries like Mexico, Chile, and Turkey. The OECD helps governments foster prosperity and fight poverty through economic growth and financial stability.

**Office of Foreign Assets Control (OFAC).** An office of the U.S. Department of the Treasury, responsible for administering and enforcing U.S. economic trade sanctions. OFAC enforces economic and trade sanctions based on U.S. foreign policy and national security goals against targeted foreign countries and regimes, terrorists, international narcotics traffickers, those engaged in activities related to the proliferation of weapons of mass destruction, and other threats to the national security, foreign policy, or economy of the United States.

**permanent establishment.** The term *permanent establishment* is used in income tax treaties to refer to the range of activities which, when conducted by an organization in a particular country, cause that organization to become subject to that country's taxing jurisdiction. Treaties vary with respect to the particular activities that give rise to a permanent establishment.

**private benefit.** Under the so-called *private benefit doctrine*, a 501(c)(3) organization is prohibited from providing more than incidental benefits to private interests. Private interests are individuals or organizations that are not the intended beneficiaries of the organization's exempt purposes.

**private foundation.** The term *private foundation* is a U.S. federal income tax term, referring to one of two types of 501(c)(3) organization. Relative to a so-called *public charity*, a private foundation is subject to more restrictions on its operations, including more onerous requirements related to international grantmaking.

**private inurement.** Under U.S. federal tax law, a 501(c)(3) organization (as well as other types of tax-exempt organization) is prohibited from providing any unearned benefits (for example, excessive compensation, or compensation for services not really performed) to certain individuals in a position to have control or influence, including directors, officers, and other individuals with significant influence, such as program heads, along with family members of these people with influence. *Private foundations* are subject to additional restrictions.

**public benefit organization.** In many countries, the term *public benefit organization* is used to designate those nonprofit organizations that are devoted to a public (rather than private) purpose, and therefore qualify for the most favored tax status. This may include the ability to attract tax-deductible (or otherwise tax-favored) contributions. The criteria for qualifying as a public benefit organization vary from country to country.

**public charity.** The term *public charity* is a U.S. federal income tax term, referring to one of two types of 501(c)(3) organization. A public charity is not subject to certain onerous restrictions, including requirements related to international grantmaking, which are imposed on private foundations.

**registered office.** As used throughout this book, the term *registered office* is interchangeable with the term *branch*, or *branch office*. When an organization establishes a legal presence in a foreign country without forming a separate *legal entity*, that legal presence is often called a registered office or branch. The administrative requirements for creating and maintaining a registered office may be very simple. Alternatively, an organization may have to comply with a cumbersome and even unpredictable application process.

**representative office.** Typically available to for-profit companies, this is a way of maintaining a minimal presence in a foreign country for purposes of marketing and communication. In China, the term representative office is used to designate an office of a non-Chinese NGO that has legal status in China but is not permitted to raise funds.

**resident alien.** An individual who, like a U.S. citizen, is required to pay U.S. federal income tax on all income he or she earns, regardless of whether the income is earned in the United States. This includes permanent residents (so-called *green card holders*) and individuals who meet certain tests for minimum time spent in the United States.

**September 11 attacks (also referred to as 9/11).** For purposes of this book, references to *September 11* mean the terrorist attacks on the New

York World Trade Center towers, the Pentagon in Washington, DC, and the state of Pennsylvania that occurred on September 11, 2001. That event was the catalyst for a wide variety of measures, in the United States and abroad, aimed at preventing international terrorism and the financing of terrorist activities.

**Specially Designated Names (SDN) list.** The SDN list is comprised of individuals and entities, designated by the U.S. Department of the Treasury, that have been identified by the U.S. government as terrorists or narcotics traffickers, or owned or controlled by certain governments. A U.S. organization that provides material support to an individual or entity found on the SDN list may face severe sanctions, including having its assets frozen. Other governmental bodies and international organizations also maintain lists of terrorists, and those lists may not overlap entirely with the SDN list.

**totalization agreement.** This is a type of bilateral agreement, between the United States and a foreign country, to avoid the problem of double social security taxes for individuals who go to work in a foreign country. As of the date of this book's publication, the United States has totalization agreements in effect with 24 foreign countries.

**trademark and service mark.** A word, name, symbol, design, or combination thereof, used to identify particular goods. The related term, service mark, is used to designate a service provider. Most nonprofit organizations will have service marks, such as a unique name, logo, and/or symbol that designates the organization.

**Unrelated Business Taxable Income (UBTI).** UBTI is a U.S. federal income tax term. It refers to income earned by a tax-exempt organization that is subject to U.S. federal (and often state) income tax because it is earned through activities that are not substantially related to the organization's tax-exempt purposes (and meets certain additional criteria).

**United Kingdom (UK).** The UK consists of England, Northern Ireland, Scotland, and Wales. There are separate government regulators for charities established in England and Wales (the Charity Commission for England and Wales), Scotland, and Northern Ireland. However, UK tax law applies to organizations established throughout the UK for purposes of obtaining tax-exempt status and eligibility for tax-favored contributions.

**United States Agency for International Development (USAID).** USAID is a U.S. federal government agency that administers foreign aid. Many nonprofit organizations (established in the United States and in foreign countries) receive grants from USAID.

**U.S. GAAP.** U.S. GAAP refers to *U.S. Generally Accepted Accounting Principles*. These are accounting standards, used in the United States, for the preparation and review of financial statements that are audited by an external *Certified Public Accountant (CPA)*. Unlike the accounting standards used in most countries, U.S. GAAP contains special rules for nonprofit (referred to in GAAP as *not-for-profit*) organizations. Many, but not all, nonprofit organizations established in the United States are required, or choose, to have their financial statements audited. Many, but not all, U.S. organizations choose to prepare financial statements using U.S. GAAP, even when they are not required to do so.

**value-added tax (VAT).** VAT, and the closely related *Goods and Service Tax*, or *GST*, is a type of tax referred to as a consumption tax. This type of tax exists in approximately 135 countries throughout the world, but not in the United States. This is a tax imposed on transactions such as sales of goods and often sales of services. Unlike sales taxes imposed by states and localities in the United States, the VAT is imposed at each stage along the chain of supply. However, the ultimate cost is borne by the consumer. A U.S. nonprofit organization that operates in foreign countries may be surprised to find itself incurring significant costs and/or administrative compliance burdens associated with VAT.

**withholding tax.** In the international context, the term *withholding tax* refers to a tax imposed on a payment made to a resident of another country. The mechanism for payment of tax is that the payor is required to withhold the amount of the tax from the payment and remit it to the payor's government. Withholding taxes are often imposed on payments of interest, royalties, dividends, and compensation for services performed (by an employee or independent contractor), to an individual or entity that is not a resident of the country from which the revenue is derived. Often, there is an ability to reduce or eliminate a withholding tax under a treaty.

# Additional Resources

## Resources for 501(c)(3) Organizations

Hopkins, Bruce R. *The Law of Tax-Exempt Organizations*. 10th ed. Hoboken, NJ: John Wiley & Sons, 2011.

Lieber, Penina Kessler, and Donald R. Levy, eds. *Complete Guide to Nonprofit Organizations: Law, Taxation, Operational Planning*. Kingston, NJ: Civic Research Institute, 2005 and 2007 Cumulative Supplement.

Rosenthal, Lesley. *Good Counsel: Meeting the Legal Needs of Nonprofits*. Hoboken, NJ: John Wiley & Sons, 2012.

Siegel, Jack B. *A Desktop Guide for Nonprofit Directors, Officers, and Advisors: Avoiding Trouble While Doing Good*. Hoboken, NJ: John Wiley & Sons, 2006.

Council on Foundations, www.cof.org.

National Council of Nonprofits, www.councilofnonprofits.org.

U.S. Internal Revenue Service, www.irs.gov/charities.

## Resources for Private Foundations

McCoy, Jerry J., and Kathryn W. Miree, *Family Foundation Handbook*. Chicago, IL: CCH, 2012.

Blazek, Jody B., and Bruce R. Hopkins. *Private Foundations: Tax Law and Compliance*. Hoboken, NJ: Wiley Nonprofit Law, Finance and Management Series, 2006 and Cumulative Supplements.
Council on Foundations, www.cof.org.

## International Activities of Nonprofit Organizations

Glassie, Jefferson C. *International Legal Issues for Nonprofit Organizations*, 2nd ed. Washington, DC: ASAE: The Center for Association Leadership, 2010.
Koenig, Bonnie. *Going Global for the Greater Good: Succeeding as a Nonprofit in the International Community*. San Francisco: Jossey-Bass, 2004.

## U.S. Intermediary Organizations for International Grantmaking

Charities Aid Foundation, www.cafamerica.org.
Give2Asia, http://give2asia.org.
Global Giving, www.globalgiving.org.
Kiva, www.kiva.org.
United Way Worldwide, http://worldwide.unitedway.org.

## Resources for Cross-Border Grantmakers

Buchanan, Rob, and Jayne Booker. *Making a Difference in Africa: Advice from Experienced Grantmakers*. Arlington, VA: Council on Foundations, 2007.
Edie, John A., Jane C. Nober, and Jacob T Clauson. *Beyond Our Borders: A Guide to Making Grants Outside the United States*, 4th ed. Arlington VA: Council on Foundations, 2012.
Lieber, Penina Kessler and Donald R. Levy eds., *Complete Guide to Nonprofit Organizations: Law, Taxation, Operational Planning*. Kingston, NJ: Civic Research Institute, 2005 and 2007 Cumulative Supplement.
McCoy, Jerry J., and Kathryn W. Miree. *Family Foundation Handbook*. Chicago, IL: CCH, 2012.
Africa Grantmakers Affinity Group, www.africagrantmakers.org.
Alliance Magazine, www.alliancemagazine.org.
Asian Philanthropy Advisory Network, http://asianphilanthropy.org.
Council on Foundations, www.cof.org.
Grantmakers Without Borders, www.gwob.net.
U.S. International Grantmakers, www.usig.org.

# Resources for Finding International Collaborators

Buchanan, Rob, and Jayne Booker. *Making a Difference in Africa: Advice from Experienced Grantmakers*. Arlington, VA: Council on Foundations, 2007.
Worldwide Initiatives for Grantmaker Support (WINGS), www.wingsweb.org.

# Resources on Foreign Country NGO Laws

## Various Countries

Hopt, Klaus J., and Thomas Von Hippel, eds, *Comparative Corporate Governance of Non-Profit Organizations*. Cambridge, UK: Cambridge University Press, 2010.
Charities Aid Foundation (CAF), www.cafamerica.org.
Give2Asia, www.give2asia.org.
Global Trends in NGO Law, www.icnl.org/knowledge/ngolawmonitor.
International Journal of Not-for-Profit Law, www.icnl.org.
U.S. International Grantmakers, www.usig.org/countryinfo.
Worldwide Initiatives for Grantmaker Support (WINGS), www.wingsweb.org/information/publications_global_institutional_philanthropy.cfm.

## Africa

Moyo, Bhekinkosi, ed. *(Dis)enabling the Public Sphere: Civil Society Regulation in Africa* (vol. 1). Johannesburg, South Africa: Southern Africa Trust and Trust Africa, 2010.

## China

China Development Brief, www.chinadevelopmentbrief.cn.

## Europe

European Foundation Centre, www.efc.be/programmes_services/resources/Pages/Legal-and-fiscal-country-profiles.aspx.

## India

Centre for Advancement of Philanthropy, www.capindia.in.

# Avoiding Participation in Corruption (Anti-Bribery)

Transparency International: The Global Coalition against Corruption, www.transparency.org.
U.S. Department of Justice, www.justice.gov/criminal/fraud/fcpa.

## Updates on Anti-Terrorism Policies and Their Impact on Nonprofit Organizations

Charity & Security Network, www.charityandsecurity.org.
United States Department of the Treasury Office of Financial Assets Control, www.treasury.gov/about/organizational-structure/offices/Pages/Office-of-Foreign-Assets-Control.aspx.

## Intellectual Property

### United States

United States Patent and Trademark Office, www.uspto.gov.
United States Copyright Office, www.copyright.gov.

### International

United States Patent and Trademark Office, www.uspto.gov/ip/iprtoolkits.jsp.
World Intellectual Property Organization (WIPO), www.wipo.int.

# U.S. Bilateral Income Tax Treaties

As of the date of this book's publication, income tax treaties are in force between the United States and the following countries:

| | |
|---|---|
| Armenia | Georgia |
| Australia | Germany |
| Austria | Greece |
| Azerbaijan | Hungary |
| Bangladesh | Iceland |
| Barbados | India |
| Belarus | Indonesia |
| Belgium | Ireland |
| Bulgaria | Israel |
| Canada | Italy |
| China | Jamaica |
| Cyprus | Japan |
| Czech Republic | Kazakhstan |
| Denmark | Korea |
| Egypt | Kyrgyzstan |
| Estonia | Latvia |
| Finland | Lithuania |
| France | Luxembourg |

Malta

Mexico

Moldova

Morocco

Netherlands

New Zealand

Norway

Pakistan

Philippines

Poland

Portugal

Romania

Russia

Slovak Republic

Slovenia

South Africa

Spain

Sri Lanka

Sweden

Switzerland

Tajikistan

Thailand

Trinidad and Tobago

Tunisia

Turkey

Turkmenistan

Ukraine

United Kingdom

Uzbekistan

Venezuela

The full text of each of these treaties is available on the IRS website at www.irs.gov/businesses/international/article/0,,id=96739,00.html.

Certain features of these treaties are summarized in IRS Publication 901, available at www.irs.gov/app/picklist/list/formsPublications.html?value=Treaties&criteria=title&submitSearch=Find.

# About the Companion Website

Please visit www.wiley.com/go/nortonglobal to access the following information to use alongside this book.

- A flowchart for deciding which point on the spectrum of international activity is right for you.
- Chapter-by-chapter checklists for organizations that operate at each point along the spectrum of international activity.

You can follow Lisa Norton on Twitter @GlobalNonprofit.

Please also visit Lisa Norton's website at www.lnortonlaw.com for more information.

# About the Author

Lisa Norton is a lawyer whose practice concentrates on nonprofit organizations with international activities. Her breadth of experience working in the nonprofit sector also includes service on boards of international nonprofits, speaking engagements, and service on Bar Association committees. Norton has also served as international tax counsel and director of international tax for several multinational corporations, including Amazon.com. She is the recipient of the President's Award for long-term distinguished service to Tax Executives Institute, an organization of 7,000 tax executives. Norton holds a Bachelor of Arts from the University of Rochester, a JD from Harvard Law School, and a Masters of Public Administration from the University of Washington. Follow her on Twitter @GlobalNonprofit.

# Index